Praise for *The Employee M*

"Winner of the 2019 Book Excellence Awards in the Real Estate Category."

— Book Excellence Awards

"Award-Winning Finalist in the Business: Personal Finance/Investing category of the 2018 Best Book Awards sponsored by American Book Fest."

— Best Book Awards

"Award Winning Finalist in the 2019 Next Generation Indie Book Awards (NGIBA)."

— Next Generation Indie Book Awards

"Honorable Mention in the Business/Sales/Economics category of the Reader Views 2018-2019 Literary Awards program."

— Reader Views

"Investing for one's own financial security is not a course taught anywhere: one learns life's hard lessons as one goes through life!! I wish I had access to his learning when I was starting out in my journey. I can strongly recommend this book to every person (employee) starting out in life and wishing to know basics of personal financial planning. It's an easy read, with simple lessons and easy-to-apply tools."

— from the foreword by NANDU NANDKISHORE, Fortune 100 CEO. Former Executive Board member for Nestlé S.A and former CEO Nestlé Nutrition. Angel VC, Mentor, Coach, Keynote Speaker, Consultant, and Faculty at B schools

"Investing in rental properties can be one of the surest ways of building wealth, but only if it is done right. H. J. Chammas has done the world a great service by writing a book that clearly explains how to "do it right" every single step of the way. Meticulous, but also enjoyable to read, The Employee Millionaire is an A to Z guide on how to acquire a portfolio of rental properties that will build wealth with every month that passes. Anyone considering investing in rental properties should begin by reading this book."

— RICHARD DUNCAN, Author, Economist and Publisher of Macro Watch

"To help you obtain financial freedom while reducing risk, read *The Employee Millionaire* — an enabling guide to achieving your goals through discipline and great self-leadership."

- BRENDA BENCE, Award-Winning Author and Top 10 Executive Coach worldwide

"*The Employee Millionaire* offers a proven methodology for creating wealth through real estate."

- THEDA DAVIDS-MULLER, UAE Advisor, Mentor, Visionary Entrepreneur, Real Estate Specialist, IT/Telecoms/ITIL Eng., Author, Writer, Keynote Speaker, Banker, Start-up Specialist, Supreme Legacy Mentor and Personal Transformational Mentor

"A solid introduction to real estate investment."

— Kirkus Review

"For those interested in investing in rental properties, this expertly written book offers the necessary guidance and support."

— Clarion Foreword Review

"Chammas lays that foundation with excellent content that includes the financial 'ins and outs' of acquiring rental properties (e.g. strategies for dealing with banks, analyzing rental property opportunities, managing properties). He also provides a thoughtful approach for analyzing less tangible considerations, such as identifying limiting beliefs, balancing lifestyle desires and pressures and managing the moving target of personal motivation. The Employee Millionaire will appeal to a broad swath of readers who appreciate this intelligent message of hope couched in helpful advice that they can leverage."

– Blueink Review

"Chammas discusses in detail all the steps needed to make smart real estate investments, including choosing location, analyzing properties and negotiating deals. It's all in this book! ... I highly recommend "The Employee Millionaire" by H. J. Chammas for anyone looking to create financial freedom through passive real estate investing. I know I will keep this as a useful reference for all my future investment opportunities. This book is a treasure that everyone should have in their library!"

- Christine Watson for Reader Views

THE
EMPLOYEE
MILLIONAIRE

*How to Use Your Day Job to Become
a Millionaire with Rental Properties*

H. J. CHAMMAS

PARTRIDGE

To order additional copies of this book, contact
Toll Free 800 101 2657 (Singapore)
Toll Free 1 800 81 7340 (Malaysia)
orders.singapore@partridgepublishing.com

www.partridgepublishing.com/singapore

LEGAL DISCLAIMER

This book is designed to provide educative information and motivation to readers. The author and publisher are not offering it as legal, accounting, or other professional services advice. The methods described in this book are the sole expression and opinion of the author. They are not intended to be a definitive set of instructions. You may discover other methods and materials that accomplish the same end result. No warranties or guarantees are expressed or implied by the publisher's choice to include any of the content in this volume. Neither the publisher nor the author shall be liable for any physical, psychological, emotional, financial, or commercial damages, including, but not limited to, special, incidental, consequential, or other damages.

Our views and rights are the same: You are responsible for your own choices, actions, and results. Seek the services of a competent professional before beginning any self-improvement program.

Characters' names and identifying details have been changed to protect the privacy of individuals. Any likeness to actual persons, either living or dead, is strictly coincidental.

References are provided for informational purposes only and do not constitute endorsement of any websites or other sources. The websites listed in this book may change.

DEDICATION AND ACKNOWLEDGMENT

The Employee Millionaire is dedicated to the men and women who work hard for their jobs and yet dream of someday achieving financial independence and freedom to finance their mission in life. It is dedicated to those who are determined to make a big financial change in their life with as few roadblocks as possible. It is dedicated to those who want to take charge of their life and take action.

This book is also dedicated to my son, Ryan. I started writing this book on the same day my wife and I received the news that we would be welcoming a baby to the world in nine months' time. It was finished and submitted to publishing when he was exactly six months old. If only one copy of this book is ever published, I wish my son, Ryan, will be the person who will read it one day and apply the learning in his life.

A big thank you to my wife, Joyce, for her patience with me for having taken yet another challenge that decreases the amount of time I could have spent with her. She accepted a big part of that sacrifice and yet kept on encouraging me all the way through writing this book.

A heartfelt appreciation to all my mentors and coaches who have taught me the lessons that have changed my life and enabled me to become better in my leadership and business skills. And I extended my gratitude to all the professionals in different part of the world, who have worked with me on each rental property acquisition.

FOREWORD

I knew H. J. Chammas when I was in the Philippines as Chairman and CEO of Nestlé Philippines Inc, between 2005 and 2009. I was heading the big multinational he refers to in the book.... he always struck me as a sincere, dedicated, strong and capable manager. I now discover he has another side, that of an avid learner and savvy investor, a side I am happy to discover through this book.

H. J. Chammas' love of storytelling, sincerity and passion shine through this book as he relates his journey to financial security. He recounts with humility, his experiences and his personal learning opportunities, and tries to present simple templates and tools for the beginner investor.

Sadly, investing for one's own financial security is not a course taught anywhere: one learns life's hard lessons as one goes through life!! I wish I had access to his learning when I was starting out in my journey.

I can strongly recommend this book to every person (employee) starting out in life and wishing to know basics of personal financial planning. It's an easy read, with simple lessons and easy-to-apply tools, even if one chooses not to apply these tools in pursuit of the investment opportunity he personally loves and recommends: real estate.

However, the reader should of course, be aware that such investments do come associated with related risks of market price fluctuations, (or even disruptions) and one should be careful of over-exposure to a single market or location.

These tools will, regardless of the specific investment opportunity or strategy one eventually follows, help challenge and sharpen one's personal savings and investment plan.

I wish you happy reading, and fruitful investing!!

-NANDU NANDKISHORE
Former Executive Board member for Nestlé S.A and former CEO
Nestlé Nutrition.
Angel VC, Mentor, Coach, Keynote Speaker, Consultant, and
Faculty at B schools

CONTENTS

PART 3: WHERE DO I WANT TO BE?

PART 4: HOW TO GET THERE?

PREFACE

Why I Wrote This Book

I have always been worried that the majority of people throughout the world fall into the trap of working hard for money just to make ends meet. When I was a teenager, I always used to wonder why my parents were so adamant about their children seeking higher education so that they would get a secure, high-paying job. Not knowing any better back then, I used to believe that my parents connived against their children. I used to see that the parents of my wealthy classmates did things quite differently from the route my parents selected for themselves. I'll never forget the landlord of the apartment building where my parents rented then. He did not have a secure, high-paying job. On the contrary, he owned many apartment buildings, with several hundred apartments, and his job was to run his business of rental properties with a large team helping him out. He used to drive the neighbourhood in the latest-model cars, sitting in the back seat in his expensive suits, while his personal chauffeur drove the car. This was quite far from the lifestyle our family was enjoying … or not enjoying!

When I grew a bit more mature, I realized that my parents had fallen in the same trap, and not knowing any other route, they wanted their children to follow the same destiny. When I graduated and started my career in the corporate world, I found myself trapped in the rat race, running from one pay cheque to the next. I came to the realization that almost all of my work colleagues, irrespective of where they fall on the corporate ladder, had accepted their fate and were trying to make the most out of the life program that their parents handed over to them. This programming is so powerful! To an extent, I have observed exactly the same trend with many fellow colleagues I have worked with in different parts of the world, from East Asia, to Europe, to South Africa, to the Middle East, to the US. I was given the opportunity to work for a giant multinational that offered me assignments throughout the world where I had the privilege of interacting with my fellow colleagues from many corners of the world.

When the world was suffering from the financial crisis of 2008, I witnessed and heard of many people being kicked out of their jobs. I couldn't imagine how millions of people could no longer sustain their standards of living when they were put out of their jobs ... the same secure, high-paying jobs they planned to count on for the rest of their lives. It was a wakeup call for me. I wanted to finally break out of this life program and write my own program. I studied many books, attended many seminars, and sought the help of coaches and mentors who have already achieved what I want to achieve in my life. I wanted to be in control of my life and refused to be like a lab rat following a set program.

The collective advice from many books, seminars, coaches, mentors, and advisors has resulted in my achieving financial freedom in fewer years than I ever imagined. Each book I read, each seminar I attended, and each mentor I worked with revealed a slightly different perspective on how to achieve success and financial freedom through rental properties. Many of the ideas in this book have been taught by others. Several key points, however, are the result of my own experiences of success and failure. This combination of learning from others, from my successes, and from my failures was the significant part of my success journey. With this book you will get inside my head and receive years of my experience and those of many others who are more successful than I am. The years of experience from myself and many others I have learned from will be offered to you in a few hours when you read this book.

The first reason I wrote this book is *responsibility*. I felt a strongly rooted feeling of responsibility to share those things that produced great results in my life. In writing this book, I hope to share with you the lessons I have learned, both the successes and the mistakes. While my goal is to share with you my experience and the collective experiences I have amassed from different mentors, your learning will not be complete if you do not go through the action steps described in this book. Those action steps are similar to the ones my mentors pushed me to accomplish. By going through those action steps, you will start to get hands on experience and therefore supercharge your ambitions to find greater success. What you will learn from this book is not only theory, but also the tools and knowledge required to achieve financial freedom through single-family rental properties. It is time for you to take action!

The second reason I wrote this book is *purpose*. My experience in life, business, and relations has helped to identify my purpose in life, which is adding value to people's lives. I was fortunate enough to learn from many others, so I wanted to pass it forward, hoping it will help you achieve financial freedom and a better quality of life. I have coached many of my colleagues on the principles taught in this program. I experience a strong sense of purpose every time someone of the people I coached contacts me to share how the learning found in this book is producing positive financial results in their lives without the need for them to leave their jobs.

Contrary to other books and coaches, this book will help you to leverage your position as an employee to achieve financial freedom. My heart breaks when I hear about people leaving their jobs in pursuit of an entrepreneurial dream and then ending up losing their jobs and their dreams. This book will guide you in achieving financial freedom while leveraging your status as an employee. When you achieve financial freedom and you generate unearned income through rental properties to a level that exceeds your total expenses, by all means you can choose to quit your job to pursue other dreams. Or you can choose to remain in a job you love. The keyword here is *choice*. When you achieve financial freedom, you have the luxury to choose your career path. On the one hand, you might choose not to work at a job you don't like. On the other hand, you might choose to keep on working at a job that fulfils you and without any fear of being kicked out of your job.

Consider this book as two books in one: one book that will guide you on achieving financial freedom, and another book on rental property investments. I've always found it difficult to follow most books about personal finances, financial freedom, and investments. But I was destined to meet great mentors and coaches who taught me those subjects in a simple way, like talking to a five-year-old. In this book, I have attempted to convey the same methods to make it easy for anyone to grasp those subjects.

I encourage you to go through all the chapters in this book, and, most importantly, not to skip any of the action steps that you will be encouraged to do for your own benefit. It is only when you go through those action steps that the learning will become engraved in your brain. Those action steps are designed to take you closer to taking action by investing in rental properties. By the time you are ready to pull the trigger, you will feel confidence that will push you to move forward.

One final word. This book will challenge the way you have always looked at life, personal finances, investments, and real estate. It will challenge you to go out of your comfort zone and stretch your brain to apprehend new ideas, new possibilities, and new opportunities. It will invite you to a new world, which is not typically encouraged or taught by your parents, friends, colleagues, school, or the media.

So it is with a sense of responsibility and purpose that I write The Employee Millionaire: How to Use Your Day Job to Become a Millionaire with Rental Properties.

A Little Bit About Me

I was raised by a middle-class family that faced many setbacks throughout the years in a country that was inflicted with civil war in the seventies and eighties. During those years, it was not only difficult for my parents to keep us safe from war, but also tough for them to see all their savings evaporate overnight when inflation went through the roof in Lebanon over the duration of the civil war, with the Lebanese pound (also called Lebanese *lira*) lost its value from an exchange rate of three pounds to one US dollar in the early eighties to a shocking 2,500 pounds in 1992, and then stabilizing back in the mid nineties to an exchange rate of 1,500 pounds to one US dollar. My parents almost had a heart attack when their bank savings lost more than a whopping five hundred times their value. My dad would complain in sorrow that his life savings could have afforded two decent houses without any mortgage before inflation kicked in. Those same savings could afford only a small piece of furniture in the nineties. Therefore, I experienced hyperinflation in action during my childhood and teenage years.

As a consequence of this major financial disaster, both my parents worked hard from early morning to late night just to provide the necessities of life for their three children. My dad had to work two jobs for about five years, with sixteen working hours per day. I highly respect his dedication to provide the best he could for his family. I can never complain about the education, food, and clothing my parents provided us. In fact, I believe both of them were fighters in life who were able to work hard, to the best of their knowledge, to provide for their family.

Throughout the years, both my parents also lost their jobs and had to eventually settle for lower-paying jobs just to pay bills and raise their family. Not having any more savings or another source of income just made them bite the bullet and work harder and harder for less and less income. I can imagine how disgraceful this could have felt to them. During this period of our life, my parents couldn't afford to buy their children the gadgets kids and teenagers would love to have. I often visited my friends so that I could play with some of the toys and gadgets that I could never have.

When people face extreme setbacks in their life in terms of their finances, health, or security, they typically do one of three things.

- Do nothing and surrender to their new reality. Those people will expect some other people or the government to help them.
- Become slaves for money and work harder and harder for little earned income.
- Challenge their situation by finding new sources of income.

The purpose of this book is to open the eyes of employees who work hard for their earned income to new streams of income, more specifically unearned income, which can be achieved by leveraging their position of being employees.

Since I was a kid, I always wanted to become rich when I grow old. At that time of my life, I never had a strong enough "why" that made me move toward something I wanted in life. In fact, my "why" was just a fearful one of ending up like my parents who were often fighting about money. I always remember my dad telling us, "Do you think I own a money press machine?"

This book comes with accompanying worksheets and templates, which are designed to allow you implement all the lessons in this book to your own personal situation. You can download those resources from:

www.employeemillionaire.com/resources.

CHAPTER 1

What Is Your "Big Why?"

During my childhood, the topic of not having enough money when I grow old intrigued me. It led me to start creating money as early as possible in my life. When I was around seven years old, I bought Kinder Surprise Eggs, which required some assembly. It was a double joy. After I enjoyed the delicious chocolate, I proceeded with my bigger joy—opening the inside plastic container and assembling the surprise toys. Some became rare collectibles my classmates were eager to acquire. When I saw my classmates were keen to own some of the rare toys I collected, I had my seven-year-old aha moment and possibly my first real-life lesson on statistics and probability. I had the brilliant idea of selling those sought-after toys for a premium price point that would enable me to go back and buy four new Surprise Eggs. In this fashion, I could increase my probability of getting those rare collectibles toys by 400 per cent. That was my first business venture.

Lo and behold, money started pouring in. I enjoyed more and more chocolate and had more and more cash. But my excitement didn't last long. My parents started to question how I had more money than what they gave me for my daily allowance. With some investigation from their end and with the school, it appeared other parents complained to the school that their children were spending their allowances on toys.

That was the end of my first business venture. I was in trouble. I was reprimanded by both the school and my parents. After my first business died, my parents, the school, and the community all successfully managed to reprogram me to study well and seek higher grades so that I would eventually become a doctor, an engineer, or be employed with a large company and become financially secure.

When I was fourteen, my parents' finances were tighter than ever after my dad has lost his job when his employer closed. As a young teenager, I didn't want to take money from my parents anymore, so I started a new business. At that time, there was still a civil war in Lebanon, and the capital, Beirut, was divided into east and west. The Christians lived in East Beirut, whereas the Muslims lived in West Beirut. Between the two parts of the capital was a long line of high sand piles. Monitored checkpoint entrances were located at both ends. Those checkpoints were guarded, not by the national police or army, but by the militias at their respective sides of the capital. Ours was one of the few Christian families living in harmony in West Beirut. My name, Habib, allowed me to be accepted by both groups.

Then came another aha moment. I had access to both ends of the capital, so I looked into selling items not readily available in West Beirut but in demand. Eureka! I found items required by engineering students but not easily available in bookstores and other specialized stores. I started my business by coming up with a company name and logo, which were affixed on a letterhead of my creation. I created a price list, printed on my company's letterhead, with high margins of around 500 per cent. I started selling those products on my small bike, with cash on delivery terms. I was so happy with money flowing in. This lasted for a few months—until my parents saw my failing grades. My bike was taken away from me, and my business venture came to an end. I used most of the cash I generated to buy Christmas gifts for my siblings and parents a few week later. It made me proud for a short while, but then it was back to being programmed to be a good student with an ambition of seeking a high-paying job on graduation.

My life went on according to the goal of succeeding at school and getting high grades. In fact, my parents and society programmed me so well that I started my employee life during my second year at university so that I could help pay my tuition fees. By the time I graduated with my master's degree, I was the perfect employee, running from one pay cheque to the other without having any savings in my bank account. This went on for about five years. Then I had an opportunity to travel to Dubai and work with a giant multinational company. I received a relatively great package as compared to the package I got in Lebanon. With a salary that was around four times as big as my previous one, my expenses got larger and larger to pay for the new lifestyle I created for myself. Over the years, my package with the same multinational grew handsomely. I climbed the corporate ladder and was expatriated to different parts of the world, but my bank account never grew at the same rate as my income. In fact, my bank account couldn't sustain the expenses of my lifestyle for more than a few weeks if I was ever without a job.

In summary, after twenty years of being an employee, I would have been broke any day I left my job. What a pity! I was navigating through life from one pay cheque to the other without any *big why* that would act as my life's purpose.

After four years of my assignment in the Philippines (still with the same multinational company), I returned to Lebanon for the first time in three years for a four-week summer vacation. In the summer of 2008, my life started to change when my *big why* started to take shape in front of my eyes. At that time, I was in my mid thirties. I never planned to get married and build a family until I laid my eyes on the most beautiful woman I had ever met in my life. Luckily, I met her the first week of my vacation. This gave me more than three weeks to get to know her. After going out together and discovering the great personality and intellect behind the obvious beauty, I knew she was the woman I wanted to marry and build my life with. But I still couldn't reveal that to her.

My *big why* started to carry with it many related whys. As per our culture, I was supposed to own a home and have a decent salary to support my family and all the other perks that came with a good salary. In theory, I had a big salary. It was around seven to eight times the average salary I would have gotten in my home country. The perception of being employed in a senior management role overseas with one of the largest multinationals was enough, for a start, to earn me enough credibility with my girlfriend's parents to be considered as a future groom, especially since they were landlords of many properties. The bar was set high for me. I needed to be perceived as a future husband who could provide the same living standards—at least—for their beloved youngest daughter.

When I started dating Joyce (now my beloved wife), she worked for a reputable bank as a wealth manager for its premium clients. I respected the banking secrecy she agreed to for this sensitive position, but I still wanted some answers. Finally, after many attempts, I managed to get an answer for this key question among others: "What do all your wealthy clients have in common?"

Her answers were made up of a few keywords: "real estate", "businesses", and for some, "the business of real estate". By digging deeper, it became obvious that the wealthy made their money with either businesses or properties. But they retained their wealth in the form of real estate, and to be more specific, rental properties that guarantee monthly unearned income with much higher returns on their invested capital as compared to stashing their money in savings accounts with interest rates that, at best, keep up with inflation rates. I needed some time to digest this information. At that time, it was a bit too much for me to assimilate.

After my summer vacation ended, I flew back to the Philippines where I worked at that time. I felt sad as I wanted to spend more time with Joyce. Every day I spent with her reaffirmed my feelings of wanting to start a new chapter of my life with her. My trip from Lebanon to the Philippines was around seventeen hours long, including a short stop in Dubai. This gave me ample time to reflect on the great time spent with Joyce during my vacation and on my future. This was the first time I seriously thought about and meditated on the things I wanted in my life. I started drafting my *big why* list. I opened my laptop and made a bullet list of whatever came to mind. I promised myself to list the things I wanted in life without any prejudice.

What I learned during this process was that long-term thinking made the process easier. The further I looked into my future, the less prejudgment

I had on whether my ambitions were achievable. I started thinking about what I wanted my life to be like in five and even ten years. The first draft of my list included my personal and financial ambitions with a time horizon of five to ten years.

Before the plane landed in Manila, I had the first draft of my *big why* list typed. But I had no clue how or where to start. With thoughts and ideas racing inside my head in all directions, I forced myself to calm down and convinced myself that I can plan my life using the same thought process I use in my professional life. I do business planning with huge budgets for the multinational I work for, so doing my personal business plan shouldn't be any different or any more difficult.

I started to look at threads on my list and how the different points related to each other. I found that the things I wanted in life can in fact be regrouped into the following areas of life:

- Home and family
- Health and fitness
- Work, career, and finances
- Personal development and education
- Social life and relationships
- Spiritual development and life contribution

With a blink of an eye, I started to attribute each item on my list to its respective area of life. I eventually saved this list on my laptop and later in my smartphone's notes. That way it acted as my daily reminder of why I needed to change my life and finances. It was a remarkable discovery that my personal ambitions came first, before my financial ambitions. What I discovered is that my financial ambitions acted like enablers for me to achieve my personal ambitions.

Chapter 1 Action Steps

Before you proceed any further with this book, I encourage you to take as much time as you require to start thinking and drafting down the things you want in life—your *big why* list. Figure 1 is a template that will help you to create your own list. You can start with writing whatever comes to your mind, without any particular order. Then you can categorize the things you want in your own life into their respective category of areas of life. The template allows you to add as many categories as you feel may specifically apply to you. Once you populate this template with the things you want in life and their respective categorization in areas of life, I highly recommend you regroup the list according to the areas of your life. This will enable you to form a clearer picture of your *big why* list. Time invested here is time well spent as it marks the first step to creating Your Personal Business Plan.

The template in figure 1 can also be downloaded from my website www.employeemillionaire.com/resources.

Things I want in life	Areas of Life *

My "Big Why" List

Name: Date: /   /

* Areas of Life Guidelines:
• Home & Family
• Health & Fitness
• Work, Career & Finances
• Personal Development & Education
• Social Life & Relationships
• Spiritual Development and Life Contribution
• Others: Please create names for the areas of life not listed above

Figure 1—My Big Why List

The giant multinational I was working with has made the processes of both the annual business planning and the business reviews quite simple. The thought process was like a storytelling with four key questions:

1. Where Are We Now?
2. Why Are We There?
3. Where Do We Want to Be?
4. How Do We Get There?

About an hour before the plane was supposed to land, I was quite exhausted from all the thoughts in my head. I wanted to type my thoughts just to have the peace of mind that I wouldn't not forget anything. So I opened my laptop again, borrowed with pride those four business reviews questions, and typed them on a new page of the same Word document I used to write my *big why* list. My questions were as follows:

1. Where Am I Now?
2. Why Am I There?
3. Where Do I Want to Be?
4. How Do I Get There?

As soon as I read those four basic questions on my laptop screen, I started to calm down as I convinced myself that it was going to be a lot of fun to start taking note of my life's situation and creating a plan that would enable me to achieve the things I wanted in life … my *big why*.

This book is divided into four parts, where each part attempts to answer each of those questions.

PART 1

Where Am I Now?

CHAPTER 2

What Is the Current State of Your Finances?

WHY A PERSONAL FINANCIAL STATEMENT?

Reflecting back on how answers to the question "Where are we now?" in a business setup lie in its financial statement, and imagining myself running the business of my life, the answer to the question of where I am I now implied that I needed a personal financial statement.

At a first glance, the thought of a personal financial statement scared me enough. The Chicken Little in me started convincing me that it was going to be tough and time-consuming; however, having my *big why* list in front of my eyes helped overcome all fears. In fact my *big why* always acted as a strong magnet that kept on attracting me to it, closer and closer. At that time the plane was approaching Manila. I was exhausted from the long trip, but at the same time energized to resume my personal business plan. I closed my laptop and tried to take a small nap until the plane landed. I was remembering all the good times I have spent with Joyce and was looking forward to calling her as soon as I land in Manila. She was already on the top of the list of my *big why*, but I couldn't have told her that yet.

The next day, I headed back to my office, back to the treadmill, racing with all my colleagues towards the next pay cheque after a lot of money had been spent during my long summer vacation. Directly after my work, although suffering from a jet lag, I headed home with lots of energy to resume my personal business plan. But first, I had to connect with Joyce via a video call. Luckily for me, she took a day off on that Monday, so with Manila being in a time zone six hours ahead of Beirut, it was in the early afternoon for her by the time I reached home at 7 p.m. I was really missing her. During my conversation with her, after chatting about personal matters, I couldn't but ask her some questions relevant to her job as wealth manager for the bank's elite clients. I used indirect questioning techniques that may confirm my hypothesis that those wealthy individuals are sleeping on seven-digit bank accounts, non-employed, and business owners, property owners, or a combination of both.

After some hesitation from her end to shift our conversation to her professional life, she realized how eager I was to learn something about those wealthy individuals. She had to correct all my assumptions before going any further by saying at the bank they do not measure the wealth of individuals based only on the size of their bank accounts. She also advised me that many of her wealthy clients do have jobs, but they own assets that pay them unearned income in amounts exceeding their monthly expenses. This information started to confuse me, and she could feel it from the tone of my voice. Thanks to her emotional intelligence, she did not allow me to feel stupid, and she consciously reiterated by explaining how wealth is measured by financial institutions that lend money to individuals.

She explained that any bank or financial institution makes money by lending money and earning interest on this money. However, the financial institution requires reassurances that the party borrowing the money is financially stable (or in a good economic position) and has a steady income to repay the loan and its interest. The two key measures of a person's financial position are net worth and cash flow. Those two measures determine the creditworthiness of the person borrowing the money, or simply said, how likely the person will pay their debt and interest on time. Any bank or financial institution will also look at the history of previous loans payments, credit card payments, and the Debt Burden Ratio (DBR), also called Debt-to-Income Ratio (DTI), which compares an individual's debt payment to his or her overall income. Not wanting me to get overwhelmed with all those financial terms, she explained to me that once I fully understand the concepts of net worth and cash flow, the other measures of an individual creditworthiness would become relatively easy to understand.

While she was talking about all those financial terms, my brain was relating them to the business financial statements I usually manage at my job. Wanting her to feel I am still on the same page with her, I intercepted her talk, saying that I believe all of those financial terms will eventually enable us to come up with a personal financial statement. She laughed while she saw (through the camera) and heard the student coming out of me.

With her determination not to lose focus, she started explaining each of those terms. *Net worth*, she continued, is the sum of a person's *total assets*, including cash, less the sum of a person's *total liabilities*. The amount by which your assets exceed your liabilities is considered your net worth. In summary, net worth measures an individual's economic position. A negative net worth can occur if you borrow too much money compared to your assets, which may indicate that your income may fall as your debt payments rise.

Net worth tells only half the story. A lending institution will also have to look at the person's cash flow position. *Cash flow* is the sum of *total income* less *total expenses*. It measures the net amount of cash moving into and out of a person's finances. If you have a positive cash flow, it means that you earn more than you spend and that you have some money left over from that period, which will enable you to settle debts and provide a buffer against future financial challenges. On the other hand, if you have a negative net cash flow, if shows that you spent more money than you brought in, which will make the financial institution look at your *balance sheet* to determine your net worth.

Joyce wanted me to write down how those two key measures are calculated since they would take us to the next topic, a *personal financial statement.* She insisted I write them down on a piece of paper, so I wouldn't interrupt our video call.

Net Worth = [Total Assets] Less [Total Liabilities]
Cash Flow = [Total Income] Less [Total Expenses]

Any bank or financial institution will definitely examine a person's personal financial statement, which consists of two related statements:

- Balance Sheet
- Income Statement

A *balance sheet* is a statement of a person's assets and liabilities. It determines that one's net worth by subtracting total liabilities from total assets.

An *income statement* lists all a person's sources of income and all types of expenses. It determines that one's net cash flow by subtracting total expenses from total income.

Joyce requested I write down the following:

Personal Balance Sheet → Net Worth
Personal Income Statement → Cash Flow

I was already tired, but I was eager to know more. I asked her if she still had some energy to share. Luckily for me, she was excited to sharing her expertise.

PERSONAL BALANCE SHEET AND NET WORTH

She reiterated that a balance sheet determines an individual's net worth by subtracting total liabilities from total assets. She then added that those two topics could become confusing if not discussed in their thorough details and thus differentiated.

Total Assets

Joyce explained that in her experience, different individuals define assets differently. Many of her clients believed that their cars, boats, or even home furniture qualify as assets, given that they may convert into cash whenever needed. Although those may be valuable items, they usually depreciate in value over time.

Jewellery is another debatable subject. Most people classify jewels as assets, but their actual value when they are sold is equal to the amount of precious metal they carry in them, which in most cases is way less than the original price tag that included a major premium related to their design.

On the other hand, financial institutions segregate assets into two major classes, either:

- Income-producing assets, or
- Non-income producing assets.

It is the income-producing assets that count the most in determining an individual's creditworthiness. They generate cash flow to their owners and generally appreciate in value. In contrast, non-income producing assets do not generate any cash flow, but they may still appreciate in value over time.

Although what I was hearing made sense, I was at first having difficulty classifying the different asset classes into either income-producing assets or non-income-producing assets. My questions regarding more clarification on how to classify some of these assets made it clear to Joyce that she needed to go into further details. She asked me to take a piece of paper and divide it into two halves by drawing a horizontal line in the middle. She had me title the upper half as income-producing assets and the lower half as non-income-producing assets. We agreed to take each common asset and discuss whether it is income generating or not. Accordingly, each asset would be classified either as an income-producing asset or a non-income-producing asset.

At the end of a good long discussion, my notes on the paper came up to be as shown below.

Income-Producing Assets

Asset Class	Definition
Bank Accounts	Interest-bearing accounts.
Stocks	Dividends-paying stocks.
Bonds	Interest-paying bonds. This could include interest paying defined contribution plans or pension plans.
Investment Real Estate	Residential or commercial properties that are rented out to tenants.
Businesses	A business that generates income to its shareholders.
Royalties	Royalties from a business franchise or from intellectual properties (e.g. books, CDs, movies, mobile applications, online business).

Non-Income Producing Assets

Asset Class	Definition
Personal Home	Personal residential property.
Motor Vehicles	Personal cars, motorcycles, and boats.
Bank Accounts	Non-interest bearing accounts.
Stocks	Stocks that do not pay dividends.
Precious Metals, Gems, Jewellery, and Art	May preserve value, but do not pay any interest or dividends.
Receivables	Money an individual will receive in the future on non-interest-paying basis. This can include life insurance or pension plans.

While talking about assets, being a visual person, I automatically started drawing sketches that visually represented the two assets classes.

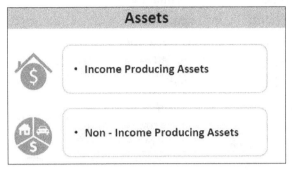

Figure 2—Assets

Total Liabilities

Liabilities are any debt or payment an individual owes to another party. It is the sum of all financial obligations for which a person is responsible and that may be satisfied out of his or her assets.

Liabilities can be classified into two types:

- Good Liability.
- Bad Liability.

Liability is no different than debt. Almost all of Joyce's wealthy clients, ones she considered to be financially smart by the size of their net worth, had good debt that far outweighed their bad debt.

People borrow from the bank so they can buy goods, services, or assets they want or need. The wealthy usually borrow from the bank to buy income-producing assets. Therefore, this debt is automatically classified as good debt. Most others carry with them the burden of large credit cards loans as well as other loans that were used towards the purchase of non-income producing assets or goods and services that are either consumable or depreciable (meaning they lose value over time).

I wanted to make sure I grasped the difference between types of debt. I repeated in my own words: "Good debt is a debt taken to purchase income-producing asset that will generate long-term income." While I was saying that, it became evident to me that good debt will increase my income-producing assets, which in turn will increase my net worth. On the other hand, I continued: "Bad debt is debt incurred to purchase things that do not generate long-term income." With Joyce's encouraging words, I managed to define the different types of debt in a simple way, and I felt a relief when I started to see the relation between good debt and income-producing assets on one hand, and between bad debt and depreciable goods and services on the other hand.

Building on what we discussed, she asked me take another new piece of paper and to divide it in two halves by drawing a horizontal line in the middle and to title the upper half Good Liability and the lower half Bad Liability. We then started to discuss our liabilities, classifying them as good or bad.

While most of the liabilities classifications were evident, the longest discussion we had was about whether a personal home mortgage is a good debt or bad debt, given that it is a non-income-producing asset. For the prudent investor and for the careful banker, any debt incurred to purchase a non-income-producing asset is a bad debt, even if the asset may appreciate in value over time, as is the case with personal residential properties.

After taking notes while engaged in this lengthy but healthy discussion, I summarized good and bad liabilities, which I've shown in the tables below.

Good Liabilities / Good Debt	
Liabilities Class	Remarks
Investment Real Estate Mortgage	Money borrowed to purchase a residential or commercial property with rental income.
Business Loan	Money borrowed to purchase equity in income- or dividend generating-business.

| Student Loans | Loan taken to pay for college education, which increases the value of an employee and raises their potential future income. |
| Other Good Debt | Money borrowed to purchase goods that can generate income. |

Bad Liabilities / Bad Debt

Liabilities Class	Remarks
Personal Home Mortgage	Money borrowed to purchase a personal home.
Credit Cards Loans	Purchases made on credit cards towards the purchase of either non-income-producing assets or goods and services that are either consumable or depreciable.
Personal Loans	Money borrowed to purchase either non-income-producing assets or goods and services that are either consumable or depreciable.
Car Loans	Money borrowed to purchase a personal car that is not used for any kind of income producing business.

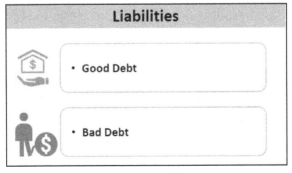

Figure 3—Liabilities

Again, I started drawing a sketch that visually represented the two types of liabilities.

Joyce took a long breath, like a marathon runner taking the last few breaths before reaching her destination. She asked me to go back to my notes where I wrote the following:

Personal Balance Sheet → Net Worth
Net Worth = [Total Assets] Less [Total Liabilities]

Joyce concluded that a personal balance sheet is nothing more than listing assets on the left side of a table, and listing liabilities on the right side.

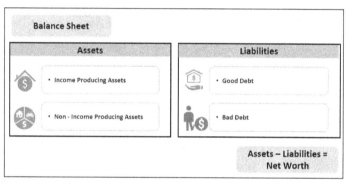

Figure 4—Balance sheet

I smiled back through the camera and thanked her. It was the first time in my life someone explained to me an important financial document in language that an average person like me could easily understand without feeling intimidated. Ever since, I have called Joyce my financial advisor. Without having to plan myself, I had started to form the first component of my *mastermind alliance.* Napoleon Hill described the mastermind alliance as the coordination of knowledge and effort in a spirit of harmony between two or more people for the attainment of a definite purpose. Later in this book, when I highlight who needs to be on your team in building your portfolio of rental properties, I will cover the principles of a mastermind alliance.

As soon as we finished our video call that evening, I started typing up on my laptop all the paper notes I had taken.

My intellectual curiosity was at its peak. I couldn't retire to bed without coming up with a balance sheet template, —according to the classifications of income-producing assets, non-income-producing assets, good liabilities, and bad liabilities. I opened a new Excel workbook on my laptop and started drafting a personal balance sheet. Finally, I came up with a personal balance sheet that I have been using ever since on a monthly basis to track the progress of my wealth-building journey.

Figure 5 below is a visual representation of the personal balance sheet. Towards the end of this chapter, I will be introducing the personal financial statement, which includes the personal balance sheet. It can be downloaded as an editable Microsoft Excel worksheet with the all the formulas from my website www.employeemillionaire.com/resources.

As soon as I created a file that can automatically compute my assets, liabilities, and net worth, I was excited to start evaluating where I was financially at the time.

It was already approaching midnight, and my body did not have enough rest after a long trip followed by a long day at the office. I convinced myself to go to bed. The next day after, leaving the office, I could start looking at my assets and liabilities.

I put myself to bed, but my brain was thinking all night long about my assets, realizing that most of the few assets I owned were non-income-producing assets. Then it was easy to also realize that my liabilities were a series of one bad debt after the other. It took me a few hours to get to sleep. By then, I was brain dead and fell asleep.

PERSONAL BALANCE SHEET			
ASSETS		LIABILITIES	
INCOME PRODUCING ASSETS		GOOD LIABILITIES / GOOD DEBT	
Bank Accounts (Interest Paying)		Investment Real Estate Mortgages	
Stocks (Dividends Paying)		Business Loans	
Bonds		Student Loans	
Investment Real Estate		Other Good Debt	
Net Business Value		Other Good Debt	
Royalties		Other Good Debt	
Other Income Producing Assets		Other Good Debt	
INCOME PRODUCING ASSETS SUBTOTAL	-	GOOD LIABILITIES / GOOD DEBT SUBTOTAL	-
NON-INCOME PRODUCING ASSETS		BAD LIABILITIES / BAD DEBT	
Personal Real Estate		Personal Home Mortgage	
Motor Vehicles		Motor Vehicles Loans	
Bank Accounts (Non Interest Paying)		Credit Cards Loans	
Stocks (Non Dividends Paying)		Personal Loans	
Precious Metals, Gems, Jewelry, and Art		Other Bad Debt	
Receivables		Other Bad Debt	
Other Non-Performing Asset		Other Bad Debt	
NON-INCOME PRODUCING ASSETS SUBTOTAL	-	BAD LIABILITIES / BAD DEBT SUBTOTAL	-
		TOTAL LIABIITIES	-
TOTAL ASSETS	-	NET WORTH	-

Figure 5—Personal balance sheet

I woke up early the next morning, after another night with few hours of sleep. I prepared my cappuccino with double shot espresso and ran to the office. After a long day in the office, I was relieved that another day had passed, putting me another day closer to my next pay cheque.

I wanted to catch up with Joyce, but with six hours difference, she was still in her office at the bank. This gave me a few hours to start working on my personal balance sheet. I opened the spreadsheet template (figure 5) that I had developed and started to list my few assets and my staggering liabilities. This was simple enough for me. I just had to go through my latest bank statements, credit card statements, and loan statements. I also had to make an online search for the fair market value of the assets I owned. In less than two hours, I was finally able to take clear stock of my assets and liabilities.

I was ashamed to look at my personal balance sheet and evaluate it in an objective manner like my financial advisor, Joyce, taught me to do. After so many years of being employed for a decent income, I had very few assets, all non-income-producing assets, consisting of a depreciating car and a defined contribution plan that I could receive only whenever I leave my job. On the other hand, all my liabilities consisted of bad debt towards a car loan, personal loans taken for vacations and leisure, and credit cards loans. All my liabilities were incurred to purchase goods that have already depreciated in value and other consumables and services that do not have any value any more.

My net worth was too small to that extent that if I ever stop working, I couldn't survive for more than a few weeks.

I needed some more time to reflect on my assets, liabilities, and net worth. I was not ready to share my discovery of my own state of affairs if inquired by Joyce on our video call later in the evening.

While waiting until about midnight so that Joyce would be back home from work (given the six-hour difference), I went online to run a search on the world's richest people, so that I could study and emulate them. The top of the list on the search engine was Forbes's World's Billionaires 2008 list. Interestingly, the only filter and measure was their net worth, which evidently had to be over a billion dollars to go on this list. I saved this list on my laptop, and was always referring to it in my quest for self-made billionaires.

As the time approached midnight, my eyes were tired from my online research. I was happy when I saw Joyce was online. I waited a bit and was excited to see a message from her, inviting me to go live on a video call. By the time we had chatted about personal matters, it was past midnight, and I was brain dead. I needed to sleep. On that night, it became evident to me that I could resume our discussion on personal financial statements only during the weekends, when we could meet at a time convenient to both of us.

The week went by with daily messages, phone calls, and short video calls. During this same week, I started reading my first-ever book on personal finances. I wanted to study and research the rich and the wealthy. My quest was specific: I wanted to study only the self-made millionaires and billionaires so that I could understand and learn how they managed to break out from being poor or middle class to become wealthy and make it on the billionaire list. Starting that week, I became a ferocious reader. I have read over three hundred books and still counting over a period of seven years. My library was not limited to paper books but included e-books and audiobooks. My audiobooks were most pleasurable during the heavy traffic of Manila. I believe I was the only person in the Philippines who was enjoying the traffic. Sometimes I would reach my destination and not set a foot out of the car until I'd completed a section of the audiobook. I never wanted to interrupt my learning.

What I will be sharing throughout this book is not limited only to learning from the books I have devoured, but most importantly how I have put that learning into practice, both to earn my first million dollars and to become financially free.

Personal Income Statement and Cash Flow

The weekend had approached. I was looking forward to continuing my education on income statements and cash flow. That Saturday, we started our video call around 6 p.m., which was noon for Joyce. I planned it at that time to have ample time not only to get closer to Joyce, but also to pick her brains and satisfy my hunger to learn more about personal finances.

After spending quality time discussing personal matters, I referred back to our previous weekend discussion on personal balance sheets. I had shared with her how much this meant to me and that I had started reading books and online articles on personal finance. When she sensed my excitement, she felt proud to be my key motivator in learning more about getting my personal finances in order. She asked if I still had my notes where I had written

Personal Income Statement $\rightarrow$ Cash Flow
Cash Flow = [Total Income] Less [Total Expenses]

When she heard that I carried on me not only the handwritten notes but that I had typed those notes on my laptop to organize my learning, she was excited to carry on.

She restated that an income statement determines an individual's net cash flow by subtracting total expenses from total income.

Total Income

While being cautious not to go into my personal finances, she asked me to share with her the source of my income. I explained that my only source of income was my salary.

Her professional experience at the bank had made her conclude that most employees depend on earned income as their primary source of income, with only a few of them having other sources of income like interest on their saving accounts. Conversely, her prime clients depended primarily on unearned income, which could be any combination of either passive income or portfolio income. Some of those prime clients still had income derived from earned income. My eyes and ears were wide open. I asked her to explain as if she was talking to a five-year-old kid. She laughed and asked me to make a note of the two major sources of income:

- Earned Income
- Unearned Income
  - o   Passive Income
  - o   Portfolio Income

While she didn't have much to say about earned income (since I was an employee and my salary was my primary source of income), she pointed out that the key to wealth is through passive income, portfolio income, or both. She shared that someone with unearned income can still settle debts and other commitments in the event of leaving his or her job for whatever reason.

I had to interrupt to ask her to shed more light on passive income and portfolio income. She continued that both types of income are generated from income-producing assets. She paused to give me time to relate the subject of income-producing assets to the topic of passive and portfolio incomes. She then suggested we take a step backward and discuss each type of income separately, starting with earned income since it is the source of income of almost every adult, at least for part of their life.

Earned Income

Simply said, earned income is money derived from paid work. It can be derived from working for someone or from a company for an agreed amount of pay or from working for oneself by running a small business that depends on the person being there.

For employees, earned income commonly includes wages, salaries, tips, and other employee pay.

For the self-employed, it is their net earnings. Joyce further explained that lawyers, doctors, or small businesses usually require the business owner to be present for the business to generate income. Hence, the term *self-employed*. So although those individuals may be their own bosses, they still work for a wage for their services or for an income by selling their products. Self-employed persons will still have to pay rent for the location of their business as well as other running expenses. Therefore their net earnings, computed by deducting their expenses from their gross income, becomes their earned income.

Earned income is the most taxed income as compared to unearned income. In most countries, the employer has to deduct the relevant income taxes and pay them to the government even before the employee gets paid. But self-employed also need to pay the government income taxes.

While talking about earned income, I couldn't resist my habit of drawing sketches. This one visually represents an employee or a self-employed person working hard for earned income.

Figure 6—Earned income

Unearned Income

The key to wealth is unearned income, whether passive income, portfolio income, or a combination of both. Before I asked Joyce to take it slowly, she suggested we list sources of income that fall under either passive or portfolio income. In the blink of an eye, like a student eager to take notes so as not to miss a detail, I took my pen and started to write.

- Passive Income
    - o Real Estate
    - o Business
- Portfolio Income
    - o Interest
    - o Dividends
    - o Royalties

Before we went any further, Joyce asked me to go back to my previous notes where we listed income-producing assets. I found my handwritten notes (so I wouldn't have to open it on my laptop and miss seeing Joyce on my screen) and waved them at the camera so she could see.

She asked me to read and reflect on the list of income-producing assets, then tested my understanding by asking me about the relationship between income-producing assets and unearned income. Like a proud student, I thought that even a five-year-old could conclude that income-producing assets are the sources of either passive or portfolio income.

She then suggested we create a table with two columns, one listing the different sources of passive and portfolio incomes and the other one listing the respective income-producing assets relevant to each of the incomes.

Unearned Income	Income-Producing Asset
Real Estate	Investment Real Estate
Business	Business
Interest	Bank Accounts (Interest-Paying)
	Bonds
Dividends	Stocks (Dividends-Paying)
Royalties	Royalties from a business franchise or from intellectual properties

With excitement, I told her that I understood why the key to wealth is unearned income. Income-producing assets work for the individual by generating income. I assertively declared that I needed to start accumulating income-producing assets that would work for me to generate unearned income.

As soon as I understood unearned income, I drew a sketch of someone having unearned income pour in while he slept. He did not have to work for money. Instead, the income-producing assets worked hard for him.

Figure 7—Unearned income

With a big smile on her face, Joyce confirmed that her wealthy prime clients follow the same routes.

She said her dad always reminds her that while it is important for individuals to focus on their income, it is also important for them to focus on how much they spend and keep. She suggested that we discuss an individual's expenses.

Total Expenses

Expenses may be classified as either essential or discretionary spending. Households incur two types of expenses. Some expenses are either enforced by law (such as income taxes and health insurance) or are essential to keeping the household running (such as personal housing, food and clothing, and transportation costs). These expenses are *essential* expenses, as the income earner does not have the option of not paying them without incurring consequences. Simply said, such expenses are essential for survival and therefore may be defined as *needs*.

On the other hand, *discretionary* expenses are optional expenses that are not necessary to run a household. In other words, the income earner can pay for these goods or services at his or her own discretion. Discretionary expenses are most often defined as things that are "wants" rather than "needs".

Joyce explained that although the definitions are clear, the concept of what is discretionary is subjective and may differ considerably among individuals. For some households, what may be classified as an essential expense in good times might be considered a discretionary expense in tough times. As an example, although a car is required for transportation, which is necessary, a household might decide to sell the car and use public transport instead to get out from a car loan.

We listed different possible expenses. I waved to the camera with my pen to indicate I was ready to start taking notes.

Expense Type
Income taxes
Food and clothing
Medical insurance

Property taxes / real estate taxes for personal home
Home mortgage or rent
Utilities
Personal home maintenance
Personal home insurance
Personal home household improvements
Student loan payments
Charity
Travel and leisure
Credit card payments
Car loan payments
Personal loan payments

When I saw the list in front of my eye, it was relatively straightforward to categorize expenses such as taxes, home mortgage, rent, utilities, home maintenance, insurance, education, food and clothing under essential expenses. Some expenses like household improvements, charity, travel and leisure were easily categorized as discretionary expenses. The remaining items on the list, which consisted of credit cards and other loans payments, required detailed examination to evaluate whether the items purchased were discretionary or essential.

On my notes I drew a small sketch that looked like this.

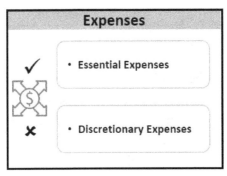

Figure 8—Expenses

Cash Flow

Joyce said that cash flow can be computed by deducting total expenses from total income. A personal income statement is nothing more than a statement that lists all income sources on one side and all expense types on the other side. She had me divide a piece of paper in half by drawing a horizontal line in the middle. The upper part would list income sources, and the lower part was to list types of expenses. At the bottom of the paper, net cash flow would be noted.

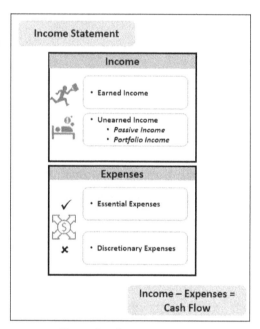

Figure 9—Income statement

I directly drew the relationship with the business profit and loss statements, at least in terms of what a personal income statement might look like. I committed to myself to come up with a template that would enable me to evaluate how my cash flows.

After we concluded my second lesson, related to my personal income statement, we came back to personal matters. On that day, I decided to visit Joyce once every three to five weeks, in spite of the long flight of seventeen hours, including a short stopover. I thought of that expense as an investment in my personal relationship. I didn't believe we could get to know each other just through messaging, daily calls, and weekly video calls. To me, the money I spent on those air tickets was money well spent in winning her heart and having her say yes when I proposed to her on New Year's Eve of the following year. Starting a family with Joyce was at the top of my *big why* list. I still remind her that she made me go around the world every few weeks to spend a good four days with her on each trip.

On that night, after we ended our video call, in spite of my wanting to go out for a drink with my friends, I wanted to control my expenses so I could afford to pay for my trips back home every three weeks, so I kept my laptop open and directly transferred my handwritten notes into my digital notes. I couldn't put my head on my pillow before I came up with a personal income statement template.

Figure 10 below is a personal income statement. It would be part of my personal financial statement. Towards the end of this chapter, I will introduce the personal financial statement, which can be downloaded in an editable Microsoft Excel worksheet with the all the formulas from my website www.employeemillionaire.com/resources.

The next day was a bright Sunday morning. I rewarded myself with a few hours' sunbathing at the pool in the condominium tower where I lived. I planned on that day to start filling up my personal income statement. Although I was not the kind of person who kept receipts for everything I spent money on, I used to charge almost all my expenses on my credit card. This made it easier to take the last three months of my credit card statements and calculate an average for each kind of expense. This enabled me to come up with my first personal income statement. In the following months, it became a habit to take each month's bank statement and list my expenses on a monthly personal income statement.

PERSONAL INCOME STATEMENT	
INCOME	
Earned Income	
Wages, Salaries, Tips	
Net Earnings from Self-Employment	
Earned Total	-
Passive Income	
Net Income from Investment Real Estate	
Net Income from Business	
Passive Total	-
Portfolio Income	
Interest	
Dividends	
Royalties	
Portfolio Total	-
TOTAL INCOME	-
EXPENSES	
Expenses	
Income Taxes	
Property Taxes / Real Estate Taxes for Personal Home	
Home Mortgage or Rent	
Utilities	
Personal Home Maintenance	
Personal Home Insurance	
Personal Home Household Improvements	
Medical Insurance	
Food and Clothing	
Charity	
Travel and Leisure	
Credit Cards Payments	
Car Loans Payments	
Personal Loans Payments	
Student Loans Payments	
Other Expenses	
TOTAL EXPENSES	-
NET MONTHLY CASH FLOW	-

Figure 10—Personal income statement sheet

During the following week, during one of our daily phone calls, Joyce reminded me that a personal financial statement consists of both the personal balance sheet and the personal income statement. She wanted to make sure I understand that seeing both statements next to each other—or even better, on the same page—would allow me to make a proper analysis of my financial situation.

Putting It All Together: The Personal Financial Statement

At that stage, having filled up both my personal balance sheet and my personal income statement, and having developed templates for each separately, it was an easy task for me to merge both templates into one statement, my personal financial statement.

Figure 11 is a simplified visual representation of a personal financial statement.

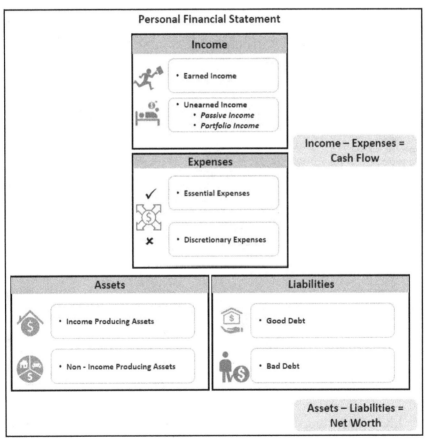

Figure 11—Personal financial statement

Figure 12 represents the full version of the personal financial statement. It can be downloaded in a Microsoft Excel format with all the formulas from my website www.employeemillionaire.com/resources.

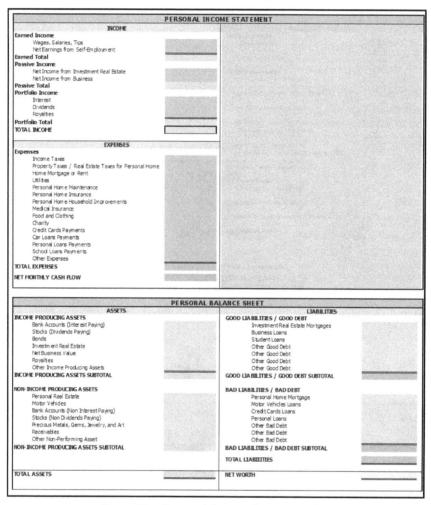

Figure 12—Personal financial statement sheet

I have intentionally covered the top right part of figure 12, which includes the financial KPIs dashboard. This will be the focus of the next chapter.

The moment I saw both statements together, the numbers started to tell me stories about my financial health. In fact, the more I started to make relations between the statements, the more indicators I developed that enabled me to evaluate my financial health. I referred to them as my financial KPIs—Key Performance Indicators. My financial KPIs started to act as my monthly dashboard on my road to wealth. In a fashion similar to the way a car's dashboard enables a driver to receive messages related to the car's performance, speed, and risks of failures, my financial KPIs dashboard enabled me to track the progress of my personal business plan.

Chapter Two Action Steps

Now it's time for you to fill up your monthly financial statements. I encourage you to complete six different statements for the previous six months. This span of time will give you a clearer picture of your financial situation. Please do not move to Part 2 of this book yet, where I will guide you on analysing those financial statements. By doing this exercise first, you will develop the habit of filling up monthly financial statements, but most importantly, you will internalize all the learning of this chapter.

The personal financial statement can be downloaded from my website www.employeemillionaire.com/resources in an editable Microsoft Excel format.

PART 2

Why Am I Here?

CHAPTER 3

The Financial KPIs Dashboard

DEVELOPING THE HABIT OF FILLING A PERSONAL FINANCIAL STATEMENT

This part of the book puts you in front of a smart mirror, one equipped with a brain scanner. It allows you to view not only to your outer reflection, but also a reflection of your inner thoughts and beliefs.

Once you start objectively analysing your current financial situation and then ask yourself daring questions, you will begin forming clear insights about your financial health, which will enable you to objectively answer the question Why am I there?

Once I filled out my personal financial statement, I was shocked to see what the numbers were telling me. I was in a situation where I had no unearned income, lots of discretionary expenses, negative cash flow, no income-producing assets, and worst of all, I was incurring more and more bad debt just to sponsor my discretionary expenses. I was headed for financial ruin.

Before taking inventory of my financial situation, although I might have felt something in my finances was going wrong, my brain never allowed me to see the real picture. This was the first stage of my financial competence: I was unconsciously incompetent.

When I completed my personal financial statements, the numbers told me a story about my financial situation. At this stage I was consciously incompetent. I was interpreting the figures in different ways and often made a wrong analysis.

The financial KPIs dashboard enabled me to clearly analyse my situation and form an objective picture of my financial situation. This right analysis of the numbers enabled me to progress to being consciously competent.

With the habit of going through the monthly exercise of looking at my financial situation, I was able to make wise decisions on how and where I wanted to spend my money. I was in control. Finally, I reached the level of unconscious competence. This is the aim of part two of this book. I would like to show you the path that will allow you to reach a level where you will be in full control of your financial situation. From this stage onward, I was able to define clear objectives for my financial situation and create a plan for myself on how to reach those objectives. It is a great feeling to know you are in control.

MY FINANCIAL KPIs DASHBOARD

My personal financial statement made me think about the key financial performance indicators discussed in this section. Eventually, I included those financial KPIs in a dashboard format in the same template of my personal financial statement. This enabled me to measure the state of my financial performance every month by just looking at one single page. I have developed the habit of filling up my personal financial statement on a monthly basis in less than an hour.

My financial KPIs dashboard allowed me to carefully examine the following areas of my finances:

A. Income Profile
B. Expenses Profile
C. Net Cash Flow
D. Assets Profile

E. Liabilities Profile
F. Net Worth
G. How Wealthy I Am

Let's go through each of those financial KPIs and measure how they will impact the financial status of any individual.

A—Income Profile

In the financial KPIs dashboard, the income profile requires you to answer two main questions:

- What is the percentage of my earned income to total income?
- What is the percentage of my unearned income to total income?

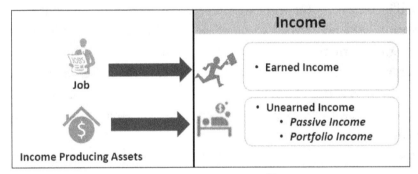

Figure 13—Income profile

Measured as per cent of earned income, the question What is the percentage of my earned income to total income? evaluates how much you work for money. In other words, what this KPI measures is how much of your total income is derived from earned income. It is computed by dividing earned income over total income.

Whenever you start to accumulate income-producing assets that will generate passive and portfolio income, the percentage of earned income contribution to total income will go down progressively since unearned income contribution to total income starts to increase at the same rate.

Inversely, per cent of unearned income helps you to answer the question What is the percentage of my unearned income to total income? This KPI measures how your money works for you. It measures the contribution of unearned income to total income in percentage. It is computed by dividing the sum of passive and portfolio incomes over total income.

On the road to wealth, as you accumulate more income-producing assets, the contribution of unearned income to total income will increase healthily over time. If you are serious about becoming financially free, you will need to keep on increasing your unearned income to a level that exceeds your total expenses.

Let's consider an example of a person called Bob, who is employed and earns a monthly income of $2,000. Before starting to invest, Bob was depending only on earned income, so his earned income contribution to total income is at 100 per cent. After reading some books on real estate investment, Bob decided to purchase rental properties. With careful investment criteria, which I cover later, he found rental properties that each will generate $200 per month in net cash flow after all expenses including mortgage have been paid. Throughout the process, Bob is still employed in the same company and for the same monthly earned income of $2,000. With each new rental property he buys, Bob will generate an incremental $200 of unearned income. Over time, sticking to the same model, Bob can achieve $2,000 of unearned income when he owns ten similar rental properties. At this stage, his total unearned income will increase to $4,000, and the contribution of unearned income to total income will increase to 50 per cent. If he continues with this same investment model, his unearned income contribution to total income will exceed that of earned income from the eleventh property onward.

Figure 14 below shows the evolution of Bob's unearned income with each rental property added to his portfolio. Figure 15 shows the same data in percentages.

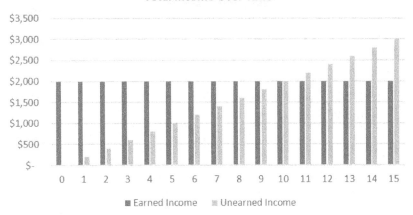

Figure 14—Evolution of unearned income with additional investments in income-producing assets

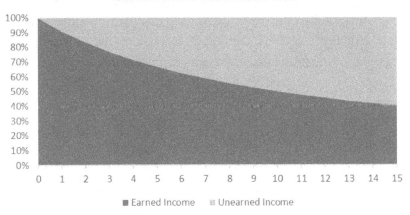

Figure 15—Evolution of unearned income in per cent with additional investments in income-producing assets

B—Expenses Profile

Any bank or financial institution that examines my creditworthiness will look at answers for the following questions:

How much do I pay for income taxes?
How much do I pay for housing?
How much do I pay for discretionary expenses?
How much do I pay for loans?

How much do I pay for income taxes?

According to Benjamin Franklin, "In this world nothing can be said to be certain, except death and taxes." This book is not intended to cover the topic of income taxes, which can be referred to in much literature and many books according to the country where you live. My simple advice is for you to understand how much you do pay in income taxes and to keep track of how much it contributes to your total income. Over time, when you start to accumulate income-producing assets, which will in turn start generating unearned income, you will experience a decline in the income taxes as a percentage to total income. The reason is due to the tax advantages of unearned income.

Certain parts of the world like the UAE and other GGC countries are still tax free on earned income; however, the income tax is already being discussed by those governments, and it might be implemented sooner rather than later.

In his book *Tax-Free Wealth*, Tom Wheelwright eloquently explains how the tax laws work. He shows how the tax law is meant to help us, not hurt us. He clarifies how the tax law is a series of financial incentives for entrepreneurs and investors. Therefore, taxes can be drastically reduced in a legal manner. That book explains how earned income is the highest taxed, whereas unearned income, generated from income-producing assets, is the least taxed. In my opinion, it is a must-read book for those who are serious about growing their wealth while reducing taxes in a legal manner.

How much do I pay for housing?

People love to live in big houses and in houses located in rich neighbourhoods. For most, it is a projection of an individual's wealth, and a lot of people like to be perceived as financially capable of affording to rent or own a good-looking house in a high-end neighbourhood. In fact, who doesn't like big, good-looking houses? But a prudent person may want to keep the amount he or she pays on a personal home, be it a mortgage or a rent, to a maximum of a third of total income.

This KPI is computed by dividing total housing expenses over total income, where total housing expenses is the sum of real estate taxes for personal home, home mortgage or rent, utilities, personal home maintenance, personal home insurance, and personal home household improvements.

In my several discussions with human resource directors of large corporations in different parts of the world, whenever I asked for guidance on how much of an employee's income should be allocated to housing, the answer was always consistent at a maximum of one third of the individual's income. According to those HR directors, the higher an employee's income, the better and larger house that one can afford. If someone wishes to live in a better or larger home, their primary objective will be to increase their total income so that the absolute value of the one third housing allowance can become bigger to afford the more expensive personal residence.

How Much Do I Pay for Discretionary Expenses?

As discussed in chapter 2, discretionary expenses are optional expenses that are not necessary for survival, and hence referred to as discretionary. This KPI is computed by dividing discretionary expenses over total income.

During my five-year assignment in the Philippines, I met a Lebanese-American businessman who lived most of his life in Asia, between China and Philippines. He was in the business of producing clothes and garments in China and the Philippines and exporting them to the US. He was also a landlord to many residential and commercial properties in the Philippines, Singapore, Hong Kong, Dubai, UK, and the US. He was well connected in the Philippines to influential people. His employees and business partners treated him and respected him like a father figure, so everyone called him Papa Joe.

Papa Joe is a self-made wealthy businessman and real estate investor who started from humble beginnings. With all the money he has, he lives in a fine home, like any other middle class person would own or rent. Due to his health conditions, he had a personal driver and a personal nurse working for him around the clock. His Type 1 diabetes obliged him to take frequent insulin shots. Therefore, a nurse was important to keep him company. I was lucky that our paths crossed on many unrelated occasions through some common acquaintances. Over time, I was approaching him with the intention of learning from him. When he saw my passion for learning, he agreed to mentor me. At a later stage, he shared with me that I reminded him of himself when he first started to change his life. Saturdays used to be days when he could dedicate some time to coaching and mentoring me, as long as I abided by two conditions: I had to book his time at least one week in advance, and I worked on any assignment he might give without any expectation in return. I didn't blink an eye and immediately agreed to his rules.

Saturday became a super-busy day for me. It was dedicated to my financial education and eventually to managing my investments. I needed to spend the mornings with Papa Joe in person in his office. The afternoons I spent with Joyce on video calls. Although at times it felt hectic, the benefits way outweighed the sacrifices.

One of Papa Joe's first lessons was that I need to study my current financial situation before I can set financial objectives for my life. This lesson was in line with what Joyce was sharing with me from her experience at the bank. When Papa Joe saw that I had a good idea about personal financial statements, it encouraged him to invest more time on my financial education. He gave me many insights about the Chinese culture, especially when it comes to personal finances. Being frugal on how you spend your money is a prerequisite for saving money that can be invested in the future on income-producing assets. His advice was never to spend more than 10 per cent of my total income on discretionary expenses. For him, this was a wise action he undertook in his early days to build his wealth from being poor to become a wealthy person.

To elaborate on this point, Papa Joe said that people like to reward themselves with spending on goods and services that might have a sentimental value but with a depreciating financial value or even zero financial value. His rule of thumb was to pay first the essential expenses, and then attempt to keep discretionary expenses to a maximum of 10 per cent of total income in the wealth building process. He insisted that I focus on increasing my unearned income. As my total income increased, the absolute value of the 10 per cent allocated to discretionary expenses would increase. Then I could afford to enjoy spending on more goods and services that are non-essential.

On that day, Papa Joe suggested we go have a coffee in a nearby coffee shop. Although his driver could have taken us, Papa Joe asked me to drive him over there. We walked to the parking lot, and I unlocked the doors of my BMW. As we entered the car, he sat next me and saw the Rolex watch on my right wrist. To divert my attention from his real intentions, he smiled and asked me if all left-handed people wear their watches on their right wrists. I said that I believed so and explained that it's more comfortable to wear my watch on the hand I don't use for writing. Then he ridiculed me, saying that he would not be surprised if I was incurring bad debt, like car loans and personal loans to pay for my car, watch, and lifestyle. He continued that he bet that my personal income statement runs on a negative cash flow. Borrowing money to spend on the appearances of wealth was not wise at all and an extreme case of discretionary expenses. He told me that this kind of spending is what brings most middle class people under water.

Papa Joe did not give a name to this type of discretionary spending on the appearance of wealth. From my eventual research on this subject, I came across with term *conspicuous consumption*, which is defined in Wikipedia as follows:

> Conspicuous consumption is the spending of money on and the acquiring of luxury goods and services to publicly display economic power—of the income or of

the accumulated wealth of the buyer. To the conspicuous consumer, such a public display of discretionary economic power is a means of either attaining or maintaining a given social status.

Papa Joe told me that many of his wealthy friends and business partners do not purchase luxury goods to display wealth, and that in the minor cases when they do purchase them, they make sure their income-producing assets can afford to buy such goods.

How much do I pay for loans?

The topic of how much of total income is spent on loans will be covered later in chapter 8.

C—Net Cash Flow

During one of my video calls with Joyce, she shared with me a story about her dad. Whenever he knows one of his family members or friends got a raise, he always asks them either of those two questions: "How much money do you keep?" or "When the end of the month approaches, do you end up with more month at the end of your money or more money at the end of the month?" Those two questions were so enlightening for me. In her dad's opinion, people too often are focused on how much money they make. As a consequence, they start to spend more to pay for more lavish lifestyles, and they lose control of how much money they keep.

I reflected on her dad's advice and came to realize that although my income kept on increasing with time, I never managed to save any money. It just meant that my expenses increased in parallel. I never focused on my net cash flow. What a mistake!

In one of my Saturday meetings with Papa Joe, he gave me my first assignment, which was to complete my monthly personal income statements over the last six months. He gave me a one-week deadline, which meant I had to be ready the following Saturday. He warned me not to come with any excuse for missing the due date. He raised his eyebrow and told me that six months' bank statements can always be fetched from online banking in case I had discarded my monthly bank statements. He told me to report back to him a story of my net cash flow by explaining to him the following:

- Monthly income
- Monthly expenses
- How much money do I keep?

What a coincidence, his request came just a few weeks after I had worked on a template for a personal financial statement with a financial KPIs dashboard. At the time of his request, I had already filled in my third monthly income statement, which made it easier for me to go for the three remaining months.

The following Saturday, I wanted to impress Papa Joe with my personal income statement template. Although he was content with me completing my assignment and working on a template, he answered me that the story behind the numbers is more important than the numbers themselves. When he was looking at my monthly statements, his face frowned. He paused, then asked me to share with him the story the numbers in my financial statements were telling. He was specific in his request for me to start with my net cash flow first, and from there I could explain my income and expenses.

Knowing that my net cash flow was averaging a negative number, with three months out of six where I barely made it to zero, I felt the same kind of shame I used to feel whenever I failed an exam during school days. I knew in advance where I was heading in this discussion. I took a deep breath to gather my composure and started to explain that my net cash flow was mostly negative, which means that I was spending much more than my income. Seeing the intimidating look on his face, I admitted that it was a disaster in the making since I might either be depleting my assets or increasing my liabilities to pay for my expenses.

Before allowing him to squeeze me into a corner, I confessed that I needed to give serious consideration to my expenses by objectively and pragmatically scrutinizing each expense to determine whether it was an essential expense or a discretionary expense, and I needed to take direct action to limit my discretionary expenses to a maximum of 10 per cent, or even lower, at least for the short term, until this KPI turned positive. With those concluding words, I saw his face becoming more relaxed. He asked me to explain to him what the story would be like if my net cash flow was positive.

I explained that if my net cash flow had been positive, it would have been a sign of a healthy financial position. The higher the percentage the better. I promised to be a more responsible person who would seek to achieve a positive net cash flow by both increasing total income and decreasing total expenses. To achieve this, I committed to evaluate my expenses with an action plan to reduce my discretionary expenses.

Papa Joe sat in silence for a moment, which felt to me like ages. He wanted to share with me some wisdom from the Chinese culture. He told me that the People's Republic of China is sometimes unofficially referred to as "the frugal republic". He reiterated that saving is a habit that's deeply rooted in the Chinese culture. The emperors and the royal families were no different. They often set good examples of frugal living. He shared a story from the Tang Dynasty, where Emperor Xuanzong said to his son, Prince Suzong: "Blessings should not be squandered! The good fortune we have in life should be treasured." Papa Joe continued to stress that we should cherish what we have and not carelessly waste it. He told me that if I manage to live by those virtues, they can guide me to develop good habits. He recommended that I limit my discretionary expenses to a maximum of 10 per cent and plan to save a minimum of 30 per cent of my total income.

Papa Joe was a great communicator. He always managed to relay information and lessons by telling stories from both the past and the present. He explained that in our current modern era, both the poor and middle class have a scarcity mentality. Their primary objective is either day-to-day survival or at best seeking comfort. As a consequence, they end up incurring liabilities to pay for the goods and services that provide them with instant gratification.

I directly related those words to my own situation. Although I had a high-paying job, my mentality and financial discipline were no different than the poor class.

Papa Joe explained that the rich, on the other hand, have an abundance mentality. They seek financial freedom. They have patience and have developed the discipline of delayed gratification. They will sacrifice short term and then reap the rewards in the long term. They focus on controlling their expenses in the short term so that they invest their savings in income-producing assets that in turn will allow them to enjoy more things later in life.

When he continued, he explained that frugality is only half of the story. I enthusiastically asked about the second half of the story. He chuckled and said: "It is what a person will do with the saved money that will make a big difference in his or her finances." Papa Joe was not a religious person, but he used to quote some stories from the Bible to make his point. He told me that even the Bible speaks about saving and investing, and then shared a quote that says: "The plans of the diligent lead to profit as surely as haste leads to poverty." (Proverbs 21:5)

He explained that money saved monthly as a result of a positive net cash flow can either go into non-income-producing assets or income-producing assets. It is the latter that will accelerate the path to wealth.

On that day, I drew a sketch that helped me visualize his advice. It looked like the one below.

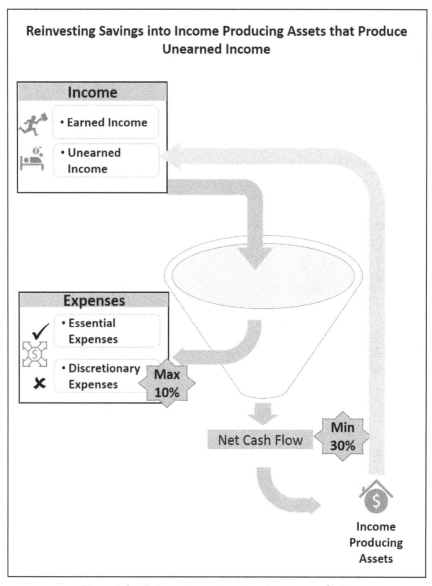

*Figure 16—Reinvesting savings into income-producing
assets that produce unearned income*

D—Assets Profile

One of the primary lessons that Joyce taught me from her experience as a wealth manager was that the wealthy keep on accumulating more and more income-producing assets. Those assets generate for them monthly, quarterly, or annual unearned income. The wealthy always ask themselves, What is the return on my invested capital? This is commonly referred to as ROI (return on investment). It is measured in percentage, and it is computed by dividing the unearned income generated from those assets over the capital invested from the investor's own funds.

The higher the unearned income and the lower the invested capital, the higher is the return on investment. The wise investor will carefully select an asset based on its ROI before acquiring it. The rule of thumb is that ROI from assets should beat inflation and the interest paid on saving accounts as a bare minimum.

Papa Joe told me that he earns double-digit returns on his investments and that it is common to get a return of 15 per cent, 25 per cent, 50 per cent, and even over 100 per cent. In one of our Saturday sessions, he informed that some assets could even deliver an infinite ROI. With those numbers, he got my attention. He explained that an infinite ROI is unearned income generated from an asset that was acquired with zero invested capital from the investor's own funds. Because I was eager to become wealthy overnight, I directly asked him to teach me how I can get infinite ROIs. He laughed and replied that this brings us the topic of *leverage*, or debt.

He again started with a quote from the book of Matthew in the Bible. The illustration talks about a man who entrusted his possessions to three of his slaves before going on a journey. To one he gave five talents, to another two, and to another one, each according to his own ability. After a long time, the master of those slaves came and settled accounts with them. Two of his slaves, the one who received five talents and the one who received two talents, returned double the amount of talents to their master. This pleased him, so he put both slaves in charge of many things. The third slave, who had received the one talent, came up and returned the same talent to his master, informing him that he dug a hole in the ground and hid the talent as he was afraid of losing it. His master was unpleased and told his slave the he could have put his money in the bank, and on his arrival he would have received his money back with interest. (Matthew 25:14–27)

While he was answering a business call, I took my notepad and drew the below sketch that visually explained to me how income-producing assets can work hard to produce unearned income.

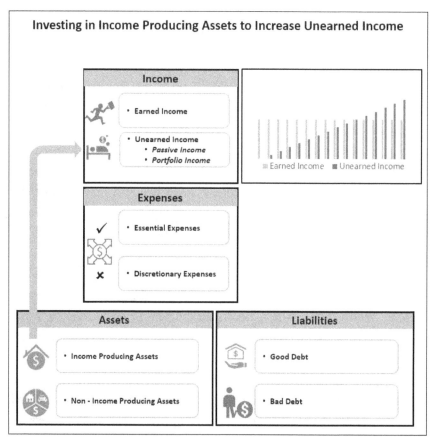

Figure 17—Investing in income-producing assets to increase unearned income

E—Liabilities Profile

Joyce paved the way for me when she explained the difference between good liabilities and bad liabilities. I was convinced that I must resolutely avoid bad debt. My financial statements revealed that to me. I had incurred bad debt to pay for goods and services that brought me instant gratification. Those goods and services depreciated, and most of them carried no financial value. On the other hand, although I understood the notion of good debt, I never had the chance to understand it in detail.

When Papa Joe finished his phone call, he came back with a high-pitched voice and told me, "The road to wealth is *good debt.*" When he saw that I thought I might have misheard him, he restated the rule: "The road to wealth is *good debt.*" He explained that good debt acquired to purchase income-producing assets will accelerate the road to wealth.

He took his usual moment of silence and then asked me how many $100,000 homes I can purchase with $100,000 cash.

With naivety, I answered that I can purchase one home worth $100,000 with $100,000 cash.

He frowned, gave me a half-hearted smile, and told me that while this is an option, other options can also be considered. He wanted to set a common set of assumptions that can be applied for all the options, so that we can easily get like-for-like comparisons. I nodded in acceptance. He took a piece of paper and wrote the following assumptions:

- Each home in each option is bought at market price of $100,000.
- The monthly rent is $1,000 (equivalent to $12,000 per year).
- The monthly expenses are $100 (equivalent $1,200 per year).

Option 1: The $100,000 home was purchased using all of the investor's $100,000 in cash.

In this scenario, the property's net cash flow, which is the rental income less total expenses, is $10,800 ($12,000 – $1,200). This results in 10.8 per cent ROI on the investor's money, computed by dividing the net cash flow of $10,800 by the investor's invested capital of $100,000.

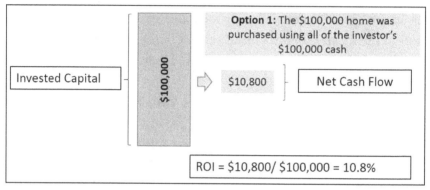

Figure 18—Property bought with 100 per cent investor's cash

Option 2: The $100,000 home was purchased using 20 per cent of the investor's cash. A mortgage loan was taken to finance 80 per cent of the property.

In this scenario, the investor has to pay a monthly mortgage to the bank towards the $80,000 loan taken. At an interest rate of 5 per cent and loan terms of 30 years, the monthly mortgage payment will be $430, which is equivalent to $5,160 per year. Mortgage payments can be calculated using many online mortgage calculators or by downloading the mortgage payments calculator in Microsoft Excel format from www. employeemillionaire.com/resources. The resulting net cash flow will be $5,640 ($12,000 – $1,200 – $5,160). The resulting ROI will be 28.2 per cent. This is computed by dividing $5,640 net cash flow over the investor's invested capital of $20,000.

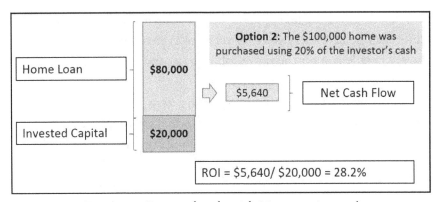

*Figure 19—Property bought with 20 per cent investor's
cash and 80 per cent mortgage loan*

Option 3: The $100,000 home was purchased using none of the investor's cash. A mortgage loan was taken to finance 100 per cent of the property.

In this scenario, the investor has to pay a monthly mortgage to the bank towards the $100,000 loan taken. At an interest rate of 5 per cent and loan terms of thirty years, the monthly mortgage payment will be $537, which is equivalent to $6,444 per year. The resulting net cash flow will be $4,356 ($12,000 − $1,200 − $6,444). The resulting ROI will be infinite. This is computed by dividing $4,356 net cash flow over the investor's invested capital of $0.

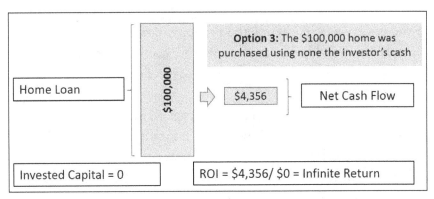

Figure 20—Property bought with 100 per cent mortgage loan

This is where magic happens. This is how infinite returns can be achieved. The investor will have a zero down payment in this deal. This was my first lesson on the power of leverage and the use of good debt. Indeed the road to wealth is good debt.

Please note that I am not promoting zero down payment deals, especially those that are bought at market price. This book will guide you on buying rental properties at a targeted 20 per cent discounted price. In that way, the price you will pay for a rental property will be equivalent to 80 per cent of its listed or market price. The difference between the price you will pay (80 per cent of the market price) and the listed price of the property will be considered as your 20 per cent down payment when you take a loan for 80 per cent of the value of the property. Your knowledge and sweat equity for finding those good deals will be equivalent to the 20 per cent down payment.

Chapter 13 covers in more details the ins and outs of financing rental properties. Warren Buffet explains how price does not equal value with his famous quote: "Price is what you pay, value is what you get."

To better illustrate my point, let's revisit scenario three above, but this time you have found a good deal at 20 per cent discount (the price of the property will be $80,000), and then upon applying for a loan, let's assume your banker will give you an 80 per cent loan on the market value of the property. So 80 per cent of the market value of $100,000 will be $80,000. In that way, the amount of the loan will be equivalent to the price you will pay for the property, namely $80,000. In that example, the monthly net cash flow will be exactly as option two above, $5,640, but the ROI will be infinite since you have invested zero from your own capital.

When he saw that I was on the same page with him, Papa Joe wanted to make it more interesting. He wanted to share with me one of the biggest secrets about good debt. With a loud and assertive voice, he said: "You will become at least as rich as the amount of good debt you take in your life." My brain started racing while trying to figure out what he meant. He explained that if I want to receive $1 million in the future, I need to borrow $1 million in good debt. He then raised the numbers and continued that if I want to receive $10 million in the future, I need to borrow $10 million in good debt. My eyes were flashing, and I believe Papa Joe could almost see a dollar sign in each of my eyes.

Papa Joe always loved round figures and usually used a $100,000 market value for a single-family house in his examples. He always reminded me that real property values may be higher or lower depending on the country and the city I wish to invest in. With a smile on his face, he told me to imagine a single-family house purchased at $100,000 with zero down payment. In this example, we would have incurred $100,000 in good debt, used to purchase the property. If this house is rented out continuously over the duration of the loan and the loan is paid back, we will own 100 per cent in equity at the end of the terms of the loan, which is thirty years in our example. Even if we disregard all positive cash flow as well as any price appreciation over the thirty-year period, we will own 100 per cent equity in that house. This means we will own a home free and clear with a value of $100,000. This is exactly equivalent to the amount of the loan taken.

Then he added that if we follow the purchase criteria of searching for properties discounted at 20 per cent, the 80 per cent loan-to-value will be exactly equal to the price of the property. This means that our equity in the property will be $20,000 on day one after we own the house. With the same logic, keeping the house rented over the thirty years duration of the loan will result in $100,000 equity, which is even higher than the loan amount. This also excludes any cash flow and capital appreciation over the thirty years. Papa Joe smiled and said, "You will become at least as rich as the amount of good debt you take in your life," and said to note that he'd said, "*at least*".

The two examples above for the same property value show that the total equity gained was at least equal to the amount of the loan taken. In reality it was much higher. Papa Joe told me to do the math by replicating the process above as many times as I wish to reach the equity I desire.

He explained that a mortgage is a long-term loan designed to help the borrower purchase a house. In addition to repaying the principal, the borrower is obligated to make interest payments to the lender, and the home around it serves as collateral. Every monthly mortgage payment is split between the principal and the interest. Loans are structured so that the amount of principal returned to the borrower starts out small and increases with each mortgage payment. The interest rate on a mortgage has a direct impact on the size of a mortgage payment, where higher interest rates mean higher mortgage payments. There is an inverse relationship between the term of the loan (the length of time within which the loan must be fully paid back) and the size of the monthly payment, with longer terms resulting in smaller monthly payments.

The graph below shows how the monthly payments of $537 (equivalent to $6,444 annual payments) are split between principal and interest over the term of thirty years. This is the same monthly mortgage payment considered in option three in the example above.

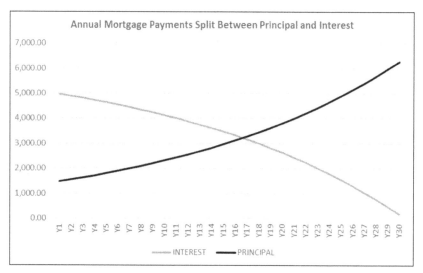

Figure 21—Annual mortgage payments split between principal and interest

Each principal paid adds to the equity accumulated for the borrower. Therefore, it reduces the remaining loan balance. The graph below visually explains how equity accumulates over the terms of the loan, when monthly mortgage payments are paid back to the bank.

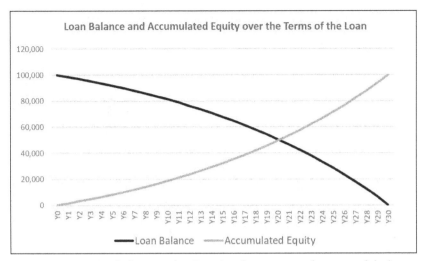

Figure 22—Loan balance and accumulated equity over the terms of the loan

Papa Joe added that the most interesting part of the story is that the investor doesn't need to wait the full thirty years, the term of the debt, to claim ownership of the full equity of $100,000. I had the exclamation mark on my face again. He claimed that in fifteen years, half of the term of the thirty-year loan, the investor can earn more than $100,000 in cash if the home appreciates at 5 per cent per year. If we add a 5 per cent appreciation for the price of the home per year, the home will more than double in value in fifteen years. To be exact, the value of the home will be $207,893 in fifteen years. (The subject of appreciation will be covered in chapter 17.)

In this example, appreciation is assumed to be a flat 5 per cent every year. In reality, property prices move up, down, or sideways during any given year, with a long-term appreciation averaging between 3 and 6 per cent in most developed markets.

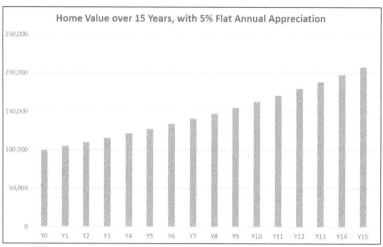

*Figure 23—Home value over fifteen years, with
5 per cent flat annual appreciation*

If the investor sells the home in fifteen years, the total money to be cashed out before tax will be $140,009, split as follows:

- All the $107,893 profit, which is the difference of the appreciated price of $207,893 less the original price of $100,000.
- All the accumulated equity resulting from the loan payment over fifteen years. This will be equivalent to $32,116.

He laughed and said that in fact, in exactly twelve years, the investor can cash in a bit over $100,000 if the house is sold.

The graph below explains how the sum of the accumulated equity and the home appreciation add up over the years to reap benefits to the investor. The assumption here is a flat 5 per cent annual appreciation over fifteen years.

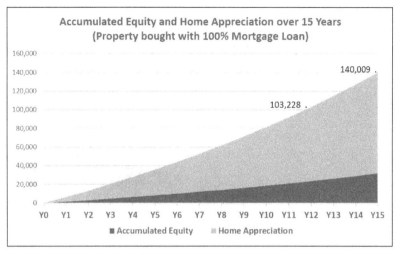

Figure 24—Accumulated equity and home appreciation over fifteen years

The investor could also chose to shorten the period to receive the full $100,000 in cash in less than twelve years. The investor could add all the $4,356 net cash flow from the property to the loan payment to accelerate the debt payment. Many banks allow a certain balloon payment per year, which could be capped to a certain percentage of the loan balance. This will speed up the payback of the loan by more than two thirds. In that way, in exactly eight years, the home could be sold at $147,746 (with 5 per cent annual appreciation) and the accumulated equity due to monthly loan payment and annual balloon payment will be $55,916. Adding both figures together will net the investor a handsome $103,662 in eight years. Not bad!

The graph below explains this scenario visually.

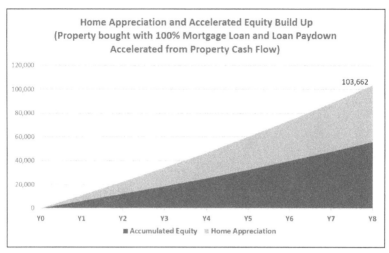

Figure 25—Home appreciation and accelerated equity build-up

Papa Joe reminded me that debt is a form of leverage, to be specific, a *financial leverage*. He added a quote from Archimedes: "Give me a lever long enough and a place to stand, and I will move the entire earth." This quote shows that the power of leverage was very highly appreciated from the days BC.

Before we ended our session on that Saturday, he told me that to be wealthy, I need to use leverage, which means not only financial leverage, like money borrowed from a financial institution. Wise investors will also leverage non-financial resources like time and knowledge. Leveraging money and time are commonly referred to as OPM and OPT, which stand for "other people's money" and "other people's time" respectively. He added that in my session with him, I was already leveraging his knowledge.

Reflecting back on my income statement, I had only bad debt and not even a dollar in good debt. This lesson on good debt was one of the best lessons I had in my entire life. In fact, this single lesson changed my life.

F—Net Worth

Papa Joe did not spend too much time on my net worth, which was negative as a reflection of too many liabilities in the form of bad debt and very little assets in the form of defined contribution plan.

He reminded me that the reason he recommended incurring good debt was to buy income-producing assets that would generate unearned income in excess of the debt payments. As a consequence, I would not only improve my net cash flow but also increase net worth.

As a reminder, net worth is measured by subtracting total liabilities from total assets. The objective of any responsible person who wishes to seek wealth is to keep on increasing income-producing assets in order to enjoy better cash flow and increased net worth.

On that Saturday I informed Papa Joe that I would see him in two weeks since the following week I had planned a trip back to Lebanon to spend some quality time with Joyce. I had already committed to visit her every three to five weeks. In return, I committed myself to limiting my day-to-day expenses to a bare minimum so that I could afford to pay for the tickets and the travel expenses. I thought of those expenses as an investment for my personal objective of building a family. This was at the top of my *big why* list.

Below is a visual representation of the process of increasing net worth through investing in income-producing assets.

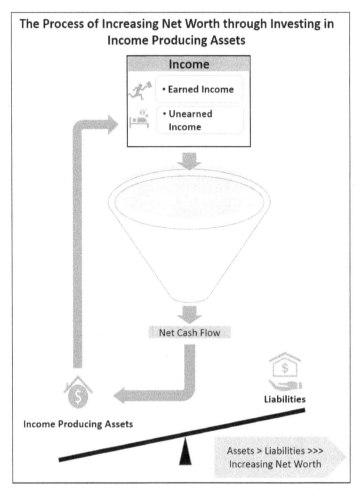

Figure 26—The process of increasing net worth through investing in income-producing assets

G—How Wealthy Am I?

I was always confused between the definitions of being rich and being wealthy. The terms are often mistakenly used interchangeably. I had to read a couple of books and do much online reading to understand the difference. While both terms involve having lots of money, wealthy people know how to *make* money while rich people only *have* money. For example, people may become rich due to high pay cheques, but the moment they stop working, they also stop making money, and eventually may end up being poor. On the other hand, being wealthy is having income-producing assets that support your expenses, even if you do not physically work to generate a recurring earned income.

From all the books I have read and the online searches I have made, the best definition of wealth was provided by Robert Kiyosaki in his best-selling book *Rich Dad Poor Dad*. According to the author, the term *rich* is measured in money, while *wealth* is measured in time. In his book, Kiyosaki defines wealth as the number of days forward that an individual can survive without working. According to this definition, wealth is measured in time and not in dollars.

Let's have a look at how wealth can be measured. According to the definition suggested above, it can be computed by dividing the net total value of income-producing assets over total monthly expenses. The resulting number will be in months. In other words, it is the number of months you can survive financially on the income-producing assets you have if you the stop working at the time this KPI is computed. This computation assumes that you maintain your current lifestyle, which is a fair assumption.

Based on that, a computation of the measure of your own wealth would take into account two major assumptions:

1. You maintain your current lifestyle.
2. The income-producing assets will be well preserved so that they generate unearned income that will support your current lifestyle.

This leads us to a logical next step of dividing total unearned income over total expenses. Let's consider here two scenarios:

- If the resulting value is over 100 per cent, this means you are financially free. In other words, if you stop working today, the income-producing assets will be generating monthly unearned income in excess of your monthly total expenses. The beauty of this scenario is that the excess money can be reinvested in acquiring more and more income-producing assets that will generate more and more unearned income. This is the formula for wealth. You are financially free when you no longer have to work for money because your income-producing assets are working hard for you. In this scenario, you can be referred to as *infinitely wealthy*.

- If the resulting value is under 100 per cent, your unearned income generated from income-producing assets will not be enough to cover expenses related to your current lifestyle. In this scenario, you will need to liquidate your total assets (income-producing assets and non-income-producing assets) on an ongoing basis to cover the difference between your unearned income and total expenses. In the worst case scenario, where total assets will be liquidated at once, the computation of dividing the net value of your total assets over your total monthly expenses will result in the number of months you are wealthy. For example, if your monthly total expenses amount to $5,000 and the net value of your total assets is $50,000, it means you are ten months wealthy.

To recap, your wealth is a measure of the number of days forward that you can survive without working. To compute your wealth, go through this process:

Divide your total unearned income by your total expenses.

1. If the resulting value is over 100 per cent, you are financially free or infinitely wealthy.
2. If the resulting value is under 100 per cent, your wealth can be computed by dividing the net value of your total assets over total monthly expenses. The resulting number is the number of months you are wealthy.

Below is a summary of how wealth can be computed:

$$Wealth = \frac{Unearned\ Income}{Total\ Expenses}$$

$$If > 100\% \rightarrow Infinitely\ Wealthy$$

$$If < 100\% \rightarrow \frac{Net\ Value\ of\ Total\ Assets}{Total\ Monthly\ Expenses} = Months\ Wealthy$$

This for me is the most important KPI on the financial KPIs dashboard. When a person's financial performance improves on each of the KPIs discussed in this section, that person's wealth is automatically increased.

In the next section, we will go through examples to put all the principles we've discussed and KPIs into perspective and allow the numbers to tell us the stories.

If made part of the personal financial statement, the financial KPIs dashboard (figure 27) can enable you to analyse the numbers and understand the story the numbers in the financial statements are telling you. The personal financial statement on the next page includes the financial KPIs dashboard. An editable Microsoft Excel format can be downloaded from www.employeemillionaire.com/resources.

Financial KPI's Dashboard	
My Income Profile	
% Earned Income	
% Unearned Income	
My Expenses Profile	
How Much do I Pay For Housing?	
How Much do I Pay For Income Taxes?	
How Much do I Pay For Charity?	
How Much Do I Pay for Discretionary Expenses? *= Discretionary Expenses / Total Income*	
How Much do I Pay For Loans? *Debt Burden Ratio (DBR) or Debt To Income Ratio (DTI)*	
How Much Money I Keep?	
My Assets Profile	
% Non-Income Producing Assets	
% Income Producing Assets	
What is My Return on Income Producing Assets?	
My Liabilities Profile	
% Good Debt	
% Bad Debt	
What is My Net Worth?	
How Wealthy Am I? *measured in months*	

Figure 27—Financial KPIs dashboard

PERSONAL INCOME STATEMENT

INCOME	Financial KPI's Dashboard
Earned Income	**My Income Profile**
Wages, Salaries, Tips	% Earned Income
Net Earnings from Self-Employment	
Earned Total	% Unearned Income
Passive Income	
Net Income from Investment Real Estate	**My Expenses Profile**
Net Income From Business	How Much do I Pay For Housing?
Passive Total	
Portfolio Income	How Much do I Pay For Income Taxes?
Interest	
Dividends	How Much do I Pay For Charity?
Royalties	
Portfolio Total	How Much Do I Pay for Discretionary Expenses?
TOTAL INCOME	= Discretionary Expenses / Total Income

EXPENSES	How Much do I Pay For Loans?
Expenses	Debt Burden Ratio (DBR) or Debt To Income Ratio (DTI)
Income Taxes	
Property Taxes / Real Estate Taxes for Personal Home	**How Much Money I Keep?**
Home Mortgage or Rent	
Utilities	**My Assets Profile**
Personal Home Maintenance	% Non-Income Producing Assets
Personal Home Insurance	
Personal Home Household Improvements	% Income Producing Assets
Medical Insurance	
Food and Clothing	What is My Return on Income Producing Assets?
Charity	
Credit Cards Payments	**My Liabilities Profile**
Car Loans Payments	% Good Debt
Personal Loans Payments	
School Loans Payments	% Bad Debt
Other Expenses	
TOTAL EXPENSES	**What is My Net Worth?**
NET MONTHLY CASH FLOW	**How Wealthy Am I?**
	measured in months

PERSONAL BALANCE SHEET

ASSETS	LIABILITIES
INCOME PRODUCING ASSETS	**GOOD LIABILITIES / GOOD DEBT**
Bank Accounts (Interest Paying)	Investment Real Estate Mortgages
Stocks (Dividends Paying)	Business Loans
Bonds	Student Loans
Investment Real Estate	Other Good Debt
Net Business Value	Other Good Debt
Royalties	Other Good Debt
Other Income Producing Assets	
INCOME PRODUCING ASSETS SUBTOTAL	**GOOD LIABILITIES / GOOD DEBT SUBTOTAL**
NON-INCOME PRODUCING ASSETS	**BAD LIABILITIES / BAD DEBT**
Personal Real Estate	Personal Home Mortgage
Motor Vehicles	Motor Vehicles Loans
Bank Accounts (Non Interest Paying)	Credit Cards Loans
Stocks (Non Dividends Paying)	Personal Loans
Precious Metals, Gems, Jewelry, and Art	Other Bad Debt
Receivables	Other Bad Debt
Other Non-Performing Asset	Other Bad Debt
NON-INCOME PRODUCING ASSETS SUBTOTAL	**BAD LIABILITIES / BAD DEBT SUBTOTAL**
	TOTAL LIABILITIES
TOTAL ASSETS	**NET WORTH**

Figure 28—Personal financial statement with financial KPIs dashboard

Once you invest the necessary time to complete your personal financial statements and then analyse your financial situation with the help of the financial KPIs dashboard, you can determine your current financial situation. At that stage, the main question for part 1 of this book—Where am I now?—will have been answered. Simply put, it is taking an honest inventory of your financial situation.

This step is a prerequisite for any person seeking financial freedom. It is a preamble for both setting new goals (Where do I want to be?) and creating a strategy to reach them (How do I get there?). If you don't know where you are and why you are where you are, you can't expect to get where you want to go.

Chapter 3 Action Steps

Before you proceed any further with this book, I strongly recommend you spend time completing your personal financial statement for the previous six months. You will need to have visibility on your income, expenses, assets, and liabilities. At first, it might seem overwhelming or time consuming. Once you go through the exercise, it will appear to be much easier than perceived. Over time, it will become a habit for you to undergo the same exercise on a monthly basis and with relatively much less time put as compared to the first few times.

Once the question Where am I now? is answered with a personal financial statement, the next step for us will be to answer the next logical question: Why am I here?

LIMITING BELIEFS

When I had a look at my first ever personal financial statement and my financial KPIs dashboard, dozens of questions and ideas came to my mind. In some instances, I comforted myself with some irrational justifications about my financial ruin. It was like covering a bad story with another bad story. Finally, I had to face reality and objectively analyse what brought me to this situation. During this same time, I looked at Forbes's list of billionaires and started to ask myself questions about how those billionaires and other wealthy people attract money like a magnet, whereas people like me and my fellow colleagues, employees in general, seem to repel it. Being determined to discover the answers, I talked to dozens of people, including ones who were poor, middle class, well off, and wealthy. As I met people who were low-, medium-, and high-paid employees, self-employed, investors, and business owners, I began to notice that people who depend on earned income, irrespective of their income level, have much in common. On the other hand, people who have acquired multiple streams of income from their income-producing assets also share a lot in common. The difference between those classes was astonishing.

People who have accumulated wealth have let go of an incredible number of misconceptions and *limiting beliefs*. In fact, the wealthy have managed to subscribe to a new set of empowering beliefs that contradict what the majority of the population still hangs onto.

It appears as if we are all programmed to believe in a set of false assumptions that become limiting beliefs. Too often the poor and the middle class hold tightly to a set of limiting beliefs about money and investing. Meanwhile, those same beliefs hold them captive and prevent them from achieving financial freedom. When I first looked at my personal financial statement, I had the same set of limiting beliefs. It was only when I understood how those beliefs were enslaving me to a state of financial ruin that I managed to let go of them. I had to understand the personal truth about my negative thoughts in order to overcome them and replace them with empowering beliefs.

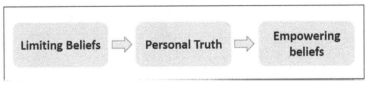

Figure 29—Limiting beliefs vs. empowering beliefs

Let's go through those beliefs and see how the poor and middle class look at them differently—actually in opposite ways. The poor and the middle class have adopted limiting personal beliefs, whereas the wealthy have adopted empowering personal beliefs. You'll never embark on the road to wealth if you let such negative thoughts constrain you. The poor and the middle class will most probably remain in the same financial situation if they conjure up any number of excuses for not choosing wealth—excuses that say more about their inner thoughts than about the difficulty of achieving wealth.

If you're embracing negative thoughts, you need to understand what they really mean. It's time to dig deep and unearth your personal truths. Jot down negative statements you whisper to yourself, and, after some honest soul searching, record the personal truth that lies beneath each. Once you become honest with yourself and accept that those beliefs are limited only to the extent you allow them to be, you will experience a transformation of those beliefs into empowering ones. Self-awareness is critical in this transformation. Before you change your life, you need to change your mind. Your thoughts and beliefs are deeply entrenched, so deeply rooted that you may not even be aware of how much they've impacted your financial situation.

Limiting Belief 1: A job provides financial security for now and at retirement

In my conversations with poor and middle-class people, I discovered that almost all of them were programmed to graduate from school to seek a high-paying job that would provide them security and eventually lead them to wealth. This might hold true for CEOs and other corporate executives with hefty pay cheques. But to the majority of employees, this remains a dream they chase until one day they retire, only to be surprised by a bank account and pension plan that can barely sustain their lifestyle for a few weeks or months. Then reality kicks in—when it is too late. The fact of the matter is that a job, for the majority of us, merely supports the basics of life, the essential expenses.

The drug that keeps all employees addicted to their job is seeing their income increasing from the day they start working till the prime of their income-earning years. This false evidence of prosperity leads to a false feeling of security. As a result, more and more of their income gets channelled to discretionary expenses, and those who can afford it start to spend on the appearances of wealth. One day their income starts to go downhill, and like a drug addict who cannot have the same high doses of drug anymore, they wake up to the fact that this fantasy is over and that they have to cut down on their expenses. The few exceptions will be corporate executives, who are only a minority of the general population. The graph below shows the earned income trend of the general population over time. If you are interested in learning more on this topic, I recommend you read books written by Harry S. Dent, an economist who specializes in generational consumer income and spending patterns.

Figure 30—Earned income over time

I encourage you to start looking at your job in a different way. Instead of seeing it as working harder and harder for the benefit of your employer, consider it as a form leverage that acts in your favor. It is about having your job work smarter for you while you work hard for your job. The objective of this book is to enable you to leverage your position as an employee to qualify for bank loans (good debt) to purchase income-producing assets that will generate unearned income in excess of your monthly expenses and therefore put you on the road to being wealthy.

As we discussed earlier, banks generate profits from lending money to people. The interest they charge the borrowers is the bank's income. Banks like to lend money to creditworthy people. They want reasonable reassurance that borrowers have steady incomes that will enable them to repay their loans. Banks will look at the length of time the borrowers were in their current jobs as their reassurance of steady income. The first step of the wealth building process is to take advantage of the fact that you have a steady income that qualifies you for a loan that you can take to purchase income-producing assets. Parts 3 and 4 of this book are dedicated to setting up your own financial objectives and then creating your own plan to achieve your objectives.

Limiting Belief	Job provides financial security for now and at retirement.
Personal Truth	I don't want to give up a regular pay cheque that provides a feeling of security, at least for the short term. In reality, I can be kicked out of my job any time.
Empowering Belief	I need to take action and be in control of my future income. I can leverage my position as an employee to qualify for good debt to purchase income-producing assets that will generate unearned income.

Limiting Belief 2: Debt is bad

It was considered a privilege to carry a credit card back in the eighties. Nowadays, credit card companies harass people who have steady incomes to offer them free-for-life credit cards. Things have evolved in a manner that you can take a cash advance with zero down payment and zero interest for a number of months. The trick here is that most people will fail to repay those credit card loans within the few months' window and then get penalized with huge interest rates that can range anywhere between 24 to 36 per cent per year. This is when the borrower becomes captive to those high-interest loans.

With good marketing campaigns that play on consumers' psychology, bankers and big companies convince us to buy goods and services that will provide instant gratification. They have also made it easy for consumers to get a suite of credit cards, personal loans, and car loans with reasonable monthly payments to make it a no-brainer to buy those goods and services even if we cannot afford them. It is normal to see offers from retailers tempting consumers to use their credit cards to buy now and pay later at zero interest over three, six, nine, or twelve months. The caveat is that by the time the debt is repaid, those goods and services are worthless.

Most of us have fallen victim to tempting instant gratification offers with delayed payment plans. We started to fear being captive to debt. Our parents, the school, and the community have each played a role in teaching us that debt is bad and that it must be avoided at any cost. And they are correct when it comes to bad debt. On the other hand, good debt, which is debt incurred to purchase income-producing assets, sets you on the road to wealth. Earlier in this book, I shared the idea that you will become as rich as the amount of good debt you take in your life. This was explained in detail under the "Liabilities" section of this chapter. I would even dare to claim that you can almost never become wealthy without incurring good debt. Think of it as borrowing yourself to wealth. Pay attention: I mentioned *good debt*, which is the kind of debt you incur to purchase income-producing assets.

Limiting Belief	Debt is bad. It signals captivity. I must avoid it at any cost.
Personal Truth	I have been captive to debt that I have taken towards the purchase of goods and services that will become worthless by the time the debt is paid.
Empowering Belief	I need to start investing in income-producing assets that will generate unearned income. I understand that debt allows for higher returns. I can never become wealthy without incurring some form of good debt in my life.

Limiting Belief 3: Saving your money is the wisest investment

Most responsible and caring parents advise their newly graduating adult children who are about to join the workforce and build their careers to make sure they save their hard-earned money in long-term savings plans that generate some kind of interest. Our parents' advice is sound, but it can never lead to wealth if the saved money is never put to hard work by having it invested in income-producing assets that generate unearned income and build wealth.

Interest rates on saving accounts vary widely across countries, especially in their respective local currencies. On average, interest earned on savings is around 3 per cent for accounts. Let's see how many years it takes for $100,000 to double if deposited in a saving bank account at 3 per cent interest.

In the 1400s, the Italians gave the world a method to estimate the doubling time of an investment, often referred to as the *rule of 72*. The rule number, 72, is divided by the annual interest percentage to obtain the approximate number of years required for doubling. Although scientific formulas and calculations do provide more accurate figures, the rule of 72 is quite useful for mental calculations and when only a basic calculator is available. Using the rule of 72 to compute how many years are required to double an amount of $100,000 deposited in a saving account at 3 per cent annual interest, we divide 72 by 3. The result is twenty-four. So it takes twenty-four years to double an amount stashed in a savings account at 3 per cent interest.

$$T = \frac{72}{R} = \frac{72}{3} = 24$$

Let's now compute how many years it takes for money invested in an income-producing asset that generates 10 per cent ROI. If we divide 72 over 10, we will get 7.2 years.

$$T = \frac{72}{R} = \frac{72}{10} = 7.2$$

If the ROI is 15 per cent, the resulting number will be 4.8 years.

You will agree with me that it will take seemingly forever to double your money when saved in the bank at low interest rates. But it can take fewer years when the money is properly invested at double-digit returns. We saw in the previous section of this book how investments can result in high double-digit ROI if properly invested in income-producing assets and with the use of leverage, good debt.

Limiting Belief	Saving my money is the wisest investment.
Personal Truth	I am cynical about investment. I let fear rule my decisions. I need to educate myself on how to invest for higher returns.
Empowering Belief	Investments can result in high double-digit ROI if properly invested in income-producing assets and with the use of leverage.

Limiting Belief 4: The government and my employer are responsible for my financial well-being

The best thing about history is that it helps us predict the future. In the last 100 years, there have been several recessions across the globe. The latest recession we witnessed was about ten years ago—the recession of 2008. The well-documented facts show us that employees were laid off and unemployment shot up to high double digits. Employers who had to let go of their employees never thought they were responsible for the financial well-being of those laid-off employees. To me, no job looks secure.

On the other hand, governments across the world have genuine obligations to improve their economies and provide jobs for their citizens. They have attempted to boost their respective economies with quantitative easing and other forms of easy money so that companies will borrow money for free to invest in their businesses and recruit people. The result of lowering unemployment did take a long time.

In most cases, although unemployment went down in percentage, the quality of the jobs created and the respective pay cheques were far from the levels before those recession hit.

The fact of the matter is that you alone are responsible for your financial well-being. I encourage you to start changing your mindset and put yourself in control. I urge you to take advantage of your current employment status and invest in income-producing assets that will work hard for you to generate income. This unearned income is what will look after your well-being in the event you ever have to (or choose to) leave your current job. Part 4 of this book will discuss the "how" in detail. It will take you through the steps of investing in single-family rental properties that will put you on the journey of being financially free.

Limiting Belief	The government and my employer are responsible for my financial well-being.
Personal Truth	When a recession hits or when my employer might pass through some tough financial situation, there is a high probability I might lose my job. If not well prepared, I will not be able to sustain my current lifestyle.
Empowering Belief	I alone am responsible for my well-being. I will learn how to invest in income-producing assets to generate unearned income that will work hard to improve my financial well-being.

Limiting Belief 5: Failure is bad, and mistakes are a reflection of my incompetence

Most of us fear failure and mistakes, which is no surprise. Throughout our years at school and university, failing an exam resulted in a feeling of shame and incompetence. Even in most of our life as employees, failure to deliver on our objectives will eventually lead to a bad performance evaluation, and in extreme cases the door will be wide open for us to leave our job. Some mature companies accept failure as part of the learning curve of their employees, but those failures need never be experienced more than once, and they should not lead to a major financial loss. In other words, those mature companies are projecting an image of a culture that welcomes failure as part of a learning organization. But when the shit hits the fan, the employee who made a mistake will be looking for a new job in a new company sooner rather than later.

In my professional life as an employee, I still fear to make large mistakes. But in my professional life as an investor, I have made rather large mistakes and realized that failure is an integral part of my success. When I learned how to convert "fear of failure" into "opportunity of failure", I developed creativity, flexibility, agility, and the ability to explore new ways of achieving my goals. In fact, the biggest mistakes I have made in my investment life have taught me lessons not only about how to avoid them in the future. The solutions to those mistakes have taught me more important lessons about how my *how-to* can become more rigid and can deliver better results.

When you fail in an important endeavour, you affiliate yourself with some of the most famous people in the world. I am confident you know two famous quotes from Thomas A. Edison, known as America's greatest inventor. One quote is "I have not failed. I've just found ten thousand ways that won't work", and the other one goes "Many of life's failures are people who did not realize how close they were to success when they gave up". The moral of the story is that you fail only when you give up.

Another impressive story is that of Abraham Lincoln, who served as the sixteenth president of the United States. After facing several failures, such as losing his job, failing in business, having a nervous breakdown, being defeated for speaker of the house, being defeated for nomination in Congress, being defeated for the US Senate, and being defeated for nomination for vice president, he overcame each of them as it was time for a better outcome, and was eventually elected president. He is also famous for saying "Always bear in mind that your own resolution to succeed is more important than any other". What those great achievers taught us is that determination for success will keep us going and trying again and again until we succeed. Who we become in the process becomes as important as success itself.

In summary, I encourage you to start "learning to learn" by learning to unlearn in order learn again and again.

Limiting Belief	Failure is bad and mistakes are a reflection of my incompetence.
Personal Truth	I am worried that people will think I am incompetent if I make mistakes. I would rather be on the safe side and avoid exploring untapped opportunities. But how can I expect different results if I keep doing the same things over and over?
Empowering Belief	Failure is an integral part of my success. Opportunities are always found when I overcome my failures. I become a better person in the process.

Limiting Belief 6: It takes money to make money

Indeed, it takes money to make money, but who said it has to be *your* money? In the section titled "Liability" in this chapter, I have shared with you the best lesson Papa Joe ever taught me: "The road to wealth is good debt". This section has explained in depth the principles of borrowing and leverage to create wealth. It is only through the wise use of good debt that returns can reach high double digits. In the best scenario—when you don't use a single dollar from your own money to purchase income-producing assets—your returns can be infinite.

Limiting Belief	It takes money to make money.
Personal Truth	A large amount of money is required for investment. I can never save that amount of money. I therefore end up spending my hard-earned money on discretionary expenses.
Empowering Belief	Indeed, it takes money to make money, but who said it has to be my money? The road to wealth is good debt. I will become as rich as the amount of good debt I take in my life. I will not need more than 20 per cent of my own money to invest in rental properties, so I shall begin managing my expenses to save money and eventually invest it and use leverage to accelerate my returns on investment.

Limiting Belief 7: Investing is complicated and risky. Others can manage my money more wisely

Among my friends and employees whom I interviewed to understand their views on investment, the majority believe that investment is complicated and risky. They eventually end up depending on their earned income and then wake up one day when their income goes lower or when they see themselves out of a job. To me, this is risky. Actually, it is riskier to keep on depending on your job until you face the reality of diminishing income or losing all your earned income later in your life.

The minority of those employees I have interviewed have sought the help of professional financial advisors to invest their money. I am not attempting to undermine the value of financial advisors—but I encourage this segment of people to ask themselves whether those financial advisors will put their customers' interest before their own.

Financial advisors are employees, agents, or brokers for financial institutions. They earn their income by selling investments to their customers. They definitely have an interest in generating high returns for their customers, but I don't believe they will place their customers' interests before their own.

What I am trying to say is that although those financial advisors might be looking after your money, you owe it to yourself to become actively engaged in your financial planning. When you become involved in the decisions on how and where to invest your own money, higher returns on your investments are more secure. You do not want to be another proof of the old saying "A fool and his money are soon parted". In the extreme case of losing your money because of bad advice, you can rest assured that your financial advisor has already received payment or commission for the advice given to you. The advisor wins in either case, whether you win or lose.

Investment is not as risky as it might appear. Actually, it is less risky than having a job, which you might lose sooner or later. I am not saying there is no risk associated with investment. Great investors minimize risk by following sound investment principles and proven models. You may have heard that investors make their money going in. This suggests that smart investors buy assets that have more value than the tag price on them. It means they are sure that their profit has actually been made when going in since they bought the asset at a discount as compared to the market price.

I would like to share a personal story that illustrates how investors make their money going in. In 2010, after I was relocated back to Dubai following my five-year assignment in the Philippines, Dubai was still experiencing the aftermath of the 2008 recession, when the stock market and real estate markets both plummeted. In a certain prime area, where all expats looked for places to live, the average price of a two-bedroom townhouse had dropped from $762,000 before 2008 to an average of $448,000 in 2010. Very few people, if any, were buying properties during this period.

When I shared with my friends and colleagues that I was planning to buy a property, they all thought I was crazy and that I was inviting risk into my door. Warren Buffet once said: "The time to get interested is when no one else is. You can't buy what is popular and do well." Following that advice together with my understanding of the market that there was higher demand for rent since no one was buying properties, I decided to search for a property that was around 20 per cent below the already-depressed market value. I contacted the bank and got a home loan preapproval. I then searched online for properties listings. I found out about five active agents, whom I managed to contact and eventually meet. When they knew how serious I was, they started searching the market for properties that were marked lower than the market price. One day one of the agents called to inform me that he found a two-bedroom townhouse for sale for $355,000. This was more than my 20 per cent discount criterion. Without a second thought, I issued an offer letter with a promise of 10 per cent down payment subject to the seller's approval of my offer. The seller was in great need to sell since he was kicked out of his job and was planning to travel back to the UK in a few weeks. We signed a contract and closed the deal in less than three weeks. At that time, I could have resold the property for market price and easily made $93,000 profit if I put the property back in the market. The only advantage I had over the previous owner was time. I had the privilege of having time to wait for the property to get sold, whereas he was working on a tight schedule and had to leave the country in less than two months.

So, with buying the property at a discounted price, I minimized the risk or even removed the risk out of the equation. The more interesting part of this investment was that the bank has agreed to lend me 80 per cent of the appraised property value. The property was appraised close to market value, to be exact at $430,000. The 80 per cent loan-to-value (LTV) was equivalent to $344,000. The total closing cost, including a 4 per cent closing fee, was $369,200 ($355,000 + $14,200). The amount paid from my pocket was only $25,200 ($369,200 - $344,000).

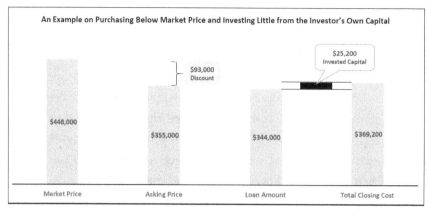

*Figure 31—An example of purchasing below market price
and investing little from the investor's own capital*

Then I lined up a tenant to rent the property from day one, after transferring the title into my name. The annual rent was $24,500. The annual mortgage payment was $19,704 ($1,642 monthly × 12 months). The annual association and maintenance fees were $2,177. Accordingly, the net cash flow was $2,619 ($24,500 - $19,704 - $2,177). This is equivalent to 10.4 per cent ROI on my invested capital of $25,200.

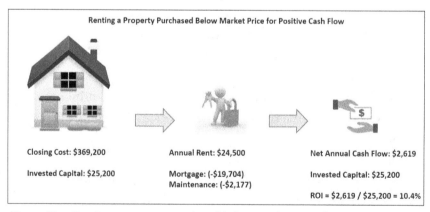

Figure 32—Renting a property purchased below market price for positive cash flow

The market in Dubai started gaining momentum in 2012, and I sold the property in 2015 for $639,500 with a capital gain of $270,300, which is equivalent to 1,072 per cent ROI on my invested capital of $25,200.

At the time I bought this property, many colleagues challenged me, saying that if the market dropped further, I would lose all my invested capital and still have to pay the bank for the amount of the loss. Thanks to one of Papa Joe's precious lessons, I was fully aware that a loss would be actualized only if I sold the property at a loss. Otherwise, it was all paper loss. So with the strategic intent of renting out the house, even with no future rent increases, at 10.4 per cent ROI, I would have returned my invested capital in 9.6 years. The worst case scenario was still much better than any interest I might get from any bank or financial institution.

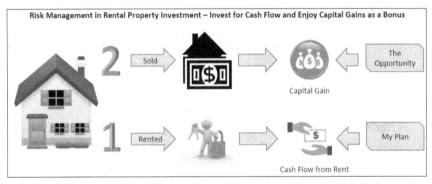

Figure 33—Risk management in rental property investment

The example above illustrates risk management. I have planned for rental income with steady income at 10.4 per cent ROI as the worst case scenario, and I would have been happy if I achieved only 10.4 per cent ROI. It beats any interest I might earn in stashing my money in a savings account. However, when the opportunity for a huge capital gain presented itself due to market cycles, I took advantage of it and sold at 1,072 per cent ROI.

The mistake most people make is that they plan for capital gain only without calculating the rental income as a cushion to fall on if the market does not go the way they wish or as they were promised by the well-spoken financial advisors or real estate agents.

Many of my friends and colleagues who challenged me and warned me really meant for my best. Almost everyone either had a personal bad experience or had a friend or relative who lost their shirt in the 2008 recession. With my curiosity to understand the details of why they lost their investments, it appeared that their negative experiences all revolved around buying a property off-plan with a promise of capital gain in three to four years, when the property would be handed over to them. So those investors were planning only for capital gains. They couldn't plan for rentals since those property purchases were off-plan.

When the recession hit in 2008, those investors saw the prices of their properties, which were still plans on paper, plummet by almost half. The developers either went bankrupt or demanded continuous payments from those investors on the contract price. Many of those investors chose to let go of their paid money, dropped their investments, and eventually lost it all. This is the opposite case of risk management. This is risk *mis*management. Those who lost such investments were all in a challenging situation. They couldn't justify continuing to pay for properties that had lost value and that could not generate any cash flow. I wish people would learn from such mistakes.

After the market started growing again in Dubai, the developers and their brilliant talkative agents managed to convince people to buy properties off-plan and that this time the market wouldn't go again into recession I wonder how those agents can read the future? I would pay millions to buy such a crystal ball that could predict the future.

One of my closest friends, for whom I have great respect, is a well-established business owner who found himself in a situation of having too much money and not knowing where to invest it. No wonder real estate agents, like wolves, will lay their eyes on prey that has too much meat and fat. They convinced my friend to buy off-plan properties in an area that was not yet developed. This area in fact was still a desert. They showed him attractive animated videos and brochures of what the development would look like when it was finished in three or four years. They showed him simulations of how he would more than double his money in three or four years. The dream of fast and easy money thoroughly tricked him, and he signed the contract and made a down payment without consulting anyone.

On the same day, he gave me a call, seeking for me to congratulate him on his new investment, which he was so proud of. He tried to convince me that his agent had saved a few other properties for some elite clients and that he could convince his agent to keep a unit for me to invest in.

Not wanting him to feel regret, I wished him good luck and explained to him my investment method and criteria. I offered my future help in case he would like to have an opinion.

Less than two months later, he signed a similar off-plan deal for a price of 1.5 million dollars with a promise to double this investment in four years. I wish him good luck and hope those agents really do have a crystal ball and that he will double his money. The agent was paid his commission regardless of whether the property appreciates or depreciates in four years.

My recommendation to you is to plan for both the risks and the opportunities for every investment you plan to make. You need to be content with the outcome of the risk. The fear and risk of failure will always be there in front of you. It is normal. The way you handle fear determines the results you will have in life. If you are equipped with knowledge, you can overcome fear. Otherwise, the lack of knowledge only makes you submit to it. Knowledge causes fear to disappear. I encourage you to read about successful people and to seek mentors and coaches in your life. This book is intended to equip you with the knowledge I have accumulated over the years from my failures and successes in real estate investment and from the books I have read and the seminars I have attended.

In his book, *The Top 10 Distinctions Between Millionaires and the Middle Class,* Keith Cameron Smith shares an empowering way to look at risks and opportunities in every investment. He recommends asking ourselves three questions:

- What's the worst thing that could happen?
- What's the best thing that could happen?
- What's the most likely thing that might happen?

After answering those questions, reflect on them. If you can live with the worst thing that could happen, and if the most likely thing that may happen will get you closer to your goals, then go for it.

Limiting Belief	Investing is complicated and risky. Others can manage my money more wisely.
Personal Truth	I am lazy. I do not want to take responsibility for my finances. I will seek the help of professionals who can manage my money.
Empowering Belief	Investment is as complicated as I think it is. With proven methods, I can be in control of my investments. I will manage risk and take advantage of opportunities. The only way out of the rat race is to take risks. If I take risk out of life, I take opportunity out of life.

Limiting Belief 8: Successful investors have a crystal ball that enables them to time the market

In the previous limiting belief about investment and risk, I explained how wise investors invest with clear criteria and plan for worst case scenarios. Once they are in the game, whenever opportunities present themselves, they will act upon them and achieve high returns. For an outsider, the image is totally different. People hold the mistaken belief that successful investors really can time the market. They do not understand that those investors were already in the market and then took advantage of opportunities.

Between 2010 and 2012, I bought three townhouses with the objective of renting them out for cash flow. I managed my risk and bought properties that are more than 20 per cent less than the market price. With the right buying price, I made my profit going in. The net cash flow from renting out those three properties was positive, with ROI's ranging between 10 to 17 per cent. I was quite happy with such returns. When the market in Dubai started to regain its 2008 losses and even started to get irrationally high, I took advantage of this window of opportunity and sold those three properties in 2015 with a total profit of a bit over a million dollars. All those agents and bankers I was working with to acquire those properties really believed that I have a crystal ball and I can time the market. I consistently explained to them that I purchased those properties for the cash flow, but I saw enormous capital gain opportunity when the market ticked up in 2015, so I immediately sold them for a handsome profit.

The funny part of the story is that my friends and colleagues who thought I was stupid to invest in properties in 2010 all thought I was smart in 2015. The fact of the matter is that I am neither stupid nor smart. I am just an investor with clear criteria and objectives who had a stake in the market when it changed course and started to grow again at very high pace.

After a strong comeback in 2015, the market in Dubai softened a bit. I immediately bought couple of properties. The banker I always work with to get loans still calls me every couple of weeks for advice on how the market is going. Every time, I tell him that I don't know. I don't think he believes me since I still receive those calls. To be transparent, I am enjoying those calls more than he is because I always ask him about the number of home loans the bank is granting. In fact, I am getting data from him that will enable me to have a feeling for where the market might be going. Please note that I said "might". I never convince myself that whatever data I read will really tell me what will *definitely* happen next or when.

In other instances, some of the agents I frequently work with also call me to ask about when the market will drop or improve. I tell them, too, that I don't know. I believe they do not believe me either, given the frequency of calls I receive from the same agents in a short span of time.

Most people think timing the market is about sitting on the sidelines and actively observing until they identify the golden moment to jump in and make a fortune. They don't understand that timing is about always being in the game, then, when opportunities show up, taking advantage of them. In other words, timing is not about being in the right place at the right time; it's about always being in that place and then leveraging any opportunity.

Warren Buffet once said: "We have long felt that the only value of stock forecasters is to make fortune-tellers look good." I'm amazed at how many investors take market forecasters seriously, even when they have no credible track records of success. Warren Buffet also advises against trying to predict the direction of the stock market, the economy, interest rates, or elections. I hope you agree with me that no one has a crystal ball to time the market.

Limiting Belief	Successful investors have a crystal ball that enables them to time the market.
Personal Truth	My fear and laziness made me believe timing the market is about sitting on the sidelines and actively observing until I identify the golden moment to jump in and make a fortune.
Empowering Belief	Timing is about always being in the game. Then, when opportunities show up, I can take advantage of them.

Limiting Belief 9: Investors have a specific knowledge that most people cannot have

It is true that investment requires some education and research on the part of the investor. Warren Buffet recommended that investors never invest in a business they cannot understand. He also added, "What counts for most people in investing is not how much they know, but rather how realistically they define what they don't know." In other words, investing in what you don't know or understand cannot be classified as investing. Actually, investing in something you do not understand is pretty much like gambling.

A good example is my friend who bought two expensive properties off-plan by following the advice of an agent that he will more than double his money in four years. My friend is counting on luck. I really do wish him all the luck.

Real investment is investing in what you know and fully understand. If you do not have deep understanding in any specific area, I encourage you to look for a topic that greatly interests you and commit yourself to studying and researching it to become an expert in it over time. Nowadays, with the fast evolution of the Internet and digital media, you can instantly get answers to any area of interest. If real estate is an area you would like to educate yourself on, this book becomes quite handy in your journey.

Limiting Belief	Investors have a specific knowledge that most people cannot have.
Personal Truth	My arrogance, ignorance, and laziness made me believe I have an idea about investment and that I am not up to it.
Empowering Belief	Real investment is investing in what I know and fully understand. I commit to studying an area of investment to become an expert in it over time.

Limiting Belief 10: Investors diversify their investments to minimize risk

"Diversify your investments" is the most common advice offered by financial advisors. Why do you think Warren Buffet believes otherwise when he said "Diversification is a protection against ignorance"? In fact, he also said that risk can be greatly reduced by concentrating on only a few holdings. This precious advice suggests that investors become deeply knowledgeable in an area of investment and then stick to what they know. It is like putting all your eggs in one basket and then watching over this basket. Think of it like a kind of protection. We cannot possibly understand all the moving parts of the economy and the countless investment choices available to us, but we can focus and become experts in one or few types of investments. In that way we minimize risk. In part 4 of this book, all the *how-to* of real estate investments will be shared with you. What you will be learning is a wealth of information I have assimilated from many books, seminars, webinars, coaching from real estate advisors, and from my personal experience. I am trying to make it simple with many illustrations to improve the chances that anyone can understand and then apply the learning.

Limiting Belief	Investors diversify their investments to minimize risk.
Personal Truth	When I do not know which investments will deliver the best returns on my invested capital, I will diversify to protect myself against ignorance.
Empowering Belief	I plan to become knowledgeable in an area of investment and then stick to what I know.

Limiting Belief 11: All the good investments are taken. Only the mediocre and bad investments are left over to the small investors

Most unknowledgeable people are cynical about investment. They often claim that all good investments are taken and that only the mediocre and bad investments are left over for small investors. Savvy investors wouldn't miss opportunities to make good investments. Why can't you join the league of those investors? In fact, the marketplace is a dynamic place, with economic forces and personal forces always at work, generating a continuous flow of investment opportunities.

Economic forces such as interest rates, employment rates, population growth, population shifts, and area developments all have major impact on the market. As a result, prices of properties might be driven up or down. Such economic forces are big and are on the news to an extent that they may often mask the impact of personal forces in putting opportunities in the market.

For example, personal situations like marriage, divorce, increase in the size of a household, relocation, death, inability to pay a mortgage, and family disputes over inheritance all present opportunities in the market. Those personal forces present more opportunities at discounted prices just because those people want to get rid of a property for personal reasons sooner rather than later. Such personal factors have always been there and will always remain there. Do you still believe opportunities at a bargain price tag are all taken?

Limiting Belief	All the good investments are taken. Only mediocre and bad investments are left over to small investors.
Personal Truth	I am lazy about searching for opportunities. If I create the excuse that all opportunities are taken, I will feel better about my inaction.
Empowering Belief	Opportunities are in the market every day. If I am in the game, opportunities will eventually present themselves for me to take advantage of them.

Chapter 3 Action Steps

Across all the limiting beliefs discussed in this chapter, the underlying personal truths were fear, cynicism, laziness, arrogance, ignorance, or bad habits. I encourage you to keep on doing those self-talks and uncover those personal truths to avoid them being obstacles between you and your empowering beliefs. Write down your own personal beliefs, unravel your personal truths, and think over their respective empowering beliefs. You can make use of the template provided below.

Limiting Beliefs	Personal Truth	Empowering Beliefs

PART 3

Where Do I Want to Be?

CHAPTER 4

Setting Objectives

If you have gone through the exercise of your *big why*, I trust you've given some good thought to what you want in your life and why you want to become wealthy. What you have written down are your dreams committed to a piece of paper and outlined in front of your eyes. Imagine your list as a large piece of magnet that will keep on attracting you towards itself. At this step you will feel energized as you start to set clear objectives and then formulate the plan that will get you there. Having this sense of clarity will keep on motivating you to achieve what you want in life.

Brian Tracy calls this your *major definite purpose*, which he defines as "The one goal that is most important to you at the moment. It is usually the one goal that will help you to achieve more of your other goals than anything else you can accomplish." From my own experience, as well as from what I have learned from other financially free people, your major definite purpose goes beyond financial goals. Your major purpose or goal is usually centred about personal matters, like home and family, health and fitness, personal development and education, social life and relationships, spiritual development, and life contribution. You will realize that your goals related to work, career, and finances will be the enablers to achieve your higher purpose.

At this stage, you might even start asking yourself powerful questions about what your life might look like if you had all the money in the world. What kind of career would you be pursuing? How would you spend your leisure time? What kind of passion would you be pursuing? How would you give back to your family, your friends, your community, your colleagues, your business associates, and your religious affiliates?

This part of the book will help you start setting your own personal financial objectives. You cannot set objectives if you do not have visibility on your current situation and an understanding of the reasons you are where you are. If you haven't filled up your personal financial statement yet, and if you haven't analysed your financial KPIs, I encourage you to go back to the previous chapters and do so. As James Burke eloquently puts it: "You can only know where you're going if you know where you've been."

To start with this section, the following documents will become handy:

- My Big Why List
- My Personal Financial Statement
- My Financial KPIs Dashboard

I suggest you have them available throughout the process of setting your own objectives.

The process I am about to share allows you to map out your goals in a measurable way.

TIME HORIZON FOR YOUR OBJECTIVES

In the "Big Why" section, I recommended you look at what you would like your life to be like five to ten years from now. During my research on the topic of building wealth, the book *The Top 10 Distinctions Between Millionaires and the Middle Class* by Keith Cameron Smith, as well as many other articles I have read, suggested that people can be categorized into poor, middle class, and rich according to the span of their future plans. Poor people plan at best for weeks, the middle class people plan for months, whereas rich people plan years in advance. The graph below visually shows the relationship between the span of future plans and accumulated wealth.

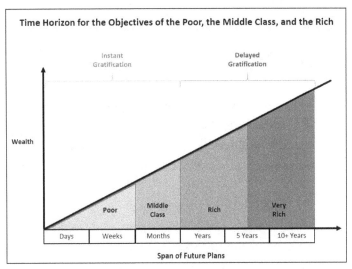

Figure 34—Time horizon for the objectives of the poor, the middle class, and the rich

What Keith Cameron Smith conveyed in this is that the poor and middle class seek instant gratification. Their impatience is their liability. They spend their money on goods and services that will have no value in the future. On the other hand, the rich develop the discipline of delayed gratification. Their patience is their asset. The rich are willing to sacrifice instant gratification by investing their money in income-producing assets and increasing their net worth and cash flow. As a result, they can enjoy later in the future a lifestyle that others cannot afford. Their discipline of delayed gratification is well rewarded in the future.

You will need to set long-term objective—five to ten years—for every area of your life, not only from a financial perspective, but also from a personal perspective, on matters related to home and family, health and fitness, personal development and education, social life and relationships, spiritual development, and life contribution. Many books can guide you to improving your life in personal matters. I recommend you also take those aspects of your life seriously. No one wants to end up financially wealthy but leading an unhappy personal life, one that may be devoid of strong family ties, relationships with friends and the community, healthy bodies, and spiritual development.

SMART OBJECTIVES

A powerful way to look at your goals is through the famous SMART model. SMART stands for the different criteria of a goal, which are Specific, Measurable, Achievable, Realistic, and Time-bound.

Let's us discuss each of the SMART goals criteria.

Specific	What is it that you want to do? Give your goal as much detail as possible. Make it crystal clear. Write it so there is no room for different interpretations. Give each goal a single focus. The road to financial freedom will be comprised of long-term and short-term goals. Have separate goals for each of the following areas: getting out of debt, real estate, business, wealth, net worth.
Measurable	This is the criterion that determines the accomplishment of success. Define the exact money amount or return on investment you want from your real estate investments, or business. If you don't know where you're going, how will you know when you've got there?

Achievable	This is the reality check. Do you possess everything necessary to reach this goal? Have you involved everyone in your mastermind alliance that needs to contribute or make a decision? Can you devote the time necessary to attain this goal?
	You know it is achievable if others have done it successfully before you, if it's theoretically possible, and if you have the necessary resources in time, people, skills, and money.
Relevant	How does this tie back to your *big why* list? Any goal must be tied back to a larger purpose. This gives the goal meaning and keeps it from being another regular task.
Time-Bound	Establish a definite date by which you intend to achieve your goal. Determine when you will start and finish. Block out the time you will work on your goal.

SETTING YOUR PRIMARY FINANCIAL OBJECTIVE

Starting with your own personal financial statements and looking into your ambitions in your *big why* list, you will need to determine your primary financial objective, whether it is security, comfort, or financial freedom. This exercise might seem a bit tricky in the beginning, since you might feel inclined to value security and put it at the top of your list, followed with comfort in the middle, and then financial freedom at the bottom.

Most of us were programmed by our parents, school, and society to value first and foremost a good job with a steady pay cheque with good health and retirement perks. This is why most people put security as their primary financial objective. As a logical next step, we start to seek comfort, with plans for a house, a car, and enough money for entertainment and vacations. This keeps the financial freedom objective at the bottom of the list. Most people will attribute this stage to luck. Most of us dream of becoming rich, but we keep it as a dream or wish and never put financial freedom at the top of our financial objectives. That's because we all find refuge in the easier objectives of security and comfort instead of bothering with the effort and education required to become financially free.

It's no wonder that the primary objectives for the poor and middle class are security and comfort respectively. Both security and comfort are short-term thinking where a pay cheque, health insurance, retirement plan, a house, a car, entertainment, and travel all offer the feeling of instant gratification. Because the poor and middle class value comfort over financial freedom, they will never become financially free unless they change their beliefs and priorities.

On the other hand, the primary goal for the rich is financial freedom. They have developed the discipline of sacrificing short-term indulgence. They invest their capital into income-producing assets. They invest time in learning about how to create wealth from books, seminars, and mentors. As a consequence, they enjoy much better and bigger things in the future. Their delayed gratification is way more rewarding. Because the rich value financial freedom over comfort, they will get both.

To better explain the benefits of self-control and delayed gratification, Papa Joe shared with me the story of the *marshmallow test*, where four-year-old children each were offered a marshmallow with a choice of either eating it immediately or receiving a second marshmallow if they waited for fifteen minutes. The researchers continued to follow up with the children for the next several decades. They found that the four-year-olds who had successfully waited for fifteen minutes differed in significant ways from the children who couldn't wait. Those children have developed better emotional coping skills, higher rates of educational attainment, healthier lifestyles, and lower divorce rates. Similar researches have reached a conclusion that self-control and delayed gratification are essential life skills, but they can be learned.

This book's primary objective is to lead you to financial freedom. Let's go a step backward to examine your current financial situation. From there you can start setting your financial freedom objectives. Referring to your financial KPIs dashboard, as a first step you will examine your income profile, your expense profile, and how much money you keep. If at this stage you haven't yet filled up your personal financial statement and your financial KPIs dashboard, I encourage you to do it now in order to get the most benefit out of this book.

Let's start with your income profile. On your journey to financial freedom, your current earned income will be crucial in the early stages. As we discussed earlier, it improves your creditworthiness and therefore will make you eligible for bank loans, which is the leverage you need to purchase your income-producing assets. In this early stage of your journey to financial freedom, you might have no or very little unearned income. Such is the case with most employees who depend on their pay cheques.

Your journey to financial freedom will include milestones. With each one you will acquire an income-producing asset that will generate unearned income. With each milestone, your total unearned income will increase. Over time, while your earned income may remain the same, with each income producing asset you acquire, your unearned income will increase; therefore your total income will increase. If you do not increase your total expenses by indulging yourself with spending the additional money on goods and services that will depreciate in value, your higher total income will make you eligible for new good debt, which in turn will make you buy more income-producing assets.

With this discipline, you will create for yourself a *virtuous cycle* in which every good action produces a good result that also causes the cycle to continue so that more good results happen. The graph below visually explains the concept of a virtuous cycle. More on this later in chapter 17.

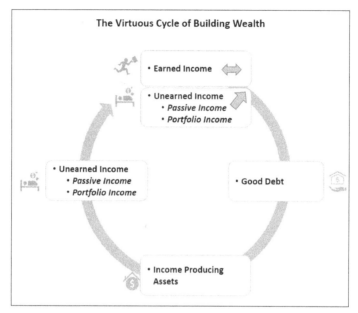

Figure 35—The virtuous cycle of building wealth

Your objective will be to increase the contribution of unearned income to total income with the acquisition of each additional income-producing asset. Over time, whenever your unearned income exceeds your total expenses, you may decide to leave your job. This will result in a scenario of 100 per cent unearned income with 0 per cent earned income.

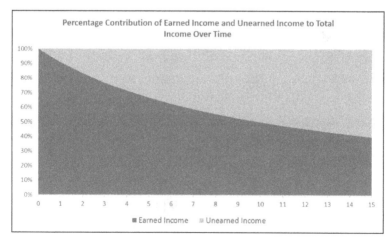

Figure 36—Percentage contribution of earned income
and unearned income to total income over time

The figure above shows the contribution in percentage of both earned income and unearned income to total income. Obviously, their sum is 100 per cent. The same data in the graph below shows what this evolution will look like in absolute values. The numbers were removed to avoid any unnecessary implication that I intend to target a specific number as a goal.

Your ultimate objective of financial freedom is to achieve a state where your unearned income exceeds your total expenses. As this stage, you will become infinitely wealthy. The black line in the graph below represent total expenses. The point of intersection between unearned income and total expenses is where financial freedom starts.

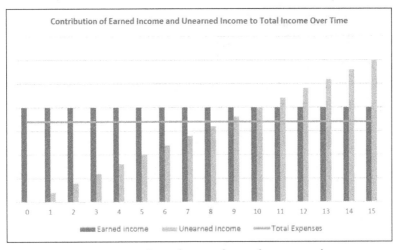

Figure 37—Contribution of earned income and unearned income to total income over time

Moving now to your expense profile in your financial KPIs dashboard, while we will consider your essential expenses as a given, I urge you to take a pragmatic approach on your discretionary expenses. Papa Joe taught me to discipline myself and to limit my discretionary expenses to a maximum of 10 per cent of total income. In the early phases of my journey to financial freedom, he urged me to set a zero target for my discretionary expenses until I achieve the milestone of my first income-producing asset. Once there, I could enjoy 2 per cent discretionary expenses out of new total income. He recommended 2 per cent incremental discretionary expenses with the acquisition of each new income-producing asset. The cap was always to be at 10 per cent discretionary expenses.

In essence, Papa Joe was reconditioning me on the discipline of delayed gratification. He was also pushing me to acquire at least five income-producing assets to reach a level where I can enjoy the indulgence of spending 10 per cent of my total income on discretionary expenses. I am not recommending you follow the same level of short-term frugality by limiting your discretionary expenses to the bare minimum. I am sharing a practice that worked well for me and many others. Although others might adopt a different threshold of 15 per cent, 20 per cent, 25 per cent, or even 30 per cent of their total expenses to be discretionary, the discipline is the same. It all depends on each individual's situation. In one of our Saturday meetings, he told me that once I achieve financial freedom and my total income is notably higher than my total expenses, from time to time I can afford to increase my discretionary expenses to enjoy things that other middle class earners won't be able to enjoy.

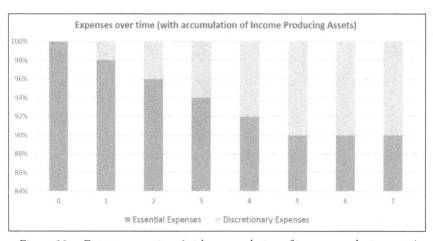

Figure 38—Expenses over time (with accumulation of income-producing assets)

THE THREE-STEP JOURNEY TO FINANCIAL FREEDOM

Putting all these principles together, your journey to financial freedom might need to undergo a three-step roadmap, starting with financial security and proceeding with financial comfort before you reach your ultimate objective of financial freedom. It all depends on your current situation. In the following paragraphs, I will lay down the three steps along the journey to financial freedom. Perhaps not all three steps apply to you since each person's situation is unique. Once you go through the three steps, you will identify where you are currently on your journey to financial freedom and then follow the roadmap.

This three-step financial freedom roadmap was one of the most life-changing lessons that Papa Joe ever taught me. In fact, this roadmap changed my life and made me achieve financial freedom in fewer years than I originally planned, even while being an employee. Let's discuss each of the stages of the financial freedom roadmap, and then connect them all together.

Stage One—Financial Security

The first stage is financial security, which will be achieved when you generate enough unearned income to cover your essential expenses. Once you achieve financial security, you will feel secure against the risk of leaving your job for whatever reason. At this stage, your unearned income still does not cover your discretionary expenses, but it ensures that you are covered on the essential expenses related to taxes, home mortgage or rent, utilities, home maintenance, insurance, education, food, and clothing. Simply put, in the first step of financial security, you will need to put a personal financial objective of achieving a sum of unearned income equal to essential expenses within a defined time frame.

Objective 1: Achieve a sum of unearned income equal to essential expenses within a defined
time frame.

If, for example, your essential expenses are $2,000, you will need to set a target of achieving a total of $2,000 from unearned income through the acquisition of income-producing assets within a defined period. It is important that you plan for this within a foreseeable time horizon. Otherwise it will become more like a wish than an objective. You will be challenged in the beginning to set a time frame since you might not yet have an idea of the net cash flow you will be generating from your income-producing assets. I recommend you start planning to achieve your financial security within a reasonable time frame. Once you start drafting your plan (see part 4 of this book on "How to Get There"), the time frame will be fine-tuned and made more realistic. In the beginning, I recommend you start with a reasonable time frame of five years. In reality, this objective may be achieved earlier. The five-year time horizon allows for some mistakes and delays while you are learning the first few baby steps in your acquisition of your first few income-producing assets. From there, you will have much more confidence and start to go at faster rates until you see yourself running quite fast. In this example, with having a monthly $2,000 essential expenses, your objective might be set as follows: Achieve $2,000 in monthly unearned income within the next five years.

At this stage, the Chicken Little in you might challenge you back with limiting beliefs about your incapability to do so. If you feel yourself getting caught in this situation, I recommend you revisit part 2 of this book, specifically the section on limiting beliefs. You need to make peace with this before you proceed any further.

Now let's get to the nitty-gritty details. For you to achieve your primary goal of generating a certain amount of unearned income per month, you will need to set secondary objectives related to your net cash flow and number of income-producing assets to be acquired. Let's go through each one of those secondary objectives in their logical order.

In step one of your journey, you will need to make sure you are reaching a set target of 30 per cent net cash flow from your total income. An increase in net cash flow can be achieved by any combination of increasing total income and decreasing total expenses. As you might be thinking right now, there is little or nothing you can do about increasing your unearned income. At this stage you have none to very limited unearned income. So you have practically no control over your income in the initial steps of stage one. Your only way to increase net cash flow is by reducing your total expenses. You need to take a pragmatic approach regarding your expenses to the extent of limiting your discretionary expenses to below 10 per cent of total income—even to zero.

Objective 1A: Achieve 30 per cent net cash flow from my total income by limiting my discretionary expenses to a maximum of 10 per cent of my total income in the next X months.

You will need to define a specific number and replace X with this number. I recommend you achieve this no later than three to six months.

Since your total income at the beginning of stage one is practically your earned income, which is more or less stable, it will be quite manageable for you to set targets of 30 per cent for net cash flow and 10 per cent for discretionary expenses. Assuming your current earned income is $2,000, your secondary objective might be written as such: Achieve $600 in monthly net cash flow by limiting my discretionary expenses to a maximum of $200 per month in the next six months. This secondary objective is usually a short-term target. With each acquisition of a new income-producing asset, your total income will change. Consequently, your absolute numbers for net cash flow and discretionary expenses will change to a higher number. Isn't that exciting? Your money engine will start to work at this stage, although at low speed in the beginning. But it will race at higher speeds later in stage one of financial security. Watch out! The speed of your money engine will go at higher speeds, beyond what you might have initially envisioned, when you move to stages two and three.

You might find yourself in a difficult situation here, where although you have limited your discretionary expenses to a maximum of 10 per cent, you are still not able to achieve your 30 per cent net cash flow target. This is where you need to take an objective look at your housing expenses. Remember, your total housing expenses must never exceed one third of your income. Can you challenge yourself and spend even 20 or 25 per cent on housing? This might imply that you are living in a house that is costing you more than what you can practically afford at this stage. The choice is yours. Do you want to enjoy a nice-looking house in an expensive neighbourhood even if it costs you more than a third of your income? If your answer is yes, you are a victim of instant gratification, and you may never achieve your objective of stage one. On the other hand, if you sacrifice the short term, your delayed gratification will be more rewarding later, in stages two and three.

Once you have secured enough monthly cash flow, you will need to save this money aside in a savings account dedicated to investment. This account will grow in the next few months until you accumulate enough to allow you to purchase income-producing assets.

This leads us to the second secondary objective of setting a number and value of rental properties to be acquired every year. The process of acquiring income-producing assets in the form of rental properties is the focus of part 4 of this book. You will learn how to use little of your money and make use of the power of leverage to acquire properties that will be rented out and generate positive cash flow after all expenses are covered.

Objective 1B: Buy X rental properties per year for the next Y years.

You will need to define a specific number of rental properties to be acquired each year. I recommend starting with one rental property per year for the first two years, and then increasing your objectives to two properties per year thereafter.

Stage Two—Financial Comfort

The second step is financial comfort. In this step you will be setting a personal financial objective of achieving a total of unearned income equal to the sum of your essential expenses plus discretionary expenses. Once you achieve this stage, you will have total relief. You can choose to leave your job to pursue other things in life. You may even choose to remain in a job that you are passionate about, but you will not have any fear of being kicked out of your job at any day in the future. Your income-producing assets can carry your total expenses as they are and without the need to reduce them.

> *Objective 2: Achieve a total of unearned income equal to the sum of your essential expenses plus discretionary expenses within a specified period of time.*

Stage Three—Financial Freedom

The final step of the journey is financial freedom. This is where your total unearned income will exceed your total expenses, both essential and discretionary expenses, by at least 30 per cent. This means your unearned income will allow you to afford keeping your life style as it is. On top of this, you will keep a 30 per cent net cash flow, which could be reinvested into more income-producing assets. This is the step where you feel your wealth is being fast-tracked and where you can start indulging yourself with things you thought you could never afford when you were at step one of your journey.

The figure below summarizes the three-step process to financial freedom.

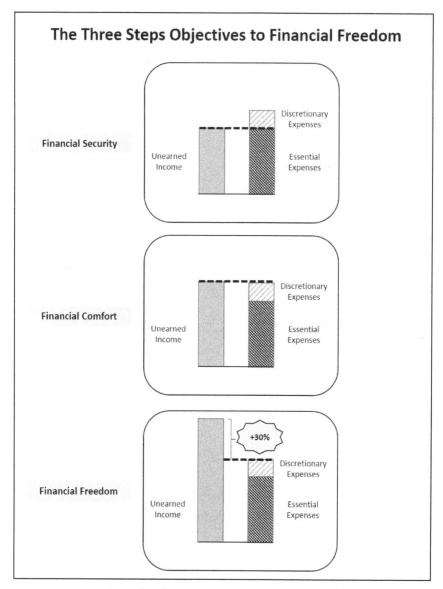

Figure 39—The three-step objectives to financial freedom

Chapter 4 Action Steps

Now it's time to set your own financial objectives for all three stages—financial security, financial comfort, and financial freedom. Your mind might trick you into taking it one step at the time, thinking that you will figure out the next stage objectives only after reaching the previous one. Don't fall victim to being short-sighted. You need to always set objectives with the end in mind—financial freedom. Papa Joe always recommended that I plan while I have the end in mind. Your ultimate objective is financial freedom, and it needs to be clear in your mind what it means to you. Stages one and two are only baby steps that lead you to the fast track, the final stage of financial freedom. Once you achieve your objectives for stages one and two, you won't feel any richer. But you will achieve a peace of mind that you can still lead a comfortable life whenever you leave your job by your own will or as an out-of-hand consequence. Only when you reach stage three, financial freedom, will you feel rich and be able to start enjoying the lifestyle that you dreamt about.

CHAPTER 5

Why Are Rental Properties the Best Investment Vehicle?

WHY ARE RENTAL PROPERTIES A BETTER INVESTMENT THAN PAPER ASSETS?

In the previous sections of this book, I've highlighted the importance of acquiring income-producing assets to build your unearned income. The golden question is, Which asset class will be the best income-producing asset? You might wonder whether paper assets (in the form of stocks, bonds, or mutual funds) will outperform real estate. Let's examine the different asset classes by comparing them from different angles, namely:

- The use of leverage
- Capital gain or loss
- Cash flow
- Control
- Liquidation of profits

The Use of Leverage

As I said earlier, when Papa Joe was explaining to me the principle of leverage, he asked me how many $100,000 homes I can purchase with $100,000 of my own cash. He explained to me how the power of leverage can allow me to purchase at least five homes, each purchased with 20 per cent down from my capital and the remaining 80 per cent financed through a bank or financial institutions. The number can even reach ten homes if each home is financed at 90 per cent loan-to-value. This means you can purchase up to $1 million worth of property with $100,000 out of your own money. The remaining $900,000 will be borrowed from the bank in the form of mortgage.

During one of our Saturday sessions, Papa Joe asked me how many hundred-thousand-dollar packages of stocks, bonds, or mutual funds I can purchase with $100,000 of my own capital. Not knowing what to answer due to my lack of information on this topic, he told me that the recommended and safe practice is to buy exactly $100,000 worth of paper assets. Some banks and financial institutions do allow buying paper assets on margins, but there are limitations related to certain selected paper assets and the amount of leverage. Not all paper assets are eligible for margin borrowing, and the available leverage for those that are eligible varies by market from 30 per cent to 60 per cent of the value of the stock.

With the evolution of online trading platforms, which are becoming more and more aggressive, the available margin on selected paper assets has reached above 90 per cent, leading the novice to suffer catastrophic losses.

But when we consider the ease with which a loan can be obtained, real estate is definitely a winner. Banks and financial institutions will be constantly competing on interest rates and offering lower financing costs to make their loans more appealing to real estate investors. Financial institutions are quite eager to lend money on properties. This makes us conclude that banks and financial institutions consider properties as a safe and secure investment. For the sake of like for like comparison, let's compare the 90 per cent leverage for both $100,000 worth of rental property and $100,000 worth of paper assets. Starting with cost comparison, you will incur a 3 per cent to 5 per cent interest rate on borrowed money for the rental property, whereas you can expect 10 per cent interest on the borrowed money for the paper asset. But this is still a minor difference as compared to our second comparison related to swings in the market.

Capital Gain or Loss

Let's compare both asset classes when their values fluctuate. If the market goes up, both assets will be winners. The major difference is when the market goes down. When paper assets on margin go down in value, the financial institution lending you the money will make a *margin call*, which forces you to top up your capital to pay a portion of the plummeted value in a way to go back to the agreed leverage, in that case 90 per cent loan-to-value. If the investor can't top up the invested capital, all the investment will be lost. To manage such disastrous risks, the investor in paper assets ends up putting almost the entire purchase price in cash. Before opening a margin account to trade paper assets or securities, consider the following:

- You can lose all the money, even more money than you invested.
- You may have to deposit additional cash or securities in your account on short notice to cover market losses and avoid margin calls.
- You may be forced to sell some or all of your securities when falling prices reduce the value of your securities.
- Your brokerage firm may sell some or all of your securities without notifying you to pay off the loan it made to you.

On the other hand, if the value of a rental property goes down, the bank will not make a margin call, you will not be obliged to add more funds to avoid losing it, and you are not obliged to sell the property to satisfy the loan. This is called *paper loss*, which is an unrealized capital loss in an investment. Losses become realized only when the asset is sold at a lower price.

Cash Flow

You will certainly be wondering why anyone would hold on to a rental property that has lost its price. The answer is cash flow. The primary reason to buy a rental property is because of its cash flow. In other words, a real estate investor carefully selects rental properties to be bought on the premise of generating positive cash flow, which means the rental income should outweigh the property expenses, including the mortgage payments. Why would anyone sell a property that is producing unearned income to its owner? As shared earlier under the section on risk management, the prudent investor buys rental property on the basis of their cash flow, not the promise of a future capital gain. For the prudent investor, capital gain is an added advantage that could be rewarding. But current decisions are never made on the basis of future capital gains. Markets can go up, down, or sideways. Cycles in the market are always there. If a rental property generates positive cash flow, the investor can weather any storm and survive any downside in the market until the cycle reverts and property prices pick up again.

Part 4 of this book will guide you on the selection criteria. A real estate investor will buy properties to ensure positive cash flow based on such criteria. In comparison, if we look at paper assets, we'll see not all of them generate positive cash flow in the form of dividends, and very few dividend-paying stocks are available on margin. The catch here is that you won't be able to collect any dividend from a stock bought on margin until you sell it. The caveat is that the broker will hold any dividends that get paid to you. The dividends held by the broker will be applied toward the debt you owe the brokerage firm. Only if you sell the stock for a profit can you pay back the broker what you borrowed and collect your dividends. In summary, cash flow in the form of dividends from stocks bought on margin is never guaranteed, whereas you are in full control of rent collected from rental properties.

Control

This takes us to the topic of control. When you buy $100,000 worth of dividend-paying stocks, you do not have any control over the initial purchase price, amount of dividends, when dividends will be paid, whether dividends will even be paid at all, or the future value of the stock. At best you can count on luck with a little bit of praying combined with some anxiety. It doesn't take much convincing here to agree that the investor will have no control at all over the current and future prices of stocks and other paper assets.

In contrast, when you buy $100,000 worth of rental property, you could have paid way more or way less than its worth, depending on how well you negotiate with the seller and the level of motivation of the seller. Most successful real estate investors whom I have studied manage to buy properties at 20 per cent discount versus their market value. They know how to negotiate, and they also know how to look for motivated sellers who want to get rid of a fine property for personal or family reasons.

Real estate investors always buy properties with money borrowed from banks or financial institutions. Those lending institutions will always ask you for an appraisal of the property to be done by a certified appraiser. This in fact acts as a protection for you not to overpay for a property, since the bank will not lend you money for something overpriced. The bank will happily lend you money for the appraised value of the property, which will act to your advantage when you buy a property at 20 per cent discount versus its appraised price. This is quite an important point that I would like to make sure you grasp. Consider a scenario where you found a property worth $100,000 that can easily be rented out. With good negotiations from your part and with good reasons for which the seller is quite motivated to close the deal, you have both agreed to close the sale at $80,000. You go to the bank and ask for a mortgage loan. The bank will send an appraiser to evaluate the property, and the report will reflect the market price or very close to it, which is $100,000. Responsible banks will lend you not more than 80 per cent of the value of the property, so with 80 per cent LTV (loan-to-value), the bank will happily lend you $80,000. As a conclusion, you would have bought this property with zero or little money down. Your cost will be limited to the agent's commissions and other closing costs. Isn't that great?

From there, you will rent out the property and generate unearned income for yourself after paying all expenses. If you are a responsible investor who looks after the investments you make, you will make sure the property is always well maintained. A combination of a good location, a well-maintained property, and positive cash flow will bring the property price higher. It will become easier for you to sell it with a proven track record of performance. This puts you in control in improving the future value of the property.

The message I am trying to share here is that you do have control over the purchase price, the rent, the expenses, and the future selling price. Many people would challenge back on the ease of selling a property in the future. This brings us to the next topic: ease of liquidation of profits.

Liquidation of Profits

Let's imagine a scenario where you bought both $100,000 worth of dividend-paying stock and a rental property worth $100,000, both with 90 per cent margin. For the sake of comparison, let's assume that after some time both investments have doubled in value. This means the current value of both investments is currently at $200,000 each. With 90 per cent margin on your initial investment, you would have invested $10,000 from your own cash to purchase each of the $100,000 stock and rental property. This means the $100,000 capital gain for each investment will result in a handsome 1000 per cent return on your invested capital. Those profits are called "paper profits" if not realized with the sale of the assets. So the main question you will be asking yourself is, Which asset is faster to liquidate to enjoy the profits? It will be a no-brainer to say definitely selling stocks is way easier and faster. In fact, with a click of a button or with a simple phone call asking your broker to sell, your stock will be sold instantaneously at market price. You will think that paper assets are definitely a winner when it comes to the ease of liquidation of profits, and I would totally agree with you.

In the case of paper assets, you can also have the choice of selling the entire portfolio or a portion of it. After paying the capital gain taxes, which depends on your country, you will still walk away with a handsome profit, but you will lose any future dividends from this stock, which is counterproductive to achieving financial freedom. Remember that to be financially free, you will need to increase your unearned income to a level that exceeds your current expenses. By selling the appreciated stocks, you will gain money now, but lose all the future unearned income in the form of dividends.

You might be wondering how rental properties can differ. The short answer is you do not need to sell your rental property to enjoy both tax-free profits and cash flow. In case you thought you read a mistake, I will repeat: You do not need to sell your rental property to enjoy both tax-free profits and cash flow.

If you got confused, don't worry. I was equally confused when Papa Joe threw this statement at me. When I asked him for an explanation, he clarified that selling such an asset would be an unwise decision for the simple fact that both the value of the property and the rental income will keep on increasing over time with inflation. Selling the property carries with it a tax burden. He explained (excitedly and in a high pitch) that the wise and educated investor can have access to the profit from the increased value of the property through refinancing.

Surprised, I sought confirmation of what I thought I understood, so I asked, "I can simply refinance the property with a new loan to enjoy the profit from the increased value?"

He advised with a smile that it is as simple as approaching the bank, asking for a new appraisal, and asking for a new mortgage on the new appraised value. The new mortgage pays off the previous one. The beauty of it all is that the investor cashes in the profit without the burden of capital gains tax. The profit is liquidated in the form of a mortgage and not in the form of a capital gain.

There is also a long-term benefit: The investor can still enjoy the rental income. This goes against the convention that says you can't have your cake and it eat it, too. Real estate, in the form of rental properties, has the magic that allows you to have your cake and eat it too ... and keep on eating from it for life. The wise investor, one who is determined to achieve financial freedom, can use this $100,000 and purchase with it five or even ten properties (each worth $100,000) with the use of leverage at 80 per cent and even 90 per cent. In that way the wealth-building process will be accelerated at rates not imagined by the investor before embarking on the journey of building wealth and achieving financial freedom. This virtuous cycle can be carried on and on with each appreciation of the price of the properties.

In this section, we have covered the advantages of real estate in the form of rental properties over paper assets. Would you be surprised if I told you that so far we are seeing just the tip of the iceberg? Let's examine the whole pack of advantages of rental properties.

RENTAL PROPERTIES GENERATE WEALTH, BUT NOT A GET-RICH-QUICK SCHEME

I recall one Saturday afternoon in the early days of my coaching with Papa Joe when I displayed my inclination to become rich practically overnight by following the same route of many people who have amassed tons of cash in short periods of time by trading paper assets and commodities. As soon as those words came out of my mouth, I saw him wearing an artificial smile. Papa Joe called his driver and asked him to prepare the car and requested me to join him for a ride in his car. While in the elevator, he asked whether I was carrying $1,000 on me.

Without a second thought, I asked him if he would instruct his driver to stop at any ATM for me to arrange to get that sum of money. While still in the elevator, which stopped on almost all the floors of this busy business tower, Papa Joe took his phone and typed a few words, which appeared to me later. It was a text message to his driver. When we reached the car, he told his driver to take us to the address that Papa Joe just texted him a few minutes back and also to stop at any ATM on our way to our destination, which I was still not aware of.

On our way, we passed by the perimeter of Manila airport runway. A few minutes later, the driver parked in front of a casino. Papa Joe opened his door and asked me to follow him inside. He informed me that he would be having a coffee in the café area while I make myself rich quick gambling. He said if I get lucky, I can become rich even much faster than trading.

I replied that I do not gamble. He asked me if day trading is any different from gambling, since success in both depends on luck.

As we sat in the café, I ordered a cappuccino. We listened to some good music and watched most of the casino guests leave with empty pockets and sorrowful faces. A rare few had happy faces after making some few winnings.

Papa Joe interrupted my contemplation and with a strong voice told me: "Rental properties are the best investment ever. I am not talking about rental properties being a *bit* better, not even *much* better, but *manifold* better than any other investment." He said that the wealthiest people throughout history made their fortunes through either real estate or businesses, but most preserve their wealth through owning real estate.

On that day, in the casino's café, Papa Joe shared with me for the first time ever his journey from poverty to wealth.

He started from humble beginnings, rarely finishing any month with money still in his pockets. He then was introduced to the benefits of owning rental properties. He invested in his ever first rental property, which allowed him to pay for the schooling of his son. Then he bought a second property a few years later to manage paying for schooling of his younger daughter. From those two properties, he repeated the same formula over and over, which seemed to accelerate more and more with the acquisition of each additional property. In less than ten years, he became financially free. He then opened his own business, which provided tons of cash, and he invested almost all of that cash into rental properties.

Then he started diversifying his rental property portfolio in major cities across the world. Based on what he learned from his first rental property investment, he replicated success hundreds of time. His story made me want to follow his steps and emulate him so I could achieve the same level of success in the future.

After we finished our coffee, he called the driver and asked him to drop us back at the office. On our way back, he told the driver to park the car on the side of a road with a clear view of Manila Airport's runway. While observing the planes taking off and landing, Papa Joe compared rental properties to a four-engine aircraft. The engines work harmoniously to lift the plane into the sky and to provide a smooth ride.

Those engines are the four wealth generators of rental properties. Papa Joe referred to those wealth generators as ACE and T.

- Appreciation
- Cash Flow
- Equity Build-up
- Tax Savings

He explained that while the engines provide the power to lift the aircraft in the air, other structural parts of the plane give it control, stability, and balance to reach its destination. Real estate is no different. Many other advantages of rental properties come into play while the four wealth engines are busy working to generate wealth to the investor. Papa Joe called those other benefits *enablers* to the wealth generation process.

The metaphor with the aircraft kept me tuned in despite some confusion on my end about what lesson Papa Joe was trying to convey. He suggested we start with the enablers first and briefly explained each as follows:

Tangible	Real estate is a physical property that anyone can see, touch, smell, and walk through. Many other investments, which can be traded online or via a phone call, are not necessarily backed up by a real physical entity behind them.
Basic need	Real estate is always in demand. People need a place to live. It is one of the most basic human needs.
Leverage-able	The fact that real estate is tangible and lovable makes it reasonably secure, which classifies it as the preferred asset to be offered as collateral by lenders against a loan. Real estate can be financed either at the front end, where it can be bought on margin, or at the back end, where existing owners can borrow money against their equity in the property. Papa

Joe often taught me that anyone can become at least as rich as the amount of good debt they take in their life. There is no better good debt than buying rental properties on margin.

Accessible   The fact that real estate is leverage-able, anyone can buy it. There are even many government-sponsored mortgages that make real estate accessible to a large segment of the population.

Stable   Real estate prices are slow to rise and slow to fall. This makes real estate a more stable and predictable investment than other investments that are subject to fluctuations in periods measured in seconds.

Reliable   Real estate has proved itself in generating and protecting wealth throughout history and across the globe. Each culture has its own stories of property ownership and wealth throughout the recorded history.

Negotiable   One of the most popular features of real estate is that its price tags (or listing prices) mean nothing. Investors can determine their real value and then can hustle and buy below listing price and below market price.

Improvable   If bought in the right location, an average property purchased at a high discount can be improved with minimal investment. This will force its price to appreciate. This kind of forced appreciation is what investors attribute to their sweat equity.

Controllable	Real estate is relatively easy to manage without too much time required by the investors. Investors with tight schedules can even assign a property management company to run the operations. The point here is that this makes real estate an asset class that can be controlled by the owner.

After we went through the enablers of rental properties, Papa Joe was excited to jump into briefly explaining the four wealth generators. He promised me to go back to this topic in due time. The four wealth generators will be explained in further details in chapter 17.

Appreciation	Real estate has witnessed many boom and bust cycles throughout history; however, the long trend is always up. The increase in value over time is slow and stable. Papa Joe referred to this benefit as the cherry on top. He told me to never buy properties for the objective of appreciation and capital gain. Appreciation can be either natural or forced. Smart investors who have experience in improving properties are at an advantage of forced appreciation.
Cash flow	Investors will buy and hold rental properties for the cash flow they generate in the form of unearned income. This will be the number one objective of buying rental properties and achieving financial freedom.

Equity build-up	The monthly rent collected from tenants will pay down the mortgage loan. With every loan instalment, a portion of the principal loan amount will be paid down, and the investor will own more equity in the mortgaged property. This means, assuming the property's market value did not change, the investor will become wealthier after each loan instalment of the mortgage.
Tax savings	Real estate owners can have access to large amounts of cash without ever needing to sell the properties and pay capital gains taxes. Papa Joe described this feature as eating the cake while still having it all. Depending on the equity level in a property, an investor can refinance the property through a mortgage and take home tax-free cash. Depending on the tax laws in your country, rental properties may have additional tax benefits. Some tax laws allow various tax deductions on expenses related to the operations of a rental property. Those tax deductions can offset the tax on unearned income from the same property and therefore can reduce the overall tax burden. Another tax advantage of real estate is depreciation. Although property values go up over time, some governments expect value depreciation (book values) to account for the wearing out over time. This allows investors in those countries to reduce their taxable income. Certain countries offer a major tax advantage of allowing investors to reinvest the capital gains from sold properties into new properties thereby deferring the taxes for later.

PART 4

How To Get There?

CHAPTER 6

Your Rental Properties' Investment Blueprint

When I was energized and ready to start investing in rental properties, I was blessed for having a great mentor who guided me throughout the journey albeit in quite an unconventional way. Papa Joe once explained to me that he would rather throw a child in a swimming pool and watch over the child fighting his way to stay afloat and survive, while staying quite close and alert as a responsible lifeguard would do, than putting that child through too much theoretical exercise. His coaching strategy worried me, but this was the deal—take it or leave it. My personality, my *big why*, and my energy level drove to jump in the swimming pool of rental property investment, without any hesitation, while I was confident that Papa Joe would always watch over me to help me, not only to stay afloat, but also to become a great swimmer.

The combination of Papa Joe's coaching style and my corporate experience in planning and following systems resulted in my systematizing what I was being coached on. The output was "My Rental property investment Blueprint". This plan has been tested and produced extraordinary results for me in my investments in East Asia, the Middle East, and Europe. I am quite confident this same blueprint will give me similar successful results in future planned investments in other European countries and the US. In fact, what Papa Joe taught me produced for him extraordinary results in his real estate empire across Asia, the Middle East, Europe, and the US. I can say with a high level of confidence that the learning from this book is not region specific, and that you can achieve great results in most countries in the world.

WHY DO YOU NEED A PROCESS?

Put simply, a process is a set of defined tasks needed to complete a given business activity, including who is responsible for completing each step, when, and how they do so. Without having a clearly defined process, your investment journey can't grow to its full potential. The closer I worked with Papa Joe, the more I realized that he had a process for all his investments. His process was never written on a piece of paper, but I concluded that he had it engraved in his brain.

Two reasons why a process is so important for success are *efficiency* and *scalability*. Having a documented process that you can use as a tool saves time, energy, and resources. Following a proven process will prevent you from losing time and money expended on trying to reinvent the wheel. Moreover, a system allows you to replicate any task over and over on each new property you will add to your portfolio.

RUN YOUR REAL ESTATE INVESTING AS A BUSINESS

In one of my Saturday coaching sessions with Papa Joe, he told me that I can choose to invest in real estate as an amateur or as a professional. Amateurs try to do it all by themselves, seldom following any proven system. Often those are the people who eventually lose their shirts in the investment game. As Papa Joe put it, amateurs end up as ignorant losers. Even if they lose their investments, they do not have a clue about the causes, and they start to blame others. They always start by playing the arrogant smart role when they go in. They end up playing the victim role when they lose it all.

On the other hand, professional investors build real estate investment businesses where they play the role of a leader who communicates a clear mission, and they surround themselves with a competent team that works together within a defined process and towards a defined set of objectives. The leader tracks the performance of each team member and measures the return on investment (ROI) and cash flow of his investments. Professional investors also carefully seek professional advice on the best legal entities to protect their investments and wealth.

There is definitely a big difference between an amateur investor and a professional one. When I learned the difference, I wanted to be only a professional investor. I understood that this means learning, following a process, having a team on board, setting objectives, and investing time to find and close deals. This book will empower you with knowledge, processes, and tools that can enable you to become a professional real estate investor.

How exciting! Let's proceed with the different steps of rental property investment. Subsequent chapters will discuss each of those steps in depth to empower you to close deals with confidence, calculated risks, and extraordinary results.

YOUR RENTAL PROPERTY INVESTMENT BLUEPRINT

In previous sections of this book, I walked you through the process of determining your current financial situation, analysing it, setting your SMART objectives, and determining your plan. You have been asked to apply the learning on your own situation with the tools presented to you in the action steps at the end of the chapters. I trust you already have a good understanding of your current financial situation and you are clear on your objectives. It is time for you now to get busy and start execution. It's the time to roll up your sleeves and go out to the marketplace, looking for team members, prospecting for deals, closing deals, and watching your cash flow and net worth grow.

Your rental property investment blueprint will consist of the following steps:

1. Build your team.
2. Get prequalified for a loan.
3. Prospect for discounted properties.
4. Analyse rental properties.
5. Negotiate and submit your offers.
6. Perform due diligence and commit.
7. Finance your rental property.
8. Transfer the title.
9. Rent your property.
10. Manage your rental property.

After reading the list above, your thoughts are most probably racing in all possible directions. You might face a feeling of anxiety. This is perfectly normal. For a novice, the blueprint might appear intimidating at first. But when you understand and follow each of the steps of this process, things will start to unfold in front of your eyes, and you will end up enjoying the process. I always compare the journey through the process to driving a car at night, where the driver can only see as far as the car's headlights allow. As the car moves forward, the driver is able to see new scenery and pass through other towns or villages until the final destination is reached. With the assistance of a navigation map or co-pilot, the driver feels more in control, confident that the car is still on the right track.

Your final destination is your set of objectives, the towns or villages along your way are the different steps of the blueprint, and your navigation map or co-pilot who will guide you throughout the way is me talking to you through the words in this book.

After you go through it at least one time and you close on a deal that makes you money, the whole process will be too much fun to repeat. It will also make you more confident on all your deals. Your confidence will project a positive vibe that makes team members want to work with you and sellers want to sell you their properties. It's a great, rewarding feeling, which gives you an equal level of satisfaction every time you close a deal, even if it's your hundredth deal.

Let's go back to the blueprint and allow me to show you the navigation map through the use of a visual roadmap. Below is a figure that represents the rental properties investment blueprint.

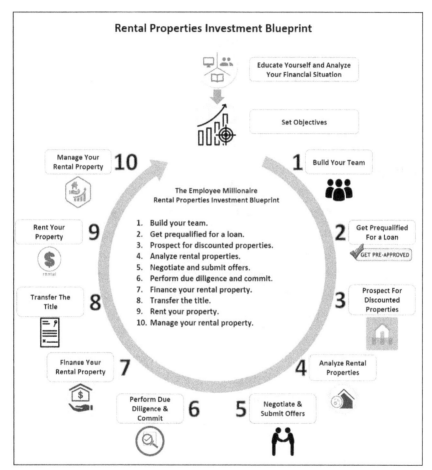

Figure 40—Rental properties investment blueprint

Each step of the blueprint is similar to a major turn onto a new major road on your navigation map. You will be given the heads-up you need to get prepared before you take each turn. You will also be receiving the information on the details of your trajectory.

So buckle up your seat belt. Your electronic navigation map is turned on. You have already have set the destination you want to reach by setting your objectives. Allow me to help you reach it using the most efficient route, while empowering you with all the information and tools you might require along the way.

A PERSONAL STORY ON BECOMING AN EMPLOYEE MULTIMILLIONAIRE BY FOLLOWING THE RENTAL PROPERTY INVESTMENT BLUEPRINT

As my financial education was on a steep curve with my Saturday coaching sessions with Papa Joe and also with my video calls with Joyce, I arrived at the realization that I needed to educate myself on real estate investment before jumping in and making costly mistakes. Whilst Papa Joe could have guided me on real estate investment, he insisted that I read books and attend seminars to learn from real estate gurus. He knew his limitations, having acquiring his knowledge from life experiences. He used to call himself "street smart" and insisted that I first learn a methodical way to which he would add using his street smart experience.

This looked to me like a fair deal, and I started reading books on real estate investing and discussing what I learned with Papa Joe. He used to add his bits of advice to my learning to add another perspective.

One day I heard about a three-day real estate seminar that had a steep price tag on it. Papa Joe insisted I invest this money in my learning. I registered online and also incurred travel and hotel costs to attend this seminar. I believe my learning from both the books and Papa Joe's advice equipped me well to benefit the most out of this seminar. I flew back to Manila and was fired up to do my first ever real estate investment.

I had reviewed my financial situation and written my SMART objectives. I chose to invest in one-bedroom apartments on the short run for the simple reason it was what I could afford back then. In retrospect, I recommend that new investors start with investing in smaller properties until they master the whole process. Eventually, with more experience and more financial strength, they will be ready to invest in larger single-family properties and eventually in multifamily properties. It's a lot of fun to climb the ladder step by step and keep a strong grip on it.

I started networking with mortgage brokers to get an idea on my loan eligibility and also with real estate agents. I carefully selected the agents who really grasped my investment criteria and conveyed the message that they could help me achieve what I wanted. Prospecting for properties took a couple of weeks. We screened more than a hundred, viewed more than a dozen that matched my investment criteria, and sent letters of intent with offer prices to a handful of owners. Bingo! One motivated seller accepted my offer to buy a one-bedroom apartment with one parking lot for $97,750. This apartment was located in a premium location condominium, and it had an excellent view overlooking the Manila Golf Course. The whole condominium was turned over by the developer at exactly the same time we sent our letter of intent. The market price of this apartment was around $120,000 at that time. The previous owners did not have the remaining 50 per cent payment that was due to the developer upon handover of the property, so they were highly motivated to sell it at 18.5 per cent below market price. Otherwise, they might have lost all their investment. As soon as my offer was accepted, I had to put a 10 per cent deposit that was contingent on the bank approving the mortgage, as stipulated in the letter of intent. The bank had asked for an appraisal report to be done by a certified party. No surprise! The property was appraised at $120,000, and the bank agreed to lend me 80 per cent of the property's value, which was $96,000, over a period of 25 years and 4 per cent interest rate. I only had to put up $1,750 from my pocket to cover the rest of the $97,750, and another $1,920 for closing costs and title registration. I immediately invested $15,000 in furniture and minor interior design, which enabled me to rent it out at a premium rate to a French expatriate who was assigned in the Philippines for three years. The monthly rent was $1,300, which was way higher than the total monthly costs of $622

($115 monthly operating expenses plus $507 monthly loan instalment). The monthly net cash flow of the property was $678, which resulted in a whopping 43.6 per cent annual ROI based on my initial investment of $18,670 (inclusive of cost of furniture and interior design).

In part 4 of this book, I will walk you through all the details of those computations. In this section, I am trying to explain the advantages of real estate, not the how-to. Since I bought this property in September 2009, it has appreciated in value to $180,000 in May 2011. I ran directly to the bank, did a new appraisal, and the bank offered me 80 per cent of the appreciated value of $60,000. I received a handsome $48,000 tax free while I still owned the property that was still providing me a monthly rental income. This sum of money has enabled me to buy more properties using the same principles. But my returns were exponential. To an extent I was able to become an employee millionaire and achieve financial freedom in less than five years. Until now I am still repeating the same formula over and over and I have become an employee multimillionaire. I enjoy the process, and I am planning on doing the same over and over. This kind of action gives me a lot of energy and keeps me going. All the while I am still an employee—by choice.

The story above is a summary of how my first investment has fuelled many other future investments and made me learn over time. In my early stages of investment, I did not have all the steps of the investment blueprint (presented in this chapter) figured out. As a result, I have made many mistakes. Some were small, and others cost me major losses. From each property I have acquired, I have jotted down the lessons, be it a success or a failure. It took me a handful of investments to fine tune the investment blueprint.

My advice is to follow all the steps in the investment blueprint, not attempting to make shortcuts. Papa Joe used to always advise me, "be smart, but don't outsmart the process and look for shortcuts". I extend to you the same advice. Every shortcut I took had its respective price tag, which was an unnecessary cost. Learn from the mistake of others and save the money you may spend on fixing unnecessary mistakes so that you will have more capital to invest in more and more rental properties.

Chapter 6 Action Steps

Have a copy of the Rental property investment Blueprint always with you in the form of either a hard copy printout or soft copy on any of your digital devices. An image of the blueprint can be downloaded from my website www.employeemillionaire.com/resources. It will become quite handy as you navigate the remaining chapters of this book. I encourage you to refer to it as often as you require when you start investing in rental properties.

CHAPTER 7

Build Your Team

WHY A TEAM?

Tell me of any person who has achieved success all alone, and you will see me raising my eyebrow with a big exclamation mark. Heads of state have large teams who give them advice behind the scenes and who help them execute their agendas. Actors have a large crew of producers, directors, trainers, prompters, and other professionals from many walks of life to help them deliver great performances in great movies or theatres. Surgeons cannot perform a surgery without the help of a team of doctors, nurses, anaesthesiologists, and other operating room staff all working together. A CEO cannot run a company without the help of a team of directors, managers, lawyers, accountants, financiers, marketers, operations, IT, sales people, supply chains, and human resources. In a similar fashion, professional real estate investors cannot succeed without a team of professionals who can help them execute their plans.

In his great book *Good to Great*, Jim Collins explains that great companies follow the mantra "first *who*, then *what*". Executives who ignite the transformation from good to great do not first figure out where to drive the bus and then get people to take it there. No, they first get the right people on the bus (and the wrong people off the bus) and then figure out where to drive it. Those leaders believe that if they get the right people on the bus, the right people in the right seats, and the wrong people off the bus, then they will figure out how to take their company someplace great. There are three mains reasons for this belief:

- If you begin with "who" rather than "what", you can more easily adapt to a changing world.
- If you have the right people on the bus, the problem on how to motivate and manage people largely goes away. The right people don't need to be tightly motivated or fired up. They will be *self*-motivated by the inner drive to produce the best results and to be part of creating something great.
- If you have the wrong people, it doesn't matter whether you discover the right direction. You still won't have a great company. Great visions without great people is irrelevant.

You should have the same philosophy when selecting your team members. In your real estate investment journey, there should be seats only for A players who are going to put forth an A-plus effort. Everyone else can look for their place on other buses. You cannot afford to spend time and energy trying to convince your team of your objectives. They need to be fully committed from day one. They need to believe that each one of them, if they do what they are good at, will make you achieve your objectives, and they will get rewarded accordingly.

After building your team and making sure you have the right people in place, you will engage with them in healthy debates to figure out the best path to greatness. You do not want to be the "genius with a thousand helpers" who sets a vision for where to drive the bus, develops a road map for driving the bus, and then enlists a crew of helpers to execute the plan. You have to share your objectives with your team members and be willing to make necessary changes based on their advice.

Who are your team members? You need to start building an alliance with a group of people for the purpose of carrying out your plans. This group is referred to as the *mastermind alliance*. You need the help of mentors and advisors who can coach you, guide you, and teach you the ropes of the trade. Without support of other people, it will be quite challenging, if not impossible, to achieve your objectives. Think of your mastermind alliance as your support team, which will be your most valuable resource.

Your mastermind alliance will consist of mentors and a team of advisors. A mentor is a successful person whom you look up to, a person whose steps you would want to follow. In my case, Papa Joe was one of my great mentors. He was a person who walked the talk. He was giving me advice on things that he had accomplished himself. In fact, Papa Joe has accomplished what I wanted to accomplish.

In addition to mentors, you will need a team of competent advisors. A well selected team of advisors will help you on your journey to financial freedom by providing both protection and technical expertise. The team members need to prove their competencies. They should practice what they preach, and their goals must be aligned with yours. Remember this team is set up to assist you achieving your objectives. A team of professional advisors will be selected on the premise that they are experts on the subject matter on which you are seeking their advice. If you are serious about starting and building your career as a professional real estate investor, your team could include mortgage bankers or brokers, real estate agents, lawyers, insurance agents, property managers, and accountants. The team list will constantly change along with different expertise you will require for the execution of the strategies and plans you have set for yourself.

Having a team of experts requires some investment. It takes time to select your team, to build a strong relationship with them, and to align them with your objectives. It also takes time and money to keep this team holding strong. The truth is that it costs much more for you *not* to have a team to support you. As my executive coach and mentor Stewart B. taught me, "The cost of having a team is way lower than the expense of not having a team." By this he meant that if you have no advice or cheap advice, it is more expensive than expert advice. Your team of experts will save you large sums of money that you could lose without expert advice. In the following paragraphs, I share two personal stories that illustrate the lessons of not building a team.

PITFALLS OF DOING IT ALL BY YOURSELF

Before I started my real estate investment career, I lost a lot of money on several failed attempts to open my own business in parallel to being an employee. At that time, I had only a vague objective of being my own boss. Not knowing any better back then, this was only a wishful thought and not a SMART objective (as you may have noticed).

In 2006, while I was based in the Philippines, I saw an opportunity to sell VoIP (voice over Internet protocol) gadgets to small businesses with business partners in other parts of the world. Those gadgets would save those businesses lots of money on international telephone bills. Given that I did not have time to go around and sell those devices to those small businesses, I recruited a salesman who visited recruiting agencies that deployed Filipino skilled labour oversees. Many of those businesses had tried those VoIP gadgets, saw the cost benefits, and started buying them and also buying credit loads to make their international calls.

In just a few weeks, the business started to perform above my humble expectations. Demand started to grow, and I started to stock up on more and more supplies. This salesman was a hell of a sales guy. He would strip you and sell you back your own clothes with a big smile on his face. My confidence in him grew daily, and in order not to miss any sales opportunities, I handed over most of the inventory I had to him so that he could make the sale on the spot without the need to go back and forth.

In the next few months, I was making a net monthly profit in excess of my salary. I started to buy more and more inventory and stock it up with my single employee. We used to meet over coffee every Saturday for about an hour to go through the sales, inventory, and the accounting. On one Saturday afternoon, this guy did not show up to our meeting. After some investigation, it appeared that he flew out of the country for good. Apparently he sold all the inventory he had on hand. On top of that, he took advance payments from some of our clients for remote credit top-up. I became liable to pay the supplier and also honor all the orders that were paid in advance by our clients. In conclusion, I paid a steep price of $35,000 due to lack of protection, both legal and insurance protection. This salesman was working with me on a part-time basis, without any legally binding documents that made him an employee of the company. Little did I know back then about building a team. If I had a lawyer or legal advisor, I would have received sound advice on how to protect my interests.

The cost of this lesson was quite expensive, not only in terms of money lost, but more importantly in terms of the stress I had to put up with to protect my reputation and pay back all my liabilities. This business did not go on for a long time. I sold it in a few months after I settled all the company's liabilities and commitments.

When I was honouring the company's commitments towards its clients and suppliers, one of my clients told me that he admired my business ethics. He thought I would run away and never imagined I would stick to the end until the matter was resolved. He called me one afternoon to invite me to visit his office. I accepted the invitation and visited him at one of his companies. This businessman owned three companies: a couple of restaurants and a hotel. I was impressed with the empire he had built, especially because he started from poverty. He told me stories of his youth stories, when he reached a stage without a single penny in his pocket. It was quite inspiring how he persevered and built up such empire with many businesses.

He offered me an opportunity to open a branch of his company as a franchise and focus on deploying skilled labour to Europe and the Middle East. Both regions were in need of nurses, waiters, and other skilled labour. This time, learning from my previous mistakes, I made my due diligence with the help of a lawyer and an auditor in order to ensure a decent level of protection. Being an employee, I did not have the luxury of time to run the day-to-day operations. I offered my brother the chance to be the managing director and run the business. It was simple, and being a franchisee kind of relationship, we were offered all the business know-hows.

Being naïve, I selected my brother as a team member to manage my business based on our family tie instead of selecting the managing director based on qualifications. A few months later, the financials of the business were in decline, and after investigation, it appeared that the good-looking secretaries were managing my brother quite well to the extent that he lost control of the business. I had to ask my brother to step out of the business.

For the next few months, I was obliged to work long nights and long weekends just to bring the business back in good shape. I couldn't continue working long hours as an employee and then equally long hours in the evenings and on weekends. Therefore, in a few months I asked my partner, the franchisor, to buy back the business. Luckily for me, I had managed to recoup my losses and walked away with a no-gain, no-loss situation. I have chalked this experience up to my education and moved on.

As you might have noticed, I was so unwise that I failed more than once in business due to not building a team of experts. Yet each failure taught me a lesson on the high cost of not having a team. I encourage you to learn from the mistakes of others instead of paying dearly for learning from your own mistakes.

When I started my real estate investment career, I was building a team of experts along the way. This team provided me the required education and guidance before I pulled the trigger on the purchase of my first one-bedroom apartment. The relatively smaller time and monetary investment I put in at the front end enabled me to reap much bigger rewards on the back end.

My simple advice is this: Build your team before you embark on your journey as a real estate investor. Your team will save you money and will prepare you to overcome challenges that you will eventually be encountering along the way. Your team will enable you to make decisions that are both right and on time because you won't have to pause and go out looking for people to help you. In the absence of a team, you will either never pull it through and invest in rental properties or settle for mediocre advice from non-professionals and will end up paying dearly for the mistakes that are inevitable from such free advice. Successful real estate investors do not wait and look for help only when they need it. They want to get the help they need, instead of the help they can get on a short notice.

YOUR TEAM MEMBERS

Having the right team members on board is crucial for your real estate investment business. The larger your objectives are, the more experienced your team must be. Each member of your team will play a key role in helping you succeed.

When you start building your team, you will need to determine the skills or expertise you require and the criteria based on which you will select your team members. Your team is to be an interconnected group of carefully selected professionals who each meet all of the following three criteria: They have an impressive track record in their area of expertise, they are currently active in the market, and they are willing to offer their professional help whenever required.

Earlier we discussed the concept of leverage. Your team is an example of leveraging talents. With their help, you can accomplish much more than you can all alone. Your role will be to build and, more importantly, maintain relationships with those team members who will mentor you, present to you opportunities, help you buy your properties, provide access to financing, and help you maintain and manage your properties. Depending on their area of expertise, your team members will fall into any of these three distinct groups:

Advisory Board	This group of people will give you advice, guidance, and wisdom. They will challenge your way of thinking. They will form your mastermind alliance.
Executive Board	This group of people will help you throughout your transactions from beginning to end. They are experts in their respective fields. They will either do the transactions on your behalf (for a fee) or advise you about the whats and hows. These people who offer you information, counsel, strategy, leads, management, and leverage.

The team members of this network are the lenders, real estate agents, property managers, and others who are called upon on every investment opportunity. Each of them will fulfil a key role in the different steps of acquiring a rental property investment.

Service Squad — These are the service providers who act on demand and will perform specific tasks and get paid for the services rendered. They perform specific works and get paid for the results. They are the lawyers, handymen, contractors, accountants, appraisers, and others you may need, depending on the situation. You will be contacting those people as often as the need arises for their services.

Do not expect to build your team all at once. You need just a few team members to get started. Your team will grow over time.

Your team members will also change over time since you will be meeting many potential team members until you find your dream team. The process is no different than recruiting employees for a company, where as soon as candidates pass the interviewing process they are placed under probation for a couple of months. During this probation period, the shortlisted candidates will demonstrate their skills and capabilities. Only when you become satisfied with the job they have done will you declare them qualified to be permanent members of your team.

BUILDING YOUR ADVISORY BOARD

When starting to build your team, among many questions that will cross your mind will be about who is the first person that needs to be on board. Before you start searching for your professional team members, you need to have your spouse or significant other on board with your *big why*, your objectives, and your plan. Your romantic partner might act either as a cheerleader or a detractor to your plan, depending on whether that one supports or opposes your mission. It makes perfect sense to have a person who has a huge impact on your emotional and mental state fully on board with your ambitions and plan. If you succeed, you've acquired yourself not just a cheerleader, but also a sounding board.

I have seen friends fail to embark on their financial freedom journey for failing to have their spouses fully aligned on their plans and not making them an integral part of their team. I have also worked with friends who got the full support of their spouses by convincing them that they had a sound plan. The following tips can help you do just that:

1. Educate yourself on rental property investment. This will help you to become an expert on that subject and will enable you to answer any question they might have. By seeing your commitment to reading books, attending seminars and webinars, attending real estate networking events, and having mentors, your significant other will have more confidence in your will to succeed and in your plans.

2. Share your *big why* and take baby steps in sharing your learning. You do not need to overwhelm your spouse with the theories, concepts, and the math of rental property investment. Instead share the big picture in a simplified way. Share how rental properties generate unearned income that will help you achieve financial freedom. Your significant other will be excited upon understanding that being financially free will enable you to spend more quality time together in the future.

3. Encourage your spouse to go through the same educational material that got you hooked. Throughout your education, you will come across a ton of educational materials. Some will be numbers and systems driven, while others will be more motivational in nature. From my experience with many friends, it is the motivational books, audiobooks, or webinars that have helped ignite the passion for real estate investing in their spouses.

4. Make them feel they are a part of your advisory board. A spouse who feels included in the decision-making will support you all the way to success. You do not need to overwhelm anyone with boring details about the numbers and the math. Sharing the bottom line of how each property will add unearned income and how it will get you closer to your financial freedom goal will make them very supportive.

I am blessed with a wife who is not only on board with my real estate investment career but also acts as my financial advisor who advocates financial freedom through rental property investment. Every day of my life I feel grateful for having her as my spouse, my friend, my mentor, my cheerleader, and my co-pilot. She often encourages me to keep my foot on the pedal when she sees me slowing down on our investments. She is also a great help in negotiating deals (a gifted negotiator), managing the properties, and bookkeeping.

After having your spouse or significant other as the first team member of your advisory board, seek other members as mentors whom you want to emulate. They will give you advice, guidance, and wisdom based on their experience and success. They will ask you the right questions to challenge your way of thinking. When you attempt to answer those questions, the best of you will show up. Those advisors will not often tell you how to perform transactions, they will guide you on what needs to be done to accomplish your goals. They will guide you in setting your objectives and fine tuning them.

It is the role of your executive board to help you on *the h*ows. If asked for referrals, your advisory board can hook you up with their own executive board members. This will give you a good head start in finding, funding, and managing your real estate purchase transactions. Papa Joe has put me in contact with many of his team members, and each of them has coached on specific aspects of real estate investing.

BUILDING YOUR EXECUTIVE BOARD

Your next step is to get started with building your executive board. As mentioned earlier, this will consist of lenders, real estate agents, property managers, and others who are called upon on every investment opportunity. Each will play a key role throughout your transactions from beginning to end.

Lender or mortgage broker: A lender or mortgage broker who understands the business of rental property investing will not only lend you money to finance the properties you want to buy but will also provide you insights on the market trends. From the volume of mortgages from their financial institutions and from their competitors, a mortgage broker can have a good feel for the market and will know whether it is trending upward or downward. Fewer people applying for mortgages means less demand on properties. Eventually prices will head down. The opposite is also true: An increasing number of mortgage applications signifies increased demand that may lead to higher property prices.

Before you go out and make offers on properties, it is wise to establish a relationship with lenders and mortgage brokers so you know how much money lenders are willing to lend you based on your creditworthiness. It's crucial to do this *before* you start searching for rental properties to invest in. The amount of money you can borrow will determine the criteria and the number of rental properties you will be buying. (More on this topic later in the book.) Remember that those professionals earn their commissions only when they sign you up for a mortgage contract. For this reason they will try their best to guide you not only on getting a loan but also on increasing the loan amount by giving you tips on restructuring your short-term debt like personal loans, car loans, and credit card loans.

Building a long-term relationship with your lender or mortgage broker is of high value for many reasons. They will keep on guiding you on getting more loans with your increased future income through rentals. They will also share with you insights on the volumes of mortgage loans being lent to both investors and end users, which will give you a kind of insider information on the current demand for rental properties in your market.

One of the most important benefits of having a mortgage broker on your team is the hints you might get on bargain buys from highly motivated (or distressed) sellers in the market. Those professionals have good insights on who from their previous customers are at risk of defaulting on their mortgage payments, which could be an opportunity for you to buy the properties that fit your criteria at a bargain price, while at the same time saving those people from losing their properties in the eventual consequence of mortgage payments default.

This topic is quite sensitive, and ethics are involved. The mortgage brokers on my team never give me hints on those financially challenged property owners who are at risk of a mortgage default. Rather, they share my contact details with those owners and leave the decision to them whether to decide to contact me to discuss the sale of their properties.

Once you start your search for lenders who can help you fund your investments, you will find yourself working with any of the following:

- Banks (large international banks, large national banks, or small community banks).
- Mortgage brokers who will find you the proper financing that fits your needs from different types of lenders.

Whether you are ready now to start your first investment or not, start engaging with lenders today. My advice is to start the process of applying for a mortgage loan with the objective of getting a loan preapproval. This will enable you to learn their requirements as early as possible in the process and to get your finances in order in the event your loan application was rejected or the loan limit was not enough to enable you to invest in your first property. Those lenders will educate you on how they computed your loan limit and will give you hints on how to structure your finances to get more loan limits moving forward. Once you have a loan preapproval (also known as a *preapproval letter*) in your hands, you can go out with strong ammunition hunting for properties that will match your investment criteria. Chapter 8 is dedicated to mortgage loans and how to get preapproved for a loan.

Real estate agent or broker: This is your key person in finding the properties that meet your criteria. You can get many insights on the rental property trend in your market from a person who specializes in a certain geography. Beware of the fast-talking real estate agents who can strip you and sell you back your own shirt! Those professionals earn their income in the form of a commission whenever a property is sold. It doesn't take too much to guess that they will try to sell you any property—regardless of whether it meets your criteria—just so they can earn their commission.

Your role is to hand-pick those agents or brokers who can understand an investor's investment criteria. As an investor, you are looking at numbers like rental income, expenses, net operating income, and cash on cash returns, which we will talk about in detail in the following chapters. You will not be convinced by a fast-talking agent who will charm you with words that make you visualize a dream home by explaining what the kitchen might look like or how the wallpaper might make your living room warm or a bedroom might make your love life happier.

Those things might convince an end user to buy a home, but your agenda is different. You want to generate unearned income through rental properties. You want the highest possible return on investment. You want to have an estimated forecast of when you can get back your invested capital so that you can reinvest in the next rental property. Please do yourself a favor and spend time meeting agents and discussing with them your investment criteria until you shortlist a handful who can help you execute your rental property investment plan. Over time, those select agents will become more educated on your criteria for rental property investing and will find you great deals. They do have a high interest in enabling you to achieve your objectives, since this will guarantee more and more future investments and eventually more and more commissions. Those professionals will also help you in negotiating with the sellers, getting the documents ready, and in registering the title. They deserve every penny of their commission.

So how much does a real estate agent cost you when buying properties? It can range from nothing up to 5 per cent, and in some countries even 6 per cent. Make sure to do the research on the practice in your city, state, or country related to the commissions to be paid to real estate agents or brokers. In some countries, the buyer does not pay anything, whereas in some other countries, the buyer pays it all. A practice I favor is splitting commission in half between the seller and the buyer. Whatever the cost is, a great real estate agent is worth every penny. This is because great real estate agents are rare gems to find in today's reality, where everyone wants to sell anything to everyone else without understanding the buyer's needs or criteria.

So what makes an agent a great real estate agent?

- **Honest and displays integrity:** It is imperative to work with an agent whose reputation precedes him as being honest. The best way to find those great real estate agents is referrals. Many salespeople are dishonest, putting their needs (earning a commission) above your own needs (buying properties that meet your investment criteria). Honesty and integrity are my first filter when meeting new real estate agents. If I encounter a dishonest agent, I just shake hands and walk on the other side of the street. This criterion should be your first selection filter. You do not want to do business with a highly skilled but dishonest agent. You will regret it big time when you find yourself losing time and money while making this dishonest agent richer.

- **Understands the investor mindset:** A great agent is someone who understands your investment criteria and can help you achieve *your* goals, not their own. After sharing your investment criteria and taking the proper time to explain your priorities, if the agent still brags about the kitchen tiles, the living room, the view, or the capital gain appreciation, shake hands, wish the person good luck, and part ways. You do not want to lose time and energy speaking an investment language to a salesperson who wants to earn a commission at any cost without even attempting to listen to your criteria. You will feel like you're speaking Chinese to a person who understands only English. Great agents can directly relate to your language when you start sharing your criteria in terms of return on investment, potential rental income, net operating income, and price negotiation. It takes time to interview many agents and end up with a few who can be classified as great agents. In my experience, great agents who understand the investor mindset are usually those who have personal investment experience. Once you find them, treat them as precious gems while building and maintaining relationships with them.

- **Has experience in the local market:** Once you set your mind on a location to invest in, you will need a great agent with hands-on experience in the same area. Your agent should be quite knowledgeable in your market. Your agent should be able to tell you of upcoming new developments (like schools, hospitals, malls, supermarkets, bridges, public transport stations). Your agent should be aware of employers moving their offices into or out of your selected market. All of those variables will have an impact on future demand for rental. An agent should have a sense for the prices in the market and give you proper advice if prices are going upward or downward.

- **Responsive, accessible, and motivated:** As an employee real estate investor, your available time to meet with real estate agents and make viewings is normally after office hours and during weekends. You will require a great agent who is accessible during those after-hours periods. In my experience, highly motivated agents who earn decent commissions by taking their profession seriously and professionally are those who make themselves accessible to your schedule and also tend to be responsive. When you find a great deal and you are ready to pull the trigger and make an offer, you need a responsive great agent who swiftly coordinates between you and the seller to close a win-win deal.

My wife and I have often found bargain properties that meet our criteria without having an agent as intermediary. Those are the direct-from-seller deals. We still called our agents on our executive board to work on closing those deals, and of course we fully paid their commissions. Those agents were able to negotiate the selling price further with the sellers on our behalf. To an extent both my wife and I have entrusted in them the full negotiation process with sellers. Our role in the negotiation process became limited to a final squeeze on the selling price before shaking hands with the sellers.

Those select agents from our executive board used to even structure the deals for us such that the difference between the negotiated price and the market value became a form of down payment in the form of sweat equity. This enabled us to pay from almost nothing to less than 10 per cent on the agreed purchase price and obtain the balance in the form of financing from the bank. In our own lingo, we often refer to this as the *art of the deal*. It is like creating money out of thin air by applying our wisdom and knowledge. More will be covered on this topic in chapter 11.

Other important team members whose role becomes important when you want to rent your vacant properties are the rental or leasing agents. In sophisticated markets or in sophisticated real estate brokerage companies, the rental or leasing agent is a different person from the real estate agent who specializes in buying and selling properties. You will need to be aware of the practices in your market so you can start looking for potential rental or leasing agents to be on your team way before you purchase a property. You do not want to end up rushing things when looking for a tenant or to be put in a situation where you offer your rental property for less than the market rate just to avoid having a vacant unit for a long time. Chapter 15 will focus on renting out properties and how a rental or leasing agent can play a crucial role in finding the right tenants, at the right time, and for the right rental income.

Insurance agent or broker: An insurance *broker* will help you place the proper protection at the right price by shopping around at different insurance companies for the best rate and coverage. Insurance *agents*, on the other hand, want to sell you the insurance provided by their affiliated insurance companies. Both insurance agents and brokers earn a living from the commissions on the insurance coverage they sell. It is a no-brainer to guess that it is in their best interest to sell you a higher coverage than you might require, which comes at a higher insurance premium, and of course higher commissions for them and lower profit for you. The caveat here is that you must not fall for the opposite mistake of chasing the lowest insurance rate or coverage. Chapter 10 covers the topic of insurance coverage in detail to enable you make the right decisions in selecting the insurance you require while managing well the property's operating expenses.

Property manager: This professional will run the operational side of your rental property business. In the beginning of your journey, I recommend you do the property management by yourself for two main reasons. First, it will give you hands-on experience on property management, which will help you better select future property managers when the number of your rental properties increases to the extent of being unmanageable, especially while you are still an employee. The second reason is to save on property managers' fees so that you secure higher returns, which will enable you to generate more cash to be used towards your next rental property investment. The sooner you invest in your next property, and your next and your next, the more energy and momentum you will maintain. There will come a time when you will definitely require professional property management. This is why it is so crucial for you to start building relationships with them early on. It will make it easier to select the fit ones whenever you require their help. Another advantage of starting to build the relationship sooner in your journey is definitely the insights you will learn from those professionals on property management.

BUILDING YOUR SERVICE SQUAD

As for your *service squad*, as mentioned earlier, it will consist of service providers who work on demand. They will perform specific tasks and get paid for the services rendered. They are the lawyers, handymen, contractors, accountants, appraisers, and others you may need, depending on the situation. You will be contacting those people as often as the need arises for their services.

Lawyers: In the early stages of your investment journey, you will need proper legal advice. But as you build wealth, you will also require legal protection against greedy persons who want to take some of your wealth away from you.

A good lawyer will help you set up your sale and purchase agreements and rental or lease contracts in a proper manner to make them legally binding, thereby protecting your interest in the purchase of properties and eventually renting them out to tenants. As the number of properties you own becomes larger, your lawyer will recommend the best legal entity for holding your properties. With the number of tenants growing with the increasing number of rental properties acquired, the risk of tenants defaulting on their rent payments will increase. Your lawyer will play an important role in the eviction process.

Lawyers provide specialized services, which do not come at a cheap rate. You have to carefully select a lawyer who has solid experience in real estate, especially in your city, state, or country. Referrals is a good way to begin selecting a lawyer to be a member of your team. You will have to interview the potential lawyers yourself, asking questions relevant to real estate and rental property investments.

Lawyers are paid by the hour, so you have to carefully determine how to best use their time. In the beginning, you will need some time with your lawyers to make sure the sale and purchase agreement as well as the rental agreement templates are legally binding in your area. Later I will offer some templates that can be shared with your lawyer, who can make any necessary adjustments that fit the legal requirements in your city, state, or country. As you acquire more properties, you will need to consult with your lawyer for protection. Your lawyer will advise you on the best legal entities for holding your properties. As you may have concluded, you may need to engage the services of a lawyer for a limited time, so do not become intimidated by the expensive rates per hour. The expense of not getting enough legal protection far outweighs the cost of a lawyer.

Contractors and Handymen: Repairs and maintenance, be it small or large jobs, are always needed for any residential property. Make sure you find someone with the right skill set, training, and licensing to do a particular task. As with the selection of most of your team members, referrals are always a safe start, followed by interviews.

In the case of handymen, I recommend you try their work on some jobs required for your personal residence. This last step is equivalent to a trade test done by some businesses in the selection of their skilled labour. Those companies want to test both the skilled labourer's attitude and skills before final selection. It shouldn't be any different for you. I am sure you have either had a bad personal experience or heard about unpleasant experiences from your parents, family members, or friends about handymen being always late for appointments, never showing up at all, not answering calls, or doing a mediocre job. You do not want to be in a situation of facing similar bad experiences when you urgently need a repair to be done. For those reasons, I recommend you start searching for handymen when you do not need them, interview them, and then test their commitment and work for jobs at your home. Finding the right contractor or handyman will be the most difficult and frustrating task when selecting your team members.

With informed expectations, you should be prepared and not surprised by any inconvenience you might face when selecting your contractor or handyman. I've often wondered why this is such a frustrating task. My experience led me to conclude that:

- Handymen possess technical skills but often lack the managerial skills required to manage their schedules, get back to clients, and plan follow-up visits.
- Handymen want to get the most income out their time, whereas real estate investors always chase better deals. While investors attempt to negotiate lower maintenance costs, contractors or handymen will probably invest their time with a client who offered them more money for their work. You guessed it! This means they will not show up to their appointments or will at best reschedule you for when they do not have other jobs.
- Real estate investors prefer to avoid working with more established contractors, ones who are good at running their business, because they assume they will charge more, are always

booked, or will not take on smaller maintenance jobs. Those assumptions are mostly not correct.

When you start looking around for contractors and handymen, you might face a dilemma regarding who you need to hire for a particular job. Should it be a handyman or a contractor? It all comes down to the list of things you want to have done. So the size of the job may determine whether you need a handyman or a contractor. If the job is small or limited to a particular skill that needs a couple of hours to do, a handyman will be your choice. For large jobs that involve multiple skills for longer periods, a contractor is necessary.

Given the complexity of the relationship between contractors and handymen, I recommend you have three on your team. Having more than one option will help you get competitive bids. And you will then have an alternate plan if a contractor does not show up. Here are a few tips for finding great contractors and handymen:

- **Ask for referrals:** I have highlighted this point often in this section of this book. Do not hesitate to ask other investors, home owners, and real estate agents for referrals.
- **Check references:** A rule of thumb is always to ask potential contractors for three references from their most recent jobs on similar tasks and then call those references and ask prudent questions about showing up on time, quality of work done, changes in actual costs versus agreed costs, and most importantly if they would ever use the same contractor again.
- **Be proactive, not reactive:** As stated earlier in this section, the best time to look for a contractor is when you do not need one. Test potential contractors or handymen on some jobs in your own residence before you give them bigger and more pressing jobs on your investments.
- **Make them compete for your business:** Once you are happy after testing them on small jobs at your own home, ask them for competitive bidding for routine maintenance required in your investment properties. Once they become aware that you have

more than one preferred contractor and that you can benchmark different quotations for similar jobs, they will try their best to compete for your business.

- **Set a *rate card* for routine repairs and maintenance:** Over time, you will develop a list of routine maintenance at your rental properties, and it will be a wise move to agree with your preferred contractors on a rate card for this list. This will save lots of time on negotiating costs each time maintenance from this list is required. I even encourage having annual maintenance contracts for both preventive maintenance and routine repairs. Those contracts help you negotiate preferred rates, whereas it secures the contractors a decent amount of income throughout the period of the contracts. Both of you will be able to forecast your respective finances.

One rarely mentioned benefit of having a contractor on your team is your ability to inspect the required maintenance on a property before you negotiate the purchase price. I often ask my preferred contractor, with whom I outsource most of the maintenance for my rental properties, to accompany me on a visit to a property I am about to purchase. He will bring to my attention required maintenance that I could never identify myself. I often use the cost of the required maintenance in my price negotiation with the seller. This helps me bring the purchase price lower and also to predict the maintenance in my financial simulations for the property.

Certified Public Accountant (CPA): A great CPA is vital in your real estate investing business. This professional's main role is to offer you and your business financial and tax advice, prepare tax returns, and create financial reports. As is the case with lawyers, CPAs are not cheap, but the money they save you in taxes far outweighs their cost. Start looking for a great CPA as early as possible, even before you start investing, so that you are equipped with the right knowledge and tax-saving strategy for buying and holding your properties. When looking for a CPA, attempt to find one who specializes in helping out investors, particularly real estate investors.

Appraiser: An appraiser who specializes in your market and the types of properties you are targeting is an important team member. This professional can help you determine the appraised value of a property before you buy it. In some countries, lenders often send their own certified appraisers to determine the value of the property on which you will be getting a loan. Lenders want to make sure they are giving you a loan for a property that has an appraised value in line with the purchase and sale agreement. In any case, whether you contract an appraiser or the lenders will assign their own appraiser, you will be responsible to pay for the appraiser's fee.

YOU PAY PEANUTS, YOU GET MONKEYS

On my first few rental property investments, in spite of many lessons from different books on team building and much advice from Papa Joe, I was still stupid enough to believe I could save a few dollars here and there on the compensation offered to my team members, especially the service squad. I ended up either employing bad team members or having good team members delivering poor results.

One of the biggest lessons I learned in my life came when I invested in a three-bedroom property on the Mediterranean Sea. It was a two-floor unit overlooking the green hills and the blue sea waters, where beautiful sunsets can be observed during spring and summer. I got a great deal on this unit, with around 30 per cent discount off the market price, for the simple reason the owner needed money urgently to settle his own financial obligations. To my novice eyes, the unit required some minimal maintenance. I closed on this deal in the summer, had it maintained (or so I believed), and then rented it out for a decent return on investment.

When the first few raindrops of the fall season hit the roof of the property, my tenants complained about the water leakage damaging the paint from the ceiling to the walls. This was a messy situation. I called some waterproofing experts, and I selected the contractor who had quoted less than half the other two. This pretending waterproofing contractor finished the job in two weeks, got paid, and departed. When the heavy rain of winter approached, the tenants called me again to complain about the same problem, but now even worse. They practically placed buckets in certain parts of the property to collect the water dripping from the ceiling.

I tried to call the same contractor to fix the problem he had caused, but he was out of business, and his phone was disconnected. Being frustrated and not wanting to pay a large amount of money to another contractor, I hired another contractor who quoted way less than the others. This contractor removed all the roof tiles, applied waterproofing materials on the concrete slabs, and replaced the roof tiles with new ones. The problem was solved for that winter.

The next winter, the same tenants complained again. I paid them a visit and saw the paint inside the house falling down from the ceiling due to moisture penetrating from the roof. I promised to get this fixed. I called Papa Joe to explain to him what was happening. With a loud laugh he told me, "You pay peanuts, you get monkeys!" He reminded me of our coaching sessions about selecting the *best* team members and paying them the *right* compensation—not a cheap one nor an expensive one. Instead of telling me how stupid I was for making the same mistake twice on the same property, he said my decisions were unwise. I think he did not want to add to my agony. He recommended I add those two incidents to my education and go search for a decent contractor who could do a professional job. I followed his advice, and the problem was solved. I've heard no complaint about water leakage for more than five years.

I called Papa Joe to thank him for his advice and informed him that the problem was solved. He pinpointed another mistake I made. If I'd had a professional contractor or an appraiser check the unit with me before buying it, they would have detected the flaws in the roof that were causing water leakage in the rainy season, and they would have prevented me from paying three times for waterproofing and repainting the house. How stupid I was for not doing my due diligence! The topic of due diligence is covered in chapter 12.

WORKING WITH FAMILY MEMBERS?

There are many conflicting opinions about having family members as part of your team. Many families have mastered that art of mixing business relationships with personal ones, while others have ended up losing both the personal and business relationships. My personal policy is not to have family members on my team, but I repeat: This is only my personal opinion. It is worth mentioning some of the main advantages and disadvantages of having family members on your team. I will leave you to choose whether to have family members on your team.

Advantages of Working with Family Members

- Saves you time in looking for referrals and interviewing potential team members.
- Keeps other family members from raising their eyebrows from wondering why you have not asked for help from the pro in the family.

Saves you cost. Often family members will volunteer their professional services for free or for small fees.

Disadvantages of Working with Family Members

- Loss of objectivity. In business, it is inevitable to have tough conversations between team members. Ask yourself if you feel at ease having an objective tough conversation with a family member and can still see that person eye-to-eye at the next family reunion.
- Loss of a family relationship as a result of a loss of a team member. As is the case in any business, team members might be asked to leave your team based on their level of commitment, work ethics, or quality of work or service they are rendering. If you have to ask a team member who happens to be a family member

to stop rendering services to your real estate business, the odds are you will lose your family relationship with this person, and sometimes even with that one's direct family members.

STRATEGY FOR BUILDING YOUR TEAM

Successful real estate investors are on top of their game. What separates them from the less successful ones is that they are always on the proactive front instead of being reactive. As mentioned earlier in this chapter, you need to start building your team before starting your investment. This means you need your team members to be on board before you need them. This makes you well prepared in terms of strategy, plan, and in addressing many of the challenges that are inevitable to happen.

Successful real estate investors follow a basic three-step team building strategy:

1. **Acquire** your team members before you need them.
2. **Retain** your team members and nurture the relationship with them so you will find them around when you need them.
3. **Appoint** your team members when you need their services.

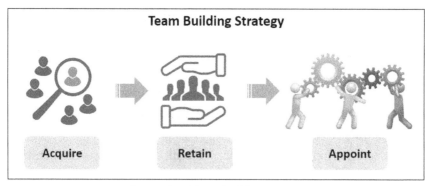

Figure 41—Team building strategy

The first step in acquiring your team members is time and energy consuming. It involves asking for referrals and then qualifying the potential team members through interviewing and checking for references.

Once you have selected who will be on your team from the different skills discussed in this chapter, the natural second step is to retain this relationship through building solid relationships and a reputation based on mutual trust. To nurture your relationships you need to touch base monthly with both your advisory board and your executive board through either face-to-face meetings or phone and video calls. The rule of thumb is to attempt to meet your advisory board in person, while a phone or video call will do fine for your executive board. As for your service squad, it is sufficient to call them or send them electronic greetings on the major holidays in your country. In essence, your service squad will be called upon for their services as needed, and this is a perfectly understood practice.

Whenever you start looking for your investment deal and throughout the process of buying the property, then renting it, and having it managed, you will appoint your team members whenever you require their respective services. This third step will be the true reputation test of both sides of the relationship. To earn their trust in you as a real estate investor and to build your reputation, you need to demonstrate the following competencies:

- **Be action oriented.** Be serious about doing deals. Remember your team members will get paid for their respective services only when you appoint them on specific deals. Do not come across as a non-serious person who has wasted their precious time.
- **Practice what you preach.** Demonstrate that you keep your word. Be a professional who walks the talk and who delivers on every commitment promised to team members. Earn your reputation as a professional who is reliable and trustworthy.
- **Don't play it smart and try to short-change anyone.** Investors lose team members for not keeping their end of the bargain. Your team members' most two precious resources are their time and the money they earn. Never appear that you disrespect their

time; give them the attention required. Never try to get out of paying them. The consequences are dire. You will not only lose your team members, but will also build a bad reputation that will be a future hindrance to building your team. The market is small, and everyone sort of knows everyone else.

- **Do not gossip and do not entertain gossip.** When I was a child, my mother used to tell me, "Whoever talks about others to you will talk about you to others." I still live by this mantra in my personal and professional life. I keep my negative emotions and opinions about others to myself. If someone demonstrates to me that they are not trustworthy, I end the relationship and never share the reasons with anyone else.

- **Refer additional business to your team members.** A powerful way to demonstrate your trust in your team is to recommend them to other investors or individuals who require services that can be provided by your team members. Who will not appreciate building their business with new leads who were offered to them on a silver platter?

Remember that you can never accomplish success without the use of the expertise, services, and guidance from your team. Do whatever needs to be done to build and maintain close and trust-based relationships with your team members.

Chapter 7 Action Steps

Start building your team right now. Begin by getting your spouse or romantic partner on board with your rental property investment plan. To complete your advisory board, look for mentors who can offer you advice and guidance.

In parallel, start looking for the most important members of your executive board whose support you will be needing in the first steps of your journey in investing in rental properties. Those are your mortgage broker and real estate agents. Finding the other members of your executive board and service squad will become easier afterward. Your real estate agents team members will play a crucial role in helping you recruit the other team members.

Once you recruit your team members, work at retaining them and building strong relationship with them. You will need to appoint them to take care of their respective area of expertise sooner rather than later.

WHAT ABOUT PARTNERSHIP IN RENTAL PROPERTY INVESTMENTS?

Often I am asked whether it is good to have a partner. My usual answer is either that I don't know or it depends. I know few investors who found great success when they partnered with like-minded investors. I have also seen many failures as a result of partnering with the wrong person. Many people have asked me to partner with them. As of the writing of this book, my only partner so far has been and always will be my wife. But the idea of partnership is not off our radar if we ever need it. And the key words here are "need it". We might consider looking into it whenever there is either a need for it or we believe we have found partners who have the same investment beliefs and strategies as we do.

Being intrigued by the question of whether a partnership may be required to invest in real estate, I have done some research by reading books and articles, attending webinars, and asking my mentors, and I have concluded that partnerships can be a great way to get you started if you need help. But they can also be a nightmare if you do not have the roles of the partners and the exit strategies clearly defined and in writing.

Before you start looking into how to go about a partnership, reflect on the true reasons behind why you need a partner. Why bring someone in to share the profits on a deal when you have the money and the knowledge about investing in rental properties? When you think about this question, it will become obvious to you that the purpose of a partner is to provide something that you cannot or do not want to provide. You give up some of the profits to spend less of your own money or to use someone's time or their expertise. If you don't need any of those things, why give up your profits?

Let's suppose you have analysed your situation and have come to the conclusion that you need a partnership for money, time, or expertise. You also need to make sure the investment strategies of all partners are aligned. Given that you are investing for the long term and holding the properties for cash flow from rentals, make sure that your potential partner's strategy is not a short-term one of cashing out in a short period for capital gains.

Suppose, too, that both of you are aligned on the investment strategy and have committed to it in a legally binding document. It is a bit tricky to figure how to split the returns on rental properties. With rentals, you have equity paydown, tax advantages, appreciation, and cash flow. Some of these returns are seen in the form of cash in your pocket like cash flow. Other returns, like appreciation and equity paydown, are not seen unless the home is sold or refinanced. Not only do you have to come up with a percentage of the actual profits (cash flow) that will be split, but you have to come up with a percentage of the equity that will be split if the properties are sold or if one partner wants to sell out and the other partner wants to keep the properties.

Here are some guidelines to be considered when partnering on rental properties:

- **Split of roles and responsibilities** throughout the whole process, from buying the properties to managing and renting them out. It does make perfect sense not to duplicate work and have each of the partners responsible for their respective roles. I am not implying that the one partner may not extend help whenever required on the role responsible by another partner.

- **What will each of the partners bring to the table?** Will one partner put in all the money and the other do all the work and receive sweat equity? Will it be a mix of money and work?

- **The decision-making process** has to be clear throughout the whole journey of buying the property, financing it, repairing it, renting it out, and managing it.

- **Split of profits among each partner.** It can be quite a challenge figuring out profits with rental properties. Although each rental property is expected to have its own projections in terms of income, expenses, mortgage, and net operating income, you will have up and down cash flow months. You also need to have reserves in place for maintenance and vacancies. You have to agree, way before your sign on a partnership agreement, what each partner's role is worth and how profits will be split.

- **What percentage of equity does each partner get?** With each monthly mortgage payment, the equity in the property will slowly increase as payments are made, and houses might appreciate as well. If you bought the property below market value, which is one of the main principles of real estate investment strategies, you also increase equity. That equity is all on paper and is never cashed out unless the property is either sold or refinanced. In that case, partners need to figure out what percentage each partner gets.

- **What happens if one partner wants to part ways?** The biggest challenge in partnerships on rental properties is when one of the partners wants to end the relationship. Partners should have a written commitment before the partnership starts that clearly states:

- o   the minimum length of time all partners plan to hold the properties to enjoy the monthly cash flow from rent,
- o   the agreed appreciation of the property below which selling the property in not an option,
- o   an action plan in case the house doesn't make as much money as planned and a partner wants out, and
- o   how the relationship can be ended.

As you can see, handling a partnership with rental properties can be tricky. Determining the amount of work each person is responsible for is tough; determining an exit strategy is tough; determining what percentages each investor gets and when is also tough. Those are among the main the reasons that keep me skeptical about partnerships in rental properties. As stated earlier, this is only my personal opinion, and I am not trying to convince you not to enter a partnership. There have been many successful partnerships. I only wanted to highlight some of the concerns that you may want to consider.

If you decide to enter a partnership, even with the closest of your family members, everything has to be in writing in a legally binding document to be drafted by your lawyer. You may feel awkward asking a friend or a sister to sign a partnership agreement. Get over it. Sign the agreement, and then go on with your daily lives, enjoying the fruits of your partnership. You will find such a document quite handy whenever any issue with partnership might surface, or when one side either forgets or does not live up to their agreed-upon obligations. Such a document will keep both partners motivated to work hard, and will make it easier to handle problems when they come up.

Some final notes in case you ever decide to enter into a partnership: You are accountable to yourself to carefully hand-pick the right partner, someone you would enjoy working with and who will bring to the table something you need (money, expertise, network, time, and so forth). Whatever you and your partner might agree on, commit your agreements to a legally binding document that will serve and protect both of you throughout the duration of the partnership. There is a great resemblance between partnerships and marriages. Both are planned for the long term, and both have a binding document protecting both partners.

WHO ARE YOUR FRIENDS?

Motivational speaker Jim Rohn famously said that "we are the average of the five people we spend the most time with". The rule suggests that the five people you spend the most time with shape who you are. It borrows from the law of averages, which is the theory that the result of any given situation will be the average of all outcomes. We might interact with many people, but the few who are closest to us have the greatest impact on our way of thinking and our decisions. When I was a teenager, whenever my mother saw something wrong in the friends I picked, she would preach to me a similar lesson, saying: "Birds of a feather flock together." All this advice suggests that people who are similar to each other or share similar interests often spend time with each other.

As we have discussed in this chapter, your team is instrumental to your success. You are most probably destined to never close a deal or to fail without the help of those professionals who each will contribute in their area of their expertise. The more time you spend with your team members, the more experience you will gain. They will also play an important role in keeping your energy and momentum towards success. Your success is their success.

As humans, we also want to socialize with friends and family who we do not choose on the basis of any skills related to business or investments. Our time with family and friends is supposed to be a break from our daily stressful work life. But be conscious of whether the people you spend most of your time with are either unintentionally dissipating your momentum and making you doubt your investment journey, or encouraging you to stay on your course. The power of association is strong, so select your friends carefully.

I am neither suggesting that you select your friends for their income level or investment acumen nor to lose friends who have selected the route of poverty. In fact I have friends from both extremes, and each one of them teaches me different lessons. What I am trying to say is that you don't want to spend too much time around financially challenged people who will question every investment or entrepreneurial opportunity you may want to take. With all good intentions, and due to their own limited experience and knowledge, they will most probably scare you off to the extent that you will lose energy and hit the brakes, leaving the road of financial freedom, and making a U-turn towards the old you. If you are really determined to become rich and achieve financial freedom, you will need to cultivate friendships with successful people who seek out and talk about opportunities. The more time you spend with those people, the more you will learn from them about how to achieve your financial goals.

In one of my coaching sessions with Papa Joe, he asked me a couple of questions aimed at learning what sort of friends I spent most of my time with. His questions revolved around my friends' career levels, their investment experience, and their financial status. When he threw those questions at me, I felt that my privacy was being invaded, and I was defensive about giving out such information.

He didn't care about the names of my friends. His questions were aimed at opening my eyes that I am indeed the average of the five people I spend the most of my time with. This lesson I understood only at a later stage, when I started to read books written by Jim Rohn. At that time, when I finally gave up and answered his questions about my friends, he said to me: "And do you still wonder why your financial situation is a challenging one?"

Chapter 7 Action Steps

List the five to ten people you spend most of your time with, then record whether they are employees, business owners, or investors, as well as an estimate of their financial status (poor, middle class, or rich). This list is for your own personal viewing. I do not recommend you share it with anyone else, except with your spouse or romantic partner.

The table below is a simple tool that will allow you to reflect on your current circle of friends. You may add as many rows you need.

Once the list is in front of your eyes, reflect on it and determine whether you agree that you are the average of the five people you spend the most of your time with.

It doesn't take a statistician to convince you that if you want to improve your average, you can make new friends who have achieved what you want to achieve. Once again, I am recommending you add new friends and spend more time with those new friends. Your old friends will always remain your friends, hopefully for a lifetime.

Name	Employee, Business Owner, or Investor?	Financial Status (poor, middle class, or rich)

One last thought about friends: You can always be the person whom your old friends want to spend time with for them to improve their average. You may become their teacher one day however, the students have to be willing ones.

CHAPTER 8

Get Prequalified for a Loan

After pushing me to build my team, Papa Joe wanted to teach me a lesson on the power of getting prequalified for a loan. He told me to go out and look for deals. Without any hesitation, I called my real estate agent for a meeting over coffee. She came to this meeting fired up and smelling the commission she was about to get paid when we closed a deal. Sitting in a Starbucks in Manila, she asked me questions related to the budget of the property I am planning to buy, the location, the size, and some other criteria related to my target investment. While I could make up some of the answers related to location and size, I couldn't answer the most important golden question, which was about the budget. Just throwing out any answer would have made me lose my credibility with this agent. Luckily for me, she had an investor mentality and was a member of an elite investor group in Makati (the financial district of Manila). She advised me to visit a lender and get myself prequalified for a loan so I would understand how much a lender would be willing to lend me for my rental property investments. I thanked her for her advice and apologized for wasting her time. I promised her that I would meet again with her soon with a bank preapproval in my hands. In fact, I closed my first one-bedroom rental property through this same agent few weeks later.

After my first meeting with the real estate agent, I went back to Papa Joe and told him furiously that I was embarrassed for not having a preapproval and a budget for my investment. He smiled and told me never to go to battle and pull the trigger without any ammunition.

▌WHY SHOULD YOU GET A LOAN PREAPPROVAL?

Papa Joe continued sharing the major advantages of securing a loan preapproval:

- You will get to know the loan amount your mortgage lender is willing to give you. This enables you to go out searching for investment properties with a budget in mind, which means you can predetermine the price ranges for properties to invest in.
- You can expedite the closing process once you find a great deal you want to invest in. The time you spend to get prequalified for a loan will be time saved when you apply for a final loan once you find an investment property that matches your criteria.
- Closing a deal faster will let the seller give you a priority before other investors who are not cash buyers and still do not have preapproved financing.

Papa Joe then asked me to go meet with my mortgage broker to get educated on the process of getting a mortgage loan approved. That day started with me being fully fired up to start looking for deals and ended up with me being out of energy like an athlete losing the game he always dreamt about winning. My scheduled video call with Joyce later in the evening was the only thing that kept me going for that day. I went home in the early evening, prepared a cappuccino, and met Joyce online. From my first hello, she directly noticed the lack of energy in my voice. Her caring personality kept her asking me in different ways what was bothering me until she succeeded in getting the words out of my mouth.

I explained how eager I was to meet with the real estate agent and close a deal in a few weeks, and how I was surprised that the agent told me to get preapproved for a mortgage loan before she would start looking for deals. Joyce made me feel better with her kind, empathetic words and promised to make an expert out of me on the topic of home mortgages. She reminded me that this is her area of expertise and that I should have never hesitated to ask for her help. My facial muscles started to relax, and I started smiling at the camera.

The teacher in Joyce started educating me on the process of applying for a home loan. She first wanted to explain the importance of getting prequalified for a loan. She said: "Whenever you apply for a loan to finance your rental property investment, any lender needs to approve both you and the property before the loan is released. This means lenders are required to make sure you are eligible for a loan before they even evaluate any property. So it makes sense to sort out the first half of that equation by getting yourself prequalified for a loan. In fact, getting yourself approved is the most difficult part of the equation. Therefore, before engaging your real estate agents or brokers to search for properties matching your criteria, it would be quite a wise move from your end to make sure you prequalify for a loan. That way you won't waste anyone's time."

PAPERWORK FOR PREAPPROVAL

Joyce clarified to me that getting a preapproval means getting a conditional approval from the lender by submitting the financial paperwork that proves the applicant's creditworthiness. She asked me to write down the list of documents the lender may require:

- **Government-issued identification** that proves your legal identity.
- **Employment certificate** that states your position within the company and the length of service with the company.
- **Salary certificate** that states your monthly income.

- **Pay cheque slips**, which are usually issued by your employer.
- **Proof of other income** that shows any unearned income you generate from dividends, rentals, and interest.
- **Bank statements**, which are usually for six months, but the period can vary by lender, city, or country. Those statements enable your lender to determine your financial strength by looking at regular monthly income, expenses, loans, savings, and other financial obligations.
- **Credit card statements**, which are usually six months, but the period can vary by lender, city, or country.
- Statements of individual retirement accounts.
- Your **credit score**, which can be pulled out by the lender to depict your creditworthiness and your ability to repay your debts. Credit score are applicable in certain developed countries and play a key role in a lender's decision to offer loans to their applicants. The higher your score, the more eligible for loans you become, and even more eligible to enjoy lower interest rates on your loans. The main factors evaluated when calculating your credit score are debt payment history, total amount owed, length of credit history, types of credit, and new credit.

When she was done with the list, she clarified that it is important to understand one basic and simple insider fact: The banks' primary business is selling loans that will secure them monthly cash flow from interest paid by their clients. This is how banks make money. They make money on the interest their clients pay on loans as well as on loan applications and processing fees. She asked me to have the confidence that any lender will do their best to help me sort out my documents in order to qualify for a loan.

Reflecting on what I had heard so far, I tried to connect the dots by figuring out the specific data that lenders will extract from this set of documents. Joyce interrupted my thinking and continued explaining that lenders will take the data from the provided documents to look at the following:

- Applicant's income (earned income and unearned income).
- Applicant's expenses.
- Applicant's loan payments.
- Applicant's assets.
- Applicant's liabilities.

She paused for a few seconds that felt like a few minutes and asked me if I recalled our earlier conversation on personal financial statements. When she learned that I was already filling out my personal financial statements monthly, she was proud that I was already practicing what she had taught me. I said that I was even analysing my financial statements by going through the financial KPIs dashboard.

When she felt we were on the same page, she said: "One of the most important ratios your lender will always study to determine your eligibility for a loan is your *debt-to-income ratio.*"

DEBT-TO-INCOME RATIO

Your *debt to income ratio* (DTI), sometimes also referred to as *debt burden ratio* (DBR) in certain countries, is as important as your credit score. In countries where credit score is not available, your DTI may be the main measure of your creditworthiness for a loan, refinancing, or credit. Debt to income ratio is exactly what it sounds like: the amount of debt you owe as compared to your overall income. Your lenders will look at this ratio when they are trying to decide whether to lend you money or extend credit. A low DTI means you have a good balance between debt and income. As you might have guessed, lenders like this number to be low, which means your debt is at a manageable level relative to your income. The lower it is, the greater the chance you will be able to get the loans or credit you seek.

Before we looked at ranges lenders consider as acceptable for your DTI ratio, Joyce suggested we go a step backward and look at how it is computed. As expected, she asked me to write down the following:

$$DTI \ (\%) = \frac{Total \ Monthly \ Debt}{Gross \ Monthly \ Income}$$

Total debt, she explained, is the total of all of your monthly debt obligations, which are considered as monthly recurring debt. It includes your home mortgage or rent, car loans, student loans, your minimum monthly payments on any credit card debt, line of credit, and any other loans that you might have. Your lender seeks to assess how comfortable you are with paying both your current debt as well as your ability to borrow more. For that reason, your new monthly mortgage payment (towards the new loan you will be applying for) will be added to your total debt computation.

Gross income is the sum of all your earned income and unearned income before tax. In the case of unearned income considerations, careful and responsible lenders need to account for a cushion in the event of any month you do not receive this unearned income from rentals, businesses, or paper assets. Those lenders are often conservative and assume about 80 per cent of unearned income. Inquire with your lender about their current practice on this topic.

DTI, expressed in percentage, is computed by dividing your total debt over gross income. It can help lenders determine how comfortable you are with current debt and assess your ability to borrow more. In other terms, lenders also want to evaluate whether you can afford to take on another payment for a new loan.

Joyce admitted that she made the computation look easy, whereas many factors come into play in the actual numbers of each of the variables mentioned. She promised me that we would go back into the details of the computation, but first she wanted to make sure I grasped the concept.

She explained that the next logical step is to understand how lenders review DTI when they're considering a loan application. Those guidelines vary slightly among lenders. She recommended asking the financial institutions about their specific guidelines when I apply for a mortgage. Nevertheless, she still shared directional guidelines to help me understand how lenders will look at DTI.

- **35 per cent or less: Green light.** You are looking good, and your lender will favor your application. Compared to your income, your debt is at a manageable level. You most likely have money left over for saving or spending after you've paid your obligations.

- **36 per cent to 49 per cent: Yellow light.** You are still eligible for a loan, but you have an opportunity to improve your situation. You're managing your debt adequately, but you may want to consider lowering your DTI. This could put you in a better position to handle unforeseen expenses. Your lender may ask you for additional eligibility criteria.

- **50 per cent or more: Red light.** You need to take action to get your finances in order. In the eyes of your lenders, you may have limited funds to save or spend. With more than half your income going toward debt payments, you may not have much money left to save, spend, or handle unforeseen expenses. With this DTI ratio, lenders may limit your borrowing options or even categorize you as not eligible for loans.

COMPUTING DEBT-TO-INCOME RATIO STEP BY STEP

Joyce next took us a step backward and asked me to look at my notes where I had written the formula to compute DTI:

$$DTI\ (\%) = \frac{Total\ Monthly\ Debt}{Gross\ Monthly\ Income}$$

She recommended we look at how total monthly debt and gross income are computed separately. Then we could figure out DTI by dividing total monthly debt by gross monthly income.

Total Monthly Debt

The current total monthly debt may include a combination of any of the following: line of credit, credit cards payments, home mortgage, personal loans payments, car loans payments, and student loans payments. We studied each loan obligation to learn how its monthly payments or instalments are computed. But first Joyce described the general categories of loans.

Loans can be either **secured loans** or **unsecured loans**. Mortgages and car loans are secured loans, as they are both secured by collateral. Loans such as credit cards and line of credit are unsecured, not backed by collateral. Unsecured loans typically have higher interest rates than secured loans as they are riskier for the lender. With a secured loan, the lender can repossess the collateral in the case of default.

- Loans can also be described as **revolving loans** or **term loans**. A revolving loan is a loan that can be spent, repaid and spent again, while a term loan is a loan paid off in equal monthly instalments over a set period called a term.

The different loans obligations are categorized as follows:

- A line of credit is an unsecured revolving loan.
- A credit card is an unsecured revolving loan.
- A home mortgage is a secured term loan.
- A personal loan is generally an unsecured term loan.
- A car loan is a secured term loan.
- A student loan is generally an unsecured term loan.

Joyce wanted me to grasp an insider tip on how banks and lending institutions look at an applicant's loan obligations. She whispered: "Responsible lenders assume that loan applicants will max out a revolving loan whenever the applicant's cash flow situation gets challenging. Therefore, lenders compute the minimum payments towards such revolving loans on the basis of the whole limit."

Line of Credit

A *line of credit*, also referred to as LOC, is an arrangement between a financial institution and a customer that establishes a maximum loan balance that the lender permits the borrower to access or maintain. In its simplest form, it is an amount of credit extended to a borrower to be taken as overdraft on a per need basis. It is an unsecured revolving loan. The borrower can access funds from the line of credit at any time. Those funds are capped by the maximum amount set in the agreement. This arrangement provides a great deal of flexibility to the borrower, where a certain amount of funds can be accessed without any obligation to use the whole amount. Borrowers can tailor what they spend to their needs, and they have to pay interest only on the amount they spend, not on the entire credit line. An additional benefit to the borrowers is flexibility of repayment of the borrowed amount based on their cash flow, on condition they pay the minimum monthly payments.

You can look at a line of credit as a revolving account, where the borrower can borrow some money, repay it, and borrow some other amount again, in a virtually never-ending, revolving cycle. This feature makes LOC behave pretty much as credit cards where only minimum monthly payments have to be paid, and not a set of equal monthly instalments as is the case with other forms of loans.

All those great features of a line of credit may play against you when you want to get prequalified for a mortgage loan. Joyce explained that financial institutions will consider that the borrower may access the whole limit of the LOC at any time, which may cause a threat to the creditworthiness of the borrower.

The idea still did not sink in my mind, so I asked Joyce to elaborate on it. She asked my candid opinion on whether I might access my total line of credit at any time in the future I might face cash flow challenges where my income would not be enough to pay my obligations. I confirmed that I would probably get my hands on as much money I need and that is available for me on my LOC. She replied that this is the reason lenders will act as though the full line of credit will be used. So they compute the minimum monthly payment based on the full amount of the LOC. Although the minimum monthly payment in theory is the monthly interest rate, responsible lenders will calculate the minimum payment as a percent of the total amount of the LOC, typically between 2 per cent and 5 per cent per month. Joyce recommended that I always base my computation of the monthly payment on the higher end of the range, which is 5 per cent. This may be the norm whenever the economy gets tough and credit gets tight.

Credit Card Payments

A credit card is a card issued by a financial institution, giving the holder an option to borrow funds within set limits, usually at the point of sale or online. Credit cards are primarily used for short-term financing. Therefore, they charge higher interest rates than most other forms of loans and lines of credit. Interest usually begins one month after a purchase is made, and borrowing limits are preset according to the borrower's creditworthiness. A credit card is an unsecured, revolving loan.

Credit cards holders usually carry multiple credit cards from different issuers and brag about higher credit limits, which gets translated into different card colours displaying status symbols. While credit cards are a convenient way to pay for purchases, and higher limits allow for payments of expensive purchases without the hassle of carrying large amount of cash, high credit limits and multiple cards may not play in your favor when applying for a mortgage loan. As is the case with a line of credit, lenders assume that credit cards holders will access the full limit of their credit for the sum of all their credit cards at some time. So they calculate the minimum payment at a range between 2 per cent and 5 per cent of the total card limits. Responsible lenders generally follow the minimum payment of 5 per cent of the total limit.

Home Mortgage, Personal Loans, Car Loans, Student Loans, and Other Term Loans

A loan is a sum of money borrowed in exchange for future repayment of the principal amount along with interest or other finance charges. The conditions of a loan are agreed to by each party in the transaction before any money is lent out. Some forms of loans require collateral to be pledged by the borrower as security for loan repayment. Loans that are secured by collateral usually have lower interest rates than non-secured loans.

Home mortgages, personal loans, car loans, and student loans are paid off in equal monthly instalments over a set period called a *term*. Loan terms extend from as little as five years or less (as is the case of personal and car loans) and extend to 25 years and even more (for home mortgages).

Depending on the loan value, the interest rate, and loan terms, the lender determines a minimum monthly payment, which is documented in a contract signed by both parties. By looking at the monthly loan statement or the loan contract, the minimum monthly payment of each loan can be easily identified. There are many online loan payment calculators. I am not recommending any special online loan payment calculator, since all of them do pretty much the same job.

Lenders also consider monthly rent payment as a debt obligation, which is treated like a mortgage payment. The reason, simply put, is that rent is considered as an obligation to be paid on a monthly basis in return for occupying a residential property.

Total Monthly Debt

Summing it all up, the formula below summarizes how total monthly debt can be computed:

$$\begin{pmatrix} Total\ Monthly \\ Debt \end{pmatrix} = \sum \begin{pmatrix} Minimum\ Montly\ Payment \\ of\ Revolving\ Loans \end{pmatrix} + \sum \begin{pmatrix} Montlhy\ Installments \\ of\ Term\ Loans \end{pmatrix}$$

In words, total monthly debt is the sum of all minimum monthly payments of revolving loans and all monthly instalments of term loans.

GROSS MONTHLY INCOME

Referring to one of our previous video calls when Joyce explained to me how personal financial statements work, she reiterated that gross income is the sum of all your earned income and unearned income before tax. While verified earned income gets accounted in full in the computation of gross monthly income, in the case of unearned income, responsible lenders will need to account for any event that the streams of cash flow from unearned income may get interrupted in the future. For this reason, careful lenders tend to be conservative and assume an average of 80 per cent of unearned income in the computation of the gross monthly income.

Summarized in an equation, gross monthly income can be computed as follows:

$$\binom{Gross\ Monthly}{Income} = \binom{100\%\ x\ Monthly}{Earned\ Income} + \binom{80\%\ x\ Monthly}{Unearned\ Income}$$

After computing separately the gross monthly income and the total monthly debt, DTI is computed by dividing total monthly debt by gross monthly income.

STRATEGIES TO LOWER YOUR DTI

As previously highlighted, financial institutions make money when they sell loans. Therefore it is in their best interest to help and guide you to lower your DTI to acceptable levels, if your debt-to-income ratio exceeds the 50 per cent threshold.

A competent mortgage broker, either on the board of your team or from the financial institute where you are applying for a home loan, will guide you on reducing your debt obligations so that your DTI is reduced to the acceptable levels set by your lender. While the strategies are quite specific to each person's case, the following section attempts to cover some main strategies to lower total debt and therefore to lower DTI. What I will be sharing in this chapter are lessons I have learned from many competent mortgage brokers and advisors I had the privilege of working with over my investment career. Please note that this information is for your educational purposes only. I recommend you always check with a competent financial advisor or mortgage broker on how to help you reduce your DTI, as your situation is quite specific to you.

As explained in the previous section, DTI is expressed in percentage and is computed by dividing your total monthly debt by gross monthly income. So to lower your DTI, you have to lower your total debt, increase your gross income, or both.

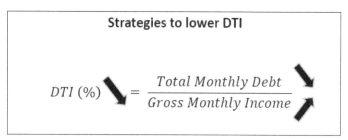

Figure 42—Strategies to lower DTI

Increasing Your Gross Monthly Income

You might have limited options to increase your gross monthly income, which would lower your DTI. That is one main strategy you will use to manage your DTI on the medium and long term. In the short term, your options are limited to finding a higher-paying job, which is not totally in your control. But later, when you have already purchased rental properties, with each in turn producing a net positive cash flow, your total unearned income will increase. Therefore, your gross monthly income will increase.

The graph below visually illustrates what I am saying. One of this book's main objectives is to educate you on how to increase your unearned income to a level that exceeds your earned income and your monthly expenses so that you achieve financial freedom.

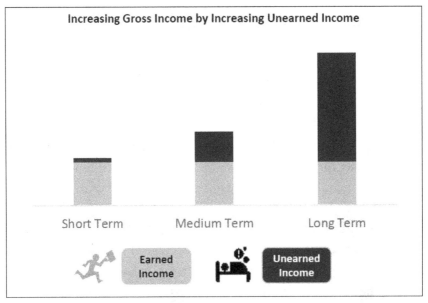

Figure 43—Increasing gross income by increasing unearned income

Decreasing Your Total Monthly Debt

A quick and pragmatic approach on the short term is to lower your current debt obligations, which will lower your debt-to-income ratio and increase your eligibility for future loans to purchase income-producing rental properties.

Let's take each loan obligation category you may currently have and look at potential strategies to manage them.

Reducing Minimum Monthly Payments of Revolving Loans

Revolving loans are non-secured and flexible by design. Therefore, they impose a bigger risk on the lender, which justifies the higher interest rates on such loans. We all love such flexibility and the instant availability of credit whenever we require it. This brings us back to the notion of instant gratification mentality, which is a main reason the general population suffers from managing its debt.

My quick advice: Kill or reduce all your revolving loans to a bare minimum. This advice may have shocked you or made you feel uncomfortable. I was quite unhappy when this advice was offered to me. I felt like something precious was taken away from me.

Because lenders assume that you will be accessing your total credit limit, they compute your minimum monthly payment at up to 5 per cent of your total limit, resulting in a high total debt payment and increasing your DTI.

My long-term advice: Kill your line of credit and reduce the number of credit cards and their respective limits to a bare minimum. Look at your situation and be pragmatic about whether a line of credit will do you any better than getting approved for a mortgage loan.

It is your call. Do you want instant credit to buy consumer goods and services that are bound to depreciate over time? Or do you want your credit to be used for good loans and to purchase income-producing assets? The fact you are reading this book tells me that you want to invest in income-producing assets.

Therefore, do yourself a favor and eliminate the lines of credit you do not need. All credit reduced towards revolving loans will mean higher eligibility for loans towards good debt. When it comes to your credit cards, have a look at their interest rates, pay off the cards with the highest interest rates first, and get rid of them. Keep a couple of cards with the lowest interest rates and ask your bank or financial institution to lower your credit card limit to the minimum that makes you feel comfortable in managing your expenses.

If you have major challenges in paying off your cards that have high interest rates, check with your financial advisor, who might recommend that you take personal loans with much lower interest and reasonable terms of up to five years to settle as much as possible of your credit card balances and get rid of this alligator that is feeding on you every month.

The rationale here is that the balance you owe on all your credit cards imposes on you very minimum monthly payments due to high interest rates. The same total balance, if owed on a personal loan with longer terms and much lower interest, will result in a lower monthly instalment. This is one of the quick fixes to credit card payments challenges. Once again, I recommend you consult with a competent financial advisor to manage your debt.

Reducing Monthly Instalments of Term Loans

Your existing term loans monthly instalments are contingent on two factors: the interest rate (in percentage) and the loan term (in years). Let's look at each of those factors separately.

- The higher the interest rate, the higher your monthly loan instalment over a fixed loan term. When a bank lends money to a borrower, the bank's return on the money lent is the interest rate of the loan. Interest is the amount the bank has earned and charges for the use of the money it has lent. When a borrower makes a loan payment in the form of a monthly instalment, the bank will first collect the interest it is owed and then apply the remainder to the loan's principal balance. So, the higher the interest rate of a loan, the more the bank charges for the money it is lending, and the higher the monthly instalments.
- The shorter the loan term, the higher your monthly loan instalment over a fixed interest rate. To simplify this point, let's consider two examples:
  o You borrow $12,000 from a relative at zero interest. If the repayment of this loan is over twelve equal monthly instalments, your monthly instalment will be $1,000. But if the repayment term is over twenty-four months, your monthly instalment will be $500. I've oversimplified this example and did not take interest into account. When interest comes into play, the math will differ, but the monthly instalments will still be lower over longer-term loans.

o   You borrow $12,000 from a bank at 10 per cent interest rate. If the repayment of this loan is over twelve equal monthly instalments, your monthly instalment will be $1,054. But if the repayment term is over twenty-four months, your monthly instalment will be $553. You can use any online monthly instalment calculator to calculate those numbers. In this example, where interest comes into play, one can always argue that the total interest paid is higher for longer terms, and this is correct. In that specific example, the interest paid over a twelve-month period is $648, whereas the interest paid over twenty-four months is $1,272. It is important to remember that the objective in this section is to lower your monthly loan instalments in order to lower your debt-to-income ratio to a level that makes you eligible for a mortgage loan on your purchase of income-producing properties.

So to lower your monthly instalment towards terms loans, you will have to get a lower interest rate or longer terms or both.

If you have an existing personal loan with an interest rate that is higher than current market rates, you can either negotiate with your existing lender to lower the interest rates or have another lender (with lower interest rates) buy out your existing loan. This means the new lender will pay your existing lender the balance of the loan you currently have outstanding. With a lower interest rate, even if you keep the same loan term, your monthly payment will get lower. The other advantages of such a loan buy-out by another lender is that the loan terms can be reset to a new four- or five-year terms, thereby, reducing your monthly instalments.

When it comes to longer-term loans, and to be more specific, I am referring to any existing home mortgage you may have, the strategy on lengthening the terms of the loan becomes more interesting. It is important to understand some guiding principles that apply for long-term mortgage loans.

- As a common practice, the maturity date, which represents the due date of the final instalment of principal on a loan, can never exceed your retirement age. In some countries, some banks are becoming more flexible and are opening their arms to welcome older borrowers. However, given that the risks are greater to the lenders, the interest rates are correspondingly higher, and the borrowers are expected to make larger down payments than the usual 20 per cent.

- Home mortgage terms vary between twenty-five and thirty years. Some banks are even open to look into forty-year terms. It all depends on your age and the laws in the country where you live.

- If you have an existing home mortgage with terms that will mature before the official retirement age in your country, this means you are not taking full advantage of the loan terms that is acceptable for your age. You can either negotiate the terms with your existing bank to extend them as much as possible or ask another lender (with interest rates equal to or lower than the rates of your existing mortgage) to buy out your mortgage. The latter scenario allows you to reset to new loan terms that can extend as long as possible, depending on your age.

To recap on this section, your objective is to reduce your DTI to levels that increase your eligibility to take on new good debt that will allow you to purchase income-producing assets. There might be some controversy on the strategies of extending loan terms that I have covered in the sections above. This is OK. It all depends on what we want to achieve. I understand that by extending your existing loan terms, you will end up paying higher interests in absolute terms over a longer period of time, but you will lower your existing loan instalments and thereby lower your DTI. Whatever contrary advice you may receive on this topic, I invite you to question the interests of the person giving the advice or their level of expertise on the subject.

My interest in this book is to help you become an employee millionaire and achieve financial freedom through investing in rental properties. The advice I have shared has worked for me and many others.

One last point: As recommended earlier, consult with a competent financial advisor to receive advice on strategies for lowering your DTI that are specific to your case. You can always bounce the ideas in this chapter off your financial advisor. This will add lots of value to your discussion.

Now that I understand how important getting prequalified for a loan before prospecting for deals is, whenever I coach others on rental property investing, I recommend that they have a mortgage broker or lender as their first team member on their advisory board. Once they have a good one, their first task is to get educated on DTI calculation, get their DTI calculated, and get an approximation on their loan eligibility.

HOW MUCH MORTGAGE LOAN WILL YOU BE ELIGIBLE FOR?

The answer to this question will feed an answer to the golden question: How many rental properties can you afford? Notice that I said *properties* and not *property*. It's the most critical question that every rental property investor needs to have an answer for. Your lender will give you the largest mortgage amount that you will be eligible for. The price tag of one rental property you will be investing in does not have to be equal to the amount of loan your lender is willing to lend you. You may opt to purchase more than one property, based on the property criteria you will be setting. The next chapter covers the topic of setting your investment criteria, which is crucial for looking out for deals.

Let's look now at how your lender will determine how much mortgage loan you will be eligible for. From a lender's perspective, loan eligibility is based on your debt-to-income ratio. As shared earlier in this chapter, your lender will allow a maximum DTI of up to 50 per cent of your gross income, and this includes all your loan obligations, including the mortgage loan instalments being considered by your bank.

In other words, your lender will compute your maximum monthly debt instalment based on the 50 per cent DTI. This computation is done by multiplying your gross monthly income by 0.50. For example, if you earn $4,000 per month in gross income, your maximum debt obligation should not exceed $2,000 per month, which would include your mortgage or rent. So let's assume you have existing loan obligations towards a home mortgage, personal loan, and car loan totaling $1,200 per month. Your eligibility for a loan will be based on the balance of your maximum debt obligation.

Going back to our example, the lender will deduct the $1,200 existing debt obligations from your $2,000 maximum debt obligation, resulting in a monthly mortgage loan instalment of $800 towards the new mortgage loan you will be eligible for. It is important to highlight that your monthly mortgage loan instalment will need to cover all four potential components of a mortgage: principal, interest, taxes, and insurance (often referred to as PITI). As you may have concluded, since your monthly instalments include the interest to be paid to the lender, the lower the interest, the higher the mortgage loan amount you will be borrowing. This is why it is so important to shop for the right mortgage loan for you. Your mortgage broker team member will play a crucial role in getting you the mortgage with the best interest and terms for you.

Let's recap what has been presented above, step by step, in a simplified mathematical model. At the end of the steps below, you will get the maximum mortgage loan that you will be eligible for.

Step 1: Compute your maximum allowed debt obligation.

Your monthly allowed debt obligation is computed by multiplying your current gross monthly income by the debt-to-income (DTI) ratio set by your lender. The DTI guideline can be easily obtained by asking your lender or mortgage broker.

This allows your lender to determine the sum of total monthly debt you will be comfortable with affording on a recurrent monthly basis based on your income. The formula below shows how the maximum allowed debt obligation is computed.

$$\binom{Maximum\ Allowed}{Debt\ Obligation} = \binom{Gross\ Monthly}{Income} \times \binom{Debt\ to\ Income}{Ratio\ Guideline}$$

Step 2: Compute your maximum monthly mortgage loan instalment.

When applying for a new mortgage loan, the lender needs to determine the maximum monthly mortgage loan instalment for the new loan. This is computed by subtracting your existing total monthly debt from your maximum allowed debt obligation. The formula below shows how the maximum monthly mortgage loan instalment is computed for a new loan.

$$\binom{Maximum\ Monthly}{Mortgage\ Loan\ Investment} = \binom{Maximum\ Allowed}{Debt\ Obligation} - \binom{Total\ Monthly}{Debt}$$

Step 3: Compute your maximum monthly mortgage instalment related to principal and interest.

Remember that your maximum monthly mortgage loan instalment must cover all four potential components of a mortgage: principal, interest, taxes, and insurance (often referred to as PITI). Instalments towards both the principal and the interest apply directly to settling your loan with your lender on a monthly basis throughout the term of the loan. On the other hand, payments towards property taxes and home insurance are obligations you owe to the government and your home insurance provider and therefore are not counted towards settling your loan. It is important to distinguish the components of your monthly mortgage instalments, since your lender will use only what counts towards directly settling your loan to compute the mortgage value you are eligible for.

Let's go in baby steps and subtract both the estimated monthly property tax and the estimated monthly home insurance payment from your maximum monthly mortgage loan instalment. The resulting number is your maximum monthly mortgage instalment related to principal and interest.

$$\begin{pmatrix} \text{Maximum Allowed Mortgage} \\ \text{Installment Related to} \\ \text{Principal and Interest} \\ (PI) \end{pmatrix} = \begin{pmatrix} \text{Maximum Monthly} \\ \text{Mortgage Loan} \\ \text{Installment} \\ (PITI) \end{pmatrix} - \begin{pmatrix} \text{Estimated} \\ \text{Monthly} \\ \text{Property Tax} \\ (T) \end{pmatrix} - \begin{pmatrix} \text{Estimated Monthly} \\ \text{Home Insurance} \\ \text{Payment} \\ (I) \end{pmatrix}$$

Otherwise stated, PI = PITI − T − I.

Step 4: Compute the mortgage value you are eligible for.

In step 3, the components of your monthly loan instalment that apply to settling both the principal and the interest of your loan have been computed. Both components, labelled as PI, when paid monthly throughout the terms of the loan, will settle the full mortgage loan by its maturity date.

So adding those PI monthly instalments over the total number of months throughout the term of the loan will determine the total amount you will be paying throughout the same period. This amount includes both the principal amount (which is mortgage value) and the total interest paid (which is the return on investment that your lender makes for lending the mortgage). This suggests that by subtracting the total interest from the total payments throughout the term of the mortgage loan, the principal value (which is the mortgage value) can be computed. The formula is quite complicated, and no one in their right mind would want to go through this whole series of formulas to compute the total mortgage value they are eligible for. I have provided a mortgage loan eligibility calculator that does all the computations on your behalf and gives you the answers you need. You just need to input a series of data that relates to your specific case. The mortgage loan eligibility calculator can be downloaded from my website www. employeemillionaire.com/resources. This tool will also help you play around with your existing debt obligations and determine how much more mortgage you will be eligible for whenever you lower any or a combination of your existing monthly debt obligations.

Mortgage Loan Calculator		
Variable	Units	Computation
Gross Monthly Income :	Local Currency	GMI
Debt-to-Income Ratio (DTI) Guideline Set by your Lender :	%	DTI
Maximum Allowed Debt Obligation :	Local Currency	M = GMI x DTI
Total Current Monthly Debt Obligations		
Line of Credit Monthly Minimum Payment :	Local Currency	
Credit Card Monthly Minimum Payment :	Local Currency	
Existing Home Mortgage or Home Rent Monthly Installment :	Local Currency	Sum of Monthly
Personal Loan Monthly Installment :	Local Currency	Debt Obligations
Car loan Monthly Installment :	Local Currency	
Student loan Monthly Installment :	Local Currency	
Other Monthly Recurring Obligations :	Local Currency	
Sum of Total Monthly Debt Payments / Installments :	Local Currency	D
Maximum Allowed Monthly New Mortgage Loan Installment :		PITI = M - D
Taxes and Insurance Components of the Maximum Monthly Mortgage Loan Installment		
Estimated Monthly Property Tax :	Local Currency	T
Estimated Monthly Home Insurance Payment :	Local Currency	I
Maximum Monthly Mortgage Installment Related to Principal and Interest :	Local Currency	PI = PITI - T - I
New Mortgage Terms (Length of Loan) :	Years	Y
New Mortgage Loan Annual Interest Rate :	%	I
New Mortgage Value :	%	= PV [(I/12), (Y*12), (-PI)]

Figure 44—Mortgage loan calculator

Chapter 8 Action Steps

Download the mortgage loan calculator from my website www. employeemillionaire.com/resources and compute the mortgage value that you might be eligible for. This exercise will enable you to discover whether you are eligible for a new mortgage loan. If you are eligible, it will compute the mortgage value that your lender might be willing to lend you.

This exercise allows you to look at your current situation. It also allows you to look at different scenarios of increasing your eligibility by playing around with the numbers related to your current debt obligations. It will help you to form an action plan to lower certain debt obligations so that you become more eligible for a new mortgage loan.

YOUR LOAN PREAPPROVAL LETTER

Mortgage preapprovals are considered the minimum level of qualification a home buyer should have. The reason this level matters is that a borrower's credit and income are verified.

After submitting all the documentation that verifies the applicant's identity, income, debt obligations, assets, and liabilities, the borrower's loan file will be evaluated by an underwriter who either approves or rejects the loan application. The underwriter will research and verify the applicant's credit and that one's capacity to repay the loan. Whenever your loan gets a thumbs-up from the underwriter, the loan officer can issue a preapproval letter.

Getting a loan preapproval means getting a conditional approval from the lender based on your creditworthiness. The final approval will be contingent on the property appraisal or title review, which can happen only when you find a home you want to buy and make an offer on it. The following chapters will walk you through the steps of prospecting for rental properties, analysing rental properties, negotiating and submitting offers, performing due diligence, and then financing your rental property through a final lender approval. Once those steps are achieved, the title can be transferred to your name. From there onward, you will rent and manage your rental properties. It will always be helpful to keep referring to your rental properties investment blueprint, (figure 40, chapter 6), which explains the whole blueprint in one single diagram.

It is worth shedding some light on loan prequalification, which is often confused with loan preapproval. The level of qualification is only a quick check at your financial situation, which is often performed by your loan officer, who in turn will submit your loan file to the underwriter for a final yes or no decision. Your loan officer is responsible for asking you about proofs of income and debt to compute your debt-to-income ratio, which serves the purpose of quick prequalification feedback. It's not the responsibility of your loan officer to verify your credit report or creditworthiness, which is performed by the underwriter. Consequently, a loan prequalification doesn't carry much weight, and sellers may not consider your offer based on a loan prequalification. Both real estate agents and sellers will ask you to get a loan preapproval letter before taking you seriously since this letter confirms to them that you are both serious and a legitimate buyer who deserves their time and resources to help you close a deal.

Let's go back to loan preapprovals, and check out what a preapproval letter is all about. When I received my first loan preapproval letter, after a couple of days of submitting the required documentation, I was excited. I couldn't wait for time to pass to reach home and read the letter carefully to understand it. I was expecting to find a simple paragraph with few words and ending with a number that quantified my mortgage eligibility. The letter consisted of a couple of pages and a series of details and conditions that went beyond just a mortgage value that I was eligible for.

Below are the main components of a loan preapproval letter, written in the form of a sample letter, which in real life is printed on the lender's official letterhead, signed, and stamped. The grey-shaded letters represent generic inputs that change with each borrower's specific case.

Mortgage Preapproval Letter

Private and Confidential

Dear Borrower's Name,

We are pleased to inform you that Lender's Name has "in principle" agreed to consider a mortgage loan facility (the "loan") for you towards the purchase of Type of Property. The details are as follows:

The Borrower:	Borrower's name
Facility Type:	Type of property
Preapproved Amount:	Mortgage loan amount
Loan-to-Value (LTV %):	The mortgage loan as a percentage of the property value or purchase price, whichever is lower.
Interest Rate Type:	Fixed or adjustable.
Interest Rate:	Interest rate percentage.

Loan Tenure or Term: Number of repayment months.

Monthly Instalment: Value of monthly instalments.

This loan preapproval is an "in principle offer" and is not considered as a commitment on the part of Lender's Name . The lender reserves the right to change the offer and conditions at its sole discretion.

Please note that the final approval will be subject to:

1. The lender's terms and conditions for the said loan must be met;
2. Property valuation by an independent valuation agency approved by the Lender's Name. The charges for the valuation will be borne by the Borrower.

This offer is valid for Number of Days from the date of issue, after which it will be automatically cancelled.

Upon reading my loan preapproval letter a couple of times, I still did not fully understand it. I had to wait a few more hours to meet Joyce over a video call and ask her a series of never-ending questions. When we finally managed to join the call after she was home, it was almost midnight in my time zone in Manila, but I still thought I was willing to sleep late instead of not sleeping at all, trying to interpret the letter. On that call, instead of allowing time to talk about personal matters, I was kind of rude and swiftly changed topics by announcing that I received my loan preapproval letter. Joyce was happy for me and promptly jumped in to motivate me to start looking for properties.

I said that I was stuck on the content of the letter and needed help in explaining it. She suggested I share a soft copy of the preapproval letter with her so she could walk me through the details. With a blink of an eye, a copy reached her halfway around the globe from the far end of East Asia to the far end of West Asia. She took a few minutes to read the letter and then suggested that she should explain what the letter meant, especially the unwritten words between the lines.

Before she went into the specifics of the numbers, the teacher in Joyce wanted to explain what a few of the subtle words in the letter suggested. I took quick notes while she covered the following points:

- Joyce wanted to make sure I understood what a mortgage is and how it works before going through the preapproval letter. In simple language, she described a mortgage as a debt, secured by the subject property as collateral, which the borrower is obliged to pay back with a predetermined set of monthly instalments over the duration of the loan. When the loan principal and the interest are paid back, the borrower will own the property free and clear. Mortgages are also referred to as *liens against the property* or *claims on the property*, which implies that the lender can foreclose on the property in the event the borrower stops paying the instalments.
- The preapproval letter is a document that states the mortgage loan amount a lender is willing to make to a borrower. It is not a guarantee to lend, since the final approval is contingent on the property to be mortgaged.
- It is not legally binding to the lender. A lender will give the borrower a final loan approval only when a valid legal purchase and sale agreement is signed on a property. A satisfactory appraisal is accomplished on the property by an independent evaluation agency approved by the lender within the timelines set by the expiry date of the letter. Until then, the borrower is expected to be careful with finances and maintain the same creditworthiness in terms of income and debt. Any anomalies will draw negative attention to the loan file. This acts as a protection for the lender to pull back without any legal obligations.
- It is not legally binding to the borrower, with no need to commit to the lender to take the loan based on the preapproval letter. Let's say, for example, no property is identified before the expiry of the letter. The borrower can either stop the process or reapply and provide a whole set of new documentation.

- The main two classes of property to be mortgaged are residential and commercial real estate. In this section, other qualifiers mentioning that the property must be complete with a title deed are clearly stated. Joyce explained that lenders want to limit their risk exposures, and residential properties that are complete with a title deed are the least risky as compared to residential properties that are either under construction or off plan. Commercial properties have their own complexities, and their mortgage loan rules are quite different from residential properties. The focus of this book is on residential properties, specifically single-family properties.

- Preapproved loan amount is often mixed up with the value of property to be purchased, which can be extrapolated using the loan-to-value (LTV) ratio. Joyce explained that LTV is often either overlooked or not fully understood by the borrower. The LTV ratio is the ratio of a loan to the value of the property being purchased. The value of the property is usually determined by a third party appraiser approved by the lender. For me to understand how LTV can help me determine the maximum property value I can purchase once the lender communicates the preapproved loan amount, she asked me to write down the following:

$$LTV\ (\%) = \frac{Mortgage\ Amount}{Property\ Value}$$

$$\rightarrow Property\ Value = \frac{Mortgage\ Amount}{LTV\ (\%)}$$

- All lenders assess the LTV ratio in relation to their risk exposure level when underwriting a mortgage. The smaller the difference between the property's appraised value and the total amount borrowed, the riskier the loan. The higher the LTV ratio, the closer the loan amount is to the appraised value and therefore, the greater is the lender's risk exposure. In such cases, lenders perceive that there is a greater chance of the loan going into default because there is little to no equity built up within the property. Should foreclosure take place, the lender may find it difficult to sell the home for an amount sufficient to cover the outstanding mortgage balance and make a profit from the transaction. For that reason, the most-often-used LTV range is between 75 and 80 per cent. Higher LTV ratios are primarily reserved for borrowers with higher credit scores and a satisfactory mortgage history. Full financing, or 100 per cent LTV, is reserved for only the most creditworthy borrowers. The loans with LTV ratios higher than 100 per cent are called *underwater mortgages* and are often allowed in some countries by lenders that have relatively loose lending conditions. In fact underwater mortgages were a key driver of the financial meltdown in 2008. I recommend you read books written by great economists such as Richard Duncan, Harry S. Dent, and Robert A. Wiedemer who wrote great books explaining the causes of the financial crisis of 2008.

- Other important components of a mortgage loan are the *interest rate type* and the *interest rate percentage*. In the broadest clarification, interest rates can be either of two types: fixed rate or adjustable rate. But creative lenders often hook the borrowers with low fixed rates for the first few years, often between two and five years, and then adopt an adjustable rate afterwards. With a fixed-rate mortgage loan, the interest rate remains the same for the term of the loan, and the loan repayment is split into equal monthly instalments. On the other hand, the interest rate on an *adjustable-rate mortgage*, often referred to as an ARM, can change from year to year. This implies that the monthly instalments of an ARM may vary significantly, which represents a level of risk for the unforeseen event of interest rates shooting over the roof. The interest rate of an adjustable-rate mortgage resets based on a benchmark or index plus an additional spread, called an ARM margin. Typically, ARMs are tied to any of the following benchmarks or indexes: LIBOR (the

London interbank offered rate), IBOR (interbank offered rate), or the maturity yield on one-year treasury bills. Those indexes represent a measure of the interest rate at which banks lend to and borrow from one another in the interbank market, which is the cost of money to the lender when borrowing money from the central bank or other banks. Although the index rate can change, the spread, or ARM margin, stays the same. Hybrid ARMs, which are prevalent, feature aspects of both adjustable-rate and fixed-rate mortgages. This creative mortgage option is intended to hook the borrower with a low fixed rate over a short period of time, usually up to five years, and then after the fixed-rate period, the loan is amortized over the balance of the term with a rate that adjusts annually according to any of the indexes followed by the central bank and the lender.

- Preapproval letters have a validity, which is usually sixty days, but may vary from one lender to the other. This acts as a layer of protection to the lender in case major changes have occurred in the borrower's credit history during such the period of validity. Until the mortgage loan is approved and disbursed, borrowers are expected to keep their same financial situation vis-à-vis keeping their income steady, staying current on their monthly debt, not taking out any new debt, not making major deposits or withdrawals from their accounts, changing banks, and opening or closing accounts.

- When Joyce explained both what is written and what is implied in a mortgage preapproval letter, she wanted to bring to my attention that the conditions of this loan are what is referred to as a *conventional loan*. There are also *government-insured home loans*, which are guaranteed by the government. The government insures the lender against losses that might result from the borrower's default. Those types of government-sponsored loans often have LTVs exceeding 90 per cent and are usually available to first-time buyers who are nationals of the country where such programs are available. Such government-sponsored programs are quite specific for each country and also specific to each individual's situation. I recommend you check with your mortgage broker on such programs. Since they are intended primarily for first-time home buyers, investors can qualify for one property, or at best for a couple. As an investor who plans to achieve financial freedom through the cash flow from rental properties, you will require much more than a couple of properties. Therefore, I recommend that you get to understand fully how conventional loans work. Government-insured home loans have conditions that may conflict with your objective of renting out the property for a positive cash flow.

HOW MANY PROPERTIES CAN I AFFORD?

I hope I have managed to clarify the difference between the preapproved loan amount and the value of the property you can purchase. The loan-to-value (LTV), which is mentioned in a loan preapproval letter, is crucial to computing the value of the property you can afford to buy. As we have seen, the property value can be computed by dividing the preapproved mortgage loan amount by the LTV.

$$Property\ Value = \frac{Mortgage\ Amount}{LTV\ (\%)}$$

So let's say you get preapproved for a $100,000 mortgage with an LTV of 80 per cent. Following the equation above, the property value you can afford to purchase will be $125,000. Let's have a closer look how this value was derived:

$$Property\ Value = \frac{Mortgage\ Amount}{LTV\ (\%)} = \frac{\$100,000}{80\%} = \$125,000$$

REAL LIFE EXAMPLES

From my experience in working one-on-one with many fellow employees with the objective of mentoring them to achieve financial freedom through investing in rental properties, I have come to learn that lessons are best conveyed through examples. In this section, I share real life examples of other employee millionaires with whom I had the privilege of working and coaching them towards their successes. Their real names have been changed into generic ones to protect their privacy and to denote their general profile. We will look at their respective financial situations, their loan eligibilities, and how many properties each could afford. Do not get distracted with the absolute figures, since the income level as well as the cost of living change by country and even by city. The important thing is to look at ratios and how their cash flows.

Joe Public: age 28, married with two children

Joe Public (aka John Q. Public) represents the average middle class man who works hard for earned income. He is employed in a medium enterprise and earns $3,200 per month. He falls in an income tax bracket of 25 per cent, spends 26 per cent of his income on housing expenses, and 28 per cent on other loan obligations. This brings his debt-to-income ratio to 51 per cent, which is higher than the threshold of 50 per cent allowed by lenders.

When he planned to start investing in rental properties, he followed advice similar to that offered in this book and started looking for his team members. As you may have expected, his first team member was his mortgage advisor. After looking at his personal financial statement, his mortgage advisor informed him that his mortgage loan application would be rejected given that his DTI was 51 per cent, higher than the 50 per cent threshold.

Upon looking at the details of his expenses, it was observed that his credit cards' outstanding balances were eating him alive. Joe and his mortgage advisor worked on a strategy to pay off his credit card loans, starting with those cards that had the highest interest. It took them a period of ten months to have his credit card debt under control and to cancel all his credit cards except the one he used often and that had the lowest interest. From that point onward, Joe established the habit of paying off all his credit card balances every month. With no outstanding credit card balances, whatever he spent using credit cards every month was reflected under food, clothing, leisure, and travel expenses, as per the receipts he kept for bookkeeping. This meant that his income statement started to reflect zeros under credit cards payments.

With this shift in managing his expenses, Joe Public reduced his DTI to a level of 38 per cent, which classified his loan file as a favourable one. As a matter of fact, after getting his expenses in order, he got preapproved for a mortgage amount of $78,500. On a standard 80 per cent LTV, Joe Public could now budget for the property he planned to purchase. He divided the preapproved mortgage loan amount by 80 per cent and obtained a budget of $98,125 for the property he could afford.

Directly afterward, he met with his second team member, his real estate agent, with the preapproval letter in his hands and with a budget in mind, which enabled the agent to start looking for properties that matched Joe's criteria.

Below is a summary of Joe Public's income statement as well as his financial KPIs dashboard, both before and after the corrective measures he took.

PERSONAL INCOME STATEMENT		
INCOME	**Before**	**After**
Earned Total	3,200	3,200
Passive Total	-	-
Portfolio Income		
EXPENSES		
Expenses		
Income Taxes	800	800
Home Mortgage or Rent	725	725
Utilities	100	100
Food and Clothing	600	850
Travel and Leisure	-	150
Credit Cards Payments	400	
Car Loans Payments	200	200
Personal Loans Payments	300	300
TOTAL EXPENSES	**3,125**	**3,125**
NET MONTHLY CASH FLOW	**75**	**75**

Figure 45—Personal income statement of Joe Public (before and after)

Financial KPI's Dashboard		
	Before	**After**
My Income Profile		
% Earned Income	**100%**	**100%**
% Unearned Income	**0%**	**0%**
My Expenses Profile		
How Much do I Pay For Housing?	**26%**	**26%**
How Much do I Pay For Income Taxes?	**25%**	**25%**
How Much do I Pay For Loans?	**51%**	**38%**
Debt Burden Ratio (DBR) or Debt To Income Ratio (DTI)		
How Much Money I Keep?	**2%**	**2%**

Figure 46—Financial KPIs dashboard of Joe Public (before and after)

The lines in both the income statement and the financial KPIs show the impact of the corrective measures taken to improve his financial situation and get preapproved for a mortgage loan. Notice that his total expenses did not change after he took the necessary measures to improve his finances. He only proved he has better control of his finances by paying off his credit cards at the end of each billing cycle. While he kept the same lifestyle, his expenses started to show on different lines on his income statement. The result was a lower DTI.

After investing in his first rental property, Joe Public was able to net $225 in the form of unearned income every month. With this incremental income and without increasing his expenses, Joe Public further improved his debt-to-income ratio to 36 per cent. With this new lower DTI, Joe Public was eligible for another new mortgage loan. He kept on following the same strategy, buying one property after another, always increasing his total income and improving his DTI. His unearned income kept on increasing over time until it reached a stage where it exceeded his expenses. Joe Public was able to achieve financial freedom in fewer years than he originally planned, thanks to a commitment from his side to keep executing the same strategy that worked for him.

Let's now look at an example of another couple who belong to a high income bracket. They lead a busy lifestyle with many social commitments. Their clothing, furniture, cars, gadgets, and even the restaurants they frequent are all carefully selected to display their wealth … or the appearance of wealth. You may have guessed who this couple is by now. Of course they are the Joneses!

William (age 35) and Elizabeth (age 31) Jones: two children

William and Elizabeth are both high-level executives who work for large corporations. Their combined income is a handsome $25,000 per month. They are in the 30 per cent tax bracket, spend $6,500 per month on housing expenses, and another $7,000 on their loan obligations. They are offered high credit card limits with all the bells and whistles as well as lines of credit. They are the perfect consumers who spend a lot of money on the latest car models, designer clothing, designer furniture, and expensive accessories and gadgets. They have a large circle of friends, and they frequently host lavish parties at their winter home, summer home, or in fine dining restaurants.

Following the financial crisis of 2008, the company where Elizabeth is the sales director failed to deliver on its sales for two years in a row. Elizabeth's job security was put at stake. This was a wakeup call for the couple that they needed to invest their money to start having new streams of income in the form of unearned income. They had always respected what William's colleague James had been doing with his investments in rental properties.

James was the CFO of the company where William works, and they were close friends. James had consistently been giving the Joneses advice to invest in rental properties so they could afford their expensive lifestyle in the event one of them was forced to leave his or her job for some unforeseen reason.

It took the Joneses a couple of years and a threat to Elizabeth's job to get them to start considering investing in rental properties.

Not knowing where to start, they sought James's advice to guide them on rental property investments. James is another successful employee millionaire who has been following sound investing strategies similar to the ones offered in this book. He recommended that the Joneses meet with a mortgage advisor who would help them in getting prequalified for a mortgage loan before they started looking for properties. James recommended a mortgage advisor who was part of his team.

The Joneses scheduled a meeting with her. They were asked to bring with them their past six months' bank statements, credit card statements, salary slips, and any proof of other sources of income. They had their documents in order in time for their meeting. They were proud of their income and went to the meeting with a strong conviction that they would easily prequalify for a large mortgage loan, which would allow them to consider buying multiple rental properties soon. Instead they were surprised to be informed that they could not qualify for a mortgage loan unless they sorted out their financial situation.

Layla, their mortgage advisor, took the information from the documents they presented and filled out an income statement, which she then explained to them. The couple had mortgages on two properties for their winter and summer residences. They spent 28 per cent of their decently large income on housing. They also had large debt obligations on their line of credit, credit cards, personal loans, and car loans amounting to $7,000 per month—another 28 per cent of their income. The Joneses' income-to-debt ratio was at 54 per cent. They were advised to bring their DTI down to below 50 per cent for them to qualify for a mortgage loan.

Layla recommended some strategies to cancel their line of credit and to lower their monthly credit card payments. With a few months of minimizing their discretionary spending, the Joneses were finally able to pay off a decent amount of their credit card balances and cancelled those credit cards they did not need. They went from a negative monthly cash flow to a positive one in less than a year and improved their DTI to 46 per cent. With those adjustments in their finances, the Joneses applied for a mortgage loan and were prequalified for a mortgage loan of $314,000 over a term of 30 years and an interest rate of 4 per cent. Below is snapshot of their income statement and financial KPIs for both before and after corrective measures were taken.

PERSONAL INCOME STATEMENT		
INCOME	Before	After
Earned Income	25,000	25,000
Passive Income	-	-
Portfolio Income	-	-
TOTAL INCOME	25,000	25,000
EXPENSES	Before	After
Expenses		
Income Taxes	7,500	7,500
Home Mortgage or Rent	6,500	6,500
Utilities	500	500
Food and Clothing	2,500	2,500
Travel and Leisure	1,500	1,500
Credit Cards Payments	3,700	1,800
Car Loans Payments	1,600	1,600
Personal Loans Payments	1,700	1,700
Line of Credit Payments	300	-
TOTAL EXPENSES	25,800	23,600
NET MONTHLY CASH FLOW	(800)	1,400

Figure 47—Personal income statement of the Joneses (before and after)

Financial KPI's Dashboard		
	Before	After
My Income Profile		
% Earned Income	100%	100%
% Unearned Income	0%	0%
My Expenses Profile		
How Much do I Pay For Housing?	28%	28%
How Much do I Pay For Income Taxes?	30%	30%
How Much do I Pay For Loans?	54%	46%
Debt Burden Ratio (DBR) or Debt To Income Ratio (DTI)		
How Much Money I Keep?	-3%	6%

Figure 48—Financial KPIs dashboard of the Joneses (before and after)

With a $314,000 preapprove mortgage loan and with some coaching from their friend James, the Joneses were able to invest in three rental properties over a period of six months. Each of the three properties have netted them $235 in cash flow after all expenses are paid. The total of $705 in unearned income has increased their total income and eventually further reduced their DTI to be eligible for more and more good debt to finance rental properties. Within around seven years, the Joneses were making $10,000 in unearned income, which could serve them well in case either of them were to leaving their job. Over the years, the Joneses have managed to maintain the lifestyle they love, but they have become smarter about how much discretionary spending do since they enjoyed reinvesting their excess cash into additional rental properties to further increase their income, cash flow, and their net worth.

Let's next consider another example that represents the blue collar working class in any society. Those people work hard in often physically demanding jobs and get paid by the hour. For this class of people, whatever extra time they put on their jobs, the little incremental income appears to never make a difference. They find it challenging to cope with the increasing cost of living.

Jane Doe: age 26, single mother with one child

Jane Doe, a hard-working beauty specialist from East Asia, planned to move to Dubai, where she thought her higher income in the Middle East would allow her to provide a better quality of life for her family than in her home country. After her divorce, she and her ex-husband parted ways, and he never looked back at supporting their daughter.

Jane Doe was in an ordeal and decided to leave her country to work in a beauty salon in Dubai. She asked her parents to look after her daughter while she traveled abroad and worked hard to remit money to provide both her parents and her daughter a much better standard of living. When she accepted a tempting offer in Dubai, she knew nothing about the high cost of living there. A few days after starting her new job, she had to begin looking for accommodations. She was surprised by the skyrocketing rental rates and settled for a bed space, sharing a house where other Asian families lived. Her total basic expenses, between housing, transportation, and food were about 47 per cent of her income. The remaining 53 per cent of her income was being remitted to her home country to provide support for her family and to save whatever remained.

Even with a small monthly income of $1,200, Jane Doe was a prudent spender and managed her finances quite well. Her salary bracket in Dubai did not qualify her for credit cards, line of credit, personal loans, or even a mortgage loan. Being ambitious and determined to improve her financial situation, in Jane Doe's job as a beautician she met rich female professionals who were real estate investors. She wanted to emulate them, and thanks to her great service and friendliness, one of her clients volunteered to coach her whenever she was having her regular weekly pedicure sessions. Jane Doe also went the extra mile and educated herself on rental property investments through online searches and reading a handful of books.

Even though Jane Doe was not qualified to apply for a home mortgage in Dubai, she was determined to become a successful real estate investor. After a year of working in Dubai, she had a good track record on her income and savings. She traveled back home for a short annual leave of three weeks and met with a local bank over there. She carried with her bank statements and income slips, and the bank officer informed her that her financial situation was favourable and that he would give her an answer within two days.

The following morning, while she was bonding with her daughter to make up for the lost time she spent working away in Dubai, Jane Doe received a call from the bank informing her that she was preapproved for a mortgage amount of $61,000 for a loan term of 30 years at 6 per cent interest rate. She never imagined she would qualify for a loan, particularly for such a large amount. Below is a summary of her financial situation.

PERSONAL INCOME STATEMENT	
INCOME	
Earned Income	**1,200**
Passive Income	-
Portfolio Income	-
TOTAL INCOME	1,200
EXPENSES	After
Expenses	
Home Mortgage or Rent	230
Utilities	30
Food and Clothing	150
Parent Support	200
Travel and Leisure	50
Credit Cards Payments	
Car Loans Payments	
Personal Loans Payments	
Transportation	100
TOTAL EXPENSES	760
NET MONTHLY CASH FLOW	440

Figure 49—Personal income statement of the blue collar working class

Financial KPI's Dashboard	
My Income Profile	
% Earned Income	**100%**
% Unearned Income	**0%**
My Expenses Profile	
How Much do I Pay For Housing?	**22%**
How Much do I Pay For Loans?	**19%**
Debt Burden Ratio (DBR) or Debt To Income Ratio (DTI)	
How Much Money I Keep?	**37%**

Figure 50—Financial KPIs dashboard of the blue collar working class

Luckily for her, her cousin was a real estate agent. She called her cousin and met to discuss investment opportunities. The preapproved mortgage amount meant that Jane Doe could invest in a property of up to $76,250 on an 80 per cent LTV.

The real estate agent lined up a couple of properties. Being properly prepared from reading books and being coached on rental property investments, Jane Doe was able to identify a great opportunity. She found a three-bedroom townhouse in a calm community that was not far from the city's centre. She planned on having her parents and daughter live in one of the bedrooms while renting out the two remaining bedrooms to executives who wanted to live in an affordable, clean place within twenty minutes' drive from the city centre. Jane Doe was able to rent out both remaining rooms for a sum of $400, which more than covered all expenses and mortgage instalments. She was still able to net $57 per month in cash flow.

This was an eye-opener for Jane Doe. From that date onward she replicated the same process for a few years. She was able to return to her home country and spend time with her growing daughter without the need to work for money for a few months. Being a motivated person, she opened a small business related to beauty to keep her busy. Her unearned income consistently exceeded her expenses. She continued working only for the fun of being productive and keeping busy.

REAL LIFE EXAMPLES COMMENTARY

The above examples represented people from different walks of life and from different income levels. Their financial situations were also quite representative of many employees, whether they are financially comfortable or struggling. I am confident you can relate to these examples. Each of those real-life scenarios teach lessons to each one of us. Allow me to summarize some of the main lessons:

- Your income level does not determine your financial health. As you may have noticed, both Joe Public and the Joneses earned a handsome income from their jobs. However, both were poor managers of their expenses and their debt—especially their bad debt, which was eating them alive like an alligator. When they were able to confine the alligator in its cage by managing their debt, their debt-to-income improved to levels that allowed their respective lenders to prequalify them for mortgage loans. On the other hand, Jane Doe belonged to the working class, with an income that would classify her under the poverty line. She was a prudent manager of her expenses and managed to prequalify for a mortgage loan without taking major steps in expenses.
- If you currently have debt obligations that increase your debt-to-income ratio above the acceptable level of 50 per cent, you can always restructure your debt and pay off those loans that have high interest rates. It sometimes makes sense to take on a personal loan with low interest to pay off outstanding credit card balances with interest rates that are manifold higher than personal loans. As recommended in the earlier examples, it always pays off to meet with a reliable financial advisor who can help in restructuring your debt and improving your DTI to levels that are acceptable to lenders in your country, state, or city.

- Earlier in this book, I shared an enlightening question Joyce's father often asked family members who were in a high income bracket. His golden question was "How much money do you keep?" Upon becoming a family member when Joyce and I got married, I met many of those family members who told me that this question, although embarrassing when he first threw it at them, made them go back home and give it thought. Many reflected on this question well and realized that they had to take actions. As a result, those who were tracking how much they keep from their income saved more, and some reinvested those savings in income-producing assets.

- Higher income level does not necessarily translate into higher eligibility for a mortgage loan. As shown in the examples above, Joe Public earns 2.7 times as much as Jane Doe earns ($3,200 vs. $1,200). But he got prequalified for a $78,500 mortgage loan, whereas Jane Doe got prequalified for $61,000. As you can see, both mortgage amounts are not miles away from each other.

Chapter 8 Action Steps

With the help of your mortgage broker, approach three different lenders and apply for a mortgage loan. Once you get prequalified, study the preapproval letter and inquire with the lender about any point that might appear unclear or confusing.

Compute the maximum property value that you can afford to purchase based on both the LTV and the approved mortgage amount. This will become your first criterion when you start working with your real estate agents to prospect for rental properties. Other criteria will be covered in the next chapter.

Now, with a preapproval letter in your hands, you can set a budget for the rental property you would like to purchase. It is time to meet with another important team member from your executive board, your real estate agent.

CHAPTER 9

Prospect for Discounted Properties

After receiving my preapproval letter, I set the budget of the rental property I would like to purchase. I was fired up to meet with my real estate agent so I could to demonstrate to her that I was a serious buyer with a loan preapproval in my hand. When sharing my excitement with Papa Joe over a casual phone call, he asked me challenging questions about whether I made up my mind on location, property type, property size, features, amenities, and potential rental income. Although I did not have too much clarity on most of those criteria, I tried to mask the truth by pretending I was on top of my game.

But I couldn't keep pretending when Papa Joe hit me with his second round of questions relating to average price of similar properties in the same neighbourhood and the potential rental income. With a furious tone, he said, "You busy fool! You plan to invest in rental properties and you do not have an idea on comparable prices? If you don't know what you are looking for, how will you know when you have found it? Will you use a crystal ball? Or will you just trust the seller or the real estate agent for the price they present to you?" He paused for a few seconds (which felt like ages) and asked me to see him in his office in a few days. Before he hung up the phone he asked me to reflect on two questions: How will I find great investment properties? How will I recognize a great deal when I find one?

All my excitement and the positive energy were squelched by Papa Joe's furious reaction. In fact, I felt like a loser. It took me a few hours to calm down and reflect on what I could possibly do in the few days before meeting Papa Joe and receiving another set of harsh words, but this time directly in my face. I started to review my notes from books I have read on rental property investments. The answer has always been under my nose. But I was a busy fool, excited to start prospecting for properties without understanding how a good deal can be identified from the non-good ones.

MY DECISION TREE (MY HIERARCHY OF CRITERIA)

My corporate life has taught me to make things repeatable by systemization. To be well prepared for my forthcoming meeting with Papa Joe, I applied for a leave from my job for the rest of that week and read my notes from the books I previously read. Some chapters I read repeatedly until I was able to connect the dots. It was a stressful week that felt like cramming for a final exam, with the only option being to pass.

This hard working week ended up being quite fruitful. I came up with a hierarchy of criteria for my rental property investments, which I categorized as follows:

Level One:	What am I looking for?
Level Two:	What will I consider viewing?
Level Three:	What will I make an offer on?
Level Four:	What will I buy?

During our office meeting, Papa Joe, was pleased to know that I least came prepared with a set of criteria in mind. This made our mentoring session constructive instead of punishing. I shared with Papa Joe my thoughts on the hierarchy of criteria I would like to follow. The lessons I received from Papa Joe and eventually with other coaches and mentors, the lessons I read in many books, the lessons taught in each seminar or webinar I have attended, the lessons from each rental property I have purchased over the years, and the lessons from my successes and failures, each enabled me to fine-tune and improve the set of criteria I am about to share in this chapter. This hierarchy of criteria acted as a *decision tree* that guided me on all the rental properties I have purchased in many countries and cities. I came to visualize this set of criteria like a funnel, which I call the *path to purchasing discounted properties*.

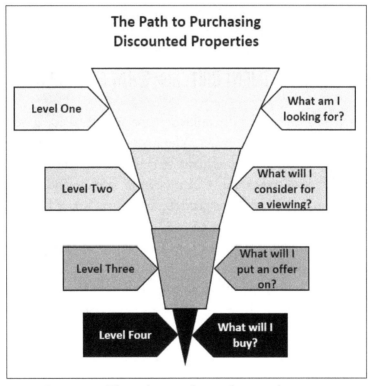

Figure 51—The path to purchasing discounted properties

The funnel shape of the path to purchasing might make you feel that you will be looking for a needle in a haystack. Trust me—this step-by-step path to purchasing will guide you on narrowing your search to fewer and fewer properties as you move along the path. The selection criteria will help eliminate properties that do not fit your benchmarks, so you will view fewer units than what you looked for before. Then you can make offers on fewer properties until you select the property that matches the criteria in all four stages. Each step of the path to purchasing will include its own criteria to help you in qualifying prospective properties and eliminating the suspect ones.

In the following sections, I will take each step of the path to purchasing and will introduce its respective categories of criteria. Each of those criteria will provide a more precise picture, describing the property from its own angle. The whole set of criteria together will determine the ideal property you may want to invest in, which will enable you to recognize it when you see it.

LEVEL ONE INVESTMENT CRITERIA: WHAT AM I LOOKING FOR?

In my prospecting for discounted properties, Papa Joe gave me a hint: Start with the end in mind. The main objective of investing in properties is to rent them to tenants to generate unearned income. A wise approach is to start looking for properties from an end user's eyes, meaning from the tenant's perspective. As an investor, if I put on the hat of an end user who wishes to live in the property, I will be in a better position to judge how easy it will be to rent out the property to prospective tenants.

The criteria in level one enable investors to answer the main question: What am I looking for? Below is the list of those criteria:

- Location
- Construction
- Type
- Features
- Amenities
- Condition
- Days on the market

Location

Location is the first criterion that allows the decision-making to be focused. It allows the search for investment properties to be narrowed down to a certain geographic area. Zooming in on a specific location allows the investor to become an expert in this area by becoming specialized in a certain city or community. This empowers the investor to better understand the factors that determine local property values and rental rates. An important lesson I learned from Papa Joe: Location determines the price of a property, all other things being equal. The wise investor will choose a location first and then pick a property.

"Location, location, location" is the slogan used in almost every reference on real estate investment and even on retail businesses. This cliché remains a mantra that is followed by the employee millionaire as the first and foremost selection criterion. Papa Joe taught me to turn this cliché into an actionable process for choosing a great location. He told me to write down the word *location* three times and to underline the letter C in each of the words. I ended up with three Cs. He told me that the Cs in location, location, location refer to country, city, and community respectively. He explained that getting clarity on those three Cs will enable me to narrow down my search criteria and start identifying great deals by looking at the different properties within my selected location. He emphasised that the most important of the three Cs is the third one, which is *community*. Investors, who become experts in a certain community, will be able to compare local property values and rental rates, which will enable them to identify great deals from the average ones.

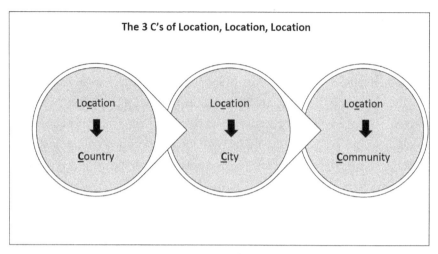

Figure 52—Location, location, location

Selecting a country

The thinking process for choosing a great location starts with selecting a country that is stable, investor friendly, allows property ownership, has a reasonable tax structure, and where there is a demand for rentals.

Investors who plan to invest in developing countries also look at the *corruption index* of those countries. Paperwork in countries with a high corruption index is usually a big headache, with many surprises draining the investors' pockets.

The table below is a simple tool to enable investors to select a country following the five-star rating system, which works in the same way you do ratings on Facebook, Yelp, TripAdvisor, and most discovery platforms. Each of the criteria can be rated as one star (worst), two stars (bad), three stars (OK), four stars (better), and five stars (best).

Country Selection Criteria		Rating (1–5 Stars)
Political Stability	A	
Security Stability	B	
Corruption Index	C	

Investor Friendly	D	
Allows Property Ownership for Non-Locals	E	
Tax Structure	F	
Total Rating (A+B+C+D+E+F)	T	
Average Rating (T/6)		

A country with an average rating of less than three will be a country to avoid if it is not the country where you live. If you are a local or a resident in the country where you wish to invest, this tool might still be useful as a guiding principle. But you will be in a situation of making an informed decision based on your experience in this country.

Selecting a City

When it comes to selecting a city, the most important selection criteria revolve around its economic prospects. We are talking here about basic economics, the laws of supply and demand. When I first heard those two words from Papa Joe, I was discouraged with the thought of going back again to a topic that I never enjoyed in college.

Papa Joe was amazing at simplifying complex matters in simple laymen's language. He defined *supply* as the number of rental properties listed in a city. Such data is easily obtained with the help of your team member who comes into play in prospecting for properties, your real estate agent or broker. Real estate agents have access to property listings with details on each property, such as type, size, number of bedrooms, dates of construction, and the date each property was listed on the market for either sale or rent.

Papa Joe explained *demand* as the number of tenants looking to rent in a specific city. Demand could become a bit trickier to estimate. The main indicators of demand are occupancy rates, move-in incentives, and future supply.

Data on occupancy rates are easily obtained in countries that publish such records. In countries where data is not available on occupancy rates, your real estate agents or property management companies can be of great help. By going through rental properties listings, your real estate agent can give you the average number of days rental properties have been listed in a certain city, or even community, without being tenanted. Locations with properties that stay on the market for a long period without being occupied may be suffering from low occupancy rates. This would signal a worrying point to the investor.

When it comes to move-in incentives, it doesn't take a genius to conclude that landlords who offer move-in incentives (such as a few months of free rent, no security deposit, or certain gifts) are competing for tenants. This is another signal that occupancy rate is quite low in your target area. You do not want to end up competing on bringing your rental prices down and giving more competitive move-in incentives to have your property rented out. Whenever you are in such a situation, you will probably end up with negative cash flow, which is counterproductive and will make you pay from your own pocket to cover the a property's total expenses.

When I asked Papa Joe how to estimate future supply, he sat back in his chair and turned it towards his office window, which is in a high-rise overlooking the city. "Have a look," he said.

I saw many other high-rise towers, and in the distance some standalone homes with green communities. When I described to him what I saw, he bluntly and straightforwardly called me blind. I figured the discussion was becoming interesting.

He let out his usual laugh and pointed his fingers towards the construction cranes lined up in the horizon over the city. He asked me to look at them and reflect on what I saw. Focusing my brain on those cranes, I saw that there were many. Below those cranes were developments under construction. I was tempted to start counting them until Papa Joe interrupted and told me that the more I see projects under construction, the greater the supply of future residential properties will be over the next few months and years.

Papa Joe explained that no rocket science or formulas measure demand and supply of rental properties. He warned me not to focus my thoughts on only the indicators of demand and supply but to look at the bigger picture to figure out what the collective set of insights indicate regarding either demand or supply. He said that if I determine that supply is greater than demand in a certain location, I may want to stay away from this location and start looking into others. My objective would be to find rent-paying tenants, translating into positive cash flow.

While taking notes, his assistant came to offer us coffee. He also had to sign some paperwork. This gap gave me time to reflect on this interesting session. While I formed a clear picture in my mind of how to estimate both demand for and supply of rental properties, something pushed me to ask more questions. I correlated high supply of properties as perhaps the result of many developers all jumping in at the same time in a certain geographical area to make profit. But I wanted more answers on what drives demand.

As Papa Joe signed something, he interrupted my thoughts and said with a loud voice, "You look like you have more questions on your mind. Ask me!"

I said I was thinking about the drivers of demand and supply and explained what I thought were drivers of rental property supply. He nodded in agreement.

"What are the drivers of demand?" I asked.

He raised his index finger to communicate visually that there is one main driver. He said one word: "Employment".

Employment might be classified as the most important indicator of demand. Cities that are established business hubs attract many people to earn their living, for example great cities like Dubai, London, New York, Sidney, Hong Kong, and Singapore. Those cities have created lots of jobs and have therefore attracted workers from around the globe to move to those cities in pursuit of careers and high-paying jobs. As a result, population in those cities grew. All this incoming population had to settle in homes, which made demand for rental properties increase, and eventually also the rental rates.

"As a matter of fact," he added, "population follows employment." He recommended I always keep updated with the economic activity of any city I invest in. The prudent investor will also look at employment stability since demand for rental will be strong, not only in the short run, but also in the longer run.

Selecting a Community

Once you choose a country and a city, the selection of communities comes into play. The problem is that most real estate investors start at this point, without giving consideration to selecting a city based on its economic dynamics.

Communities that are the best picks for real estate investors are those that are emerging and have an established reputation as desirable. Communities that are sought after by end users who want to live there are often close to work, schools, hospitals, retail, and recreational centres. Some communities are even more distinguished from the others by earning a character for being safe, calm, and with a great quality of life. Select communities that have earned an attractive brand identity draw population and consequently command higher rental rates (and higher property values). There are two types of those highly desirable communities: those that are established and those that are emerging.

An investor should be aware that it might be challenging to find great deals in established communities. Prices are generally inflated because everyone wants to live there; hence demand is high. But emerging communities are considered the investor's sweet spot because they are often overlooked and undervalued, which makes them ideal for investors. Emerging communities that have earned an attractive brand character are able to command high property prices, which puts the purchase price out of reach for most people. This high cost of home ownership forces people who want to live in those attractive emerging communities to rent.

Another determining factor for the property prices of emerging communities is their distance to the city centre, where most businesses are located. I have seen in many countries that rental rates and property values go down the greater the travel distance from the city centre.

Selecting a Street

Once a community has been selected, an investor can be more precise with the choice of a lot or street. This decision is fairly intuitive.

It will as much as possible be determined by any of the combination of being private, accessible, and with a great view.

Summary on Location

To recap the above: the set of criteria related to location allows any investor to plan with the end in mind. Locations that are sought after by end users are those that will rent easier and faster and can command a premium rental rate.

As you will see later in this book, it is the rental income of a property that plays the biggest role in determining its value. The higher the rental income, the higher the value of the property. This is why many investors follow a strategy of purchasing average properties in the most sought-after communities. They know that they can easily improve the property with a little investment and then improve its value for a gain that far exceeds the cost of improvement.

The figure below summarizes the zooming-in process for choosing a great location.

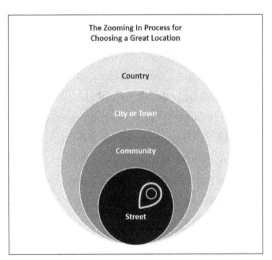

Figure 53—The zooming-in process for choosing a great location

Construction

The second defining selection criterion is whether the property is finished (with a ready title deed) or still under construction. The employee millionaire strategy focuses on rental properties and therefore, by default, investing for cash flow requires properties that are finished and ready to be occupied by tenants who will pay rent. It is quite a simple and straightforward strategy. Once you understand the demand for rent and the rental rates in a certain community, it doesn't require a crystal ball to forecast the future rental income, the expenses, and the net cash flow.

On the other hand, investors who do not want to bother to find discounted properties, rent them out, and receive positive cash flow often get bought on the Ponzi scheme of buying planned properties, thinking wishfully that they can resell those same properties at much higher prices in a few years. They are practically betting on the unknown. They are being carried away by false promises made by fast-talking real estate agents who claim that prices of those off-plan properties will double or even triple in a few years ... as if they had a crystal ball.

Many of my colleagues fell in the same trap in the mid-2000s and used their life savings to off-plan properties in the hope of doubling their money. I have seen photos of those friends proudly taken in front of giant hoardings that had impressive visuals of the design of the master development where they bought their off-plan units. When the financial crisis hit Dubai in 2008, those hoardings fencing the perimeter of the planned development ended up fencing a large piece of desert land with at best some partial construction. Those friends and colleagues lost their life savings and never were able to get their money back from those bankrupted developers.

The situation got worse when those investors were still asked to make payments as scheduled in their sales agreements, given that those agreements did not tie up the payments to the construction progress. When those investors were hesitant to continue making payments for a development that would never see the light, those developers legally foreclosed on whatever payments were made by those investors. The investors got greedy when they were promised huge capital gains in a few years, when those projects would be handed over. They accepted great risks and as a result have paid a high price for their bad decisions.

The bigger problem is that those lessons are never learned. The majority of the real estate investors in Dubai still invest in off-plan properties with the hope of major capital gains. I receive more than a dozen calls and emails every week from developers and real estate agents who want to convince me to buy properties off-plan with their assertive promises of huge capital gains. I always answer them politely and ask them if they can lend me their crystal ball. I end up explaining to them why I am not interested. Those guys are sales dogs. They never give up. They will try to call again and again, even if sometimes I say loud and bluntly: "I am not interested!" My advice is to beware of agents like that. They will make their commissions when you sign the purchase agreement. On the other hand, you might never see either your money back or the development built up. I use my smartphone to block those irritating agents from calling, texting, or even emailing me.

Lenders want to minimize risks when they finance properties through mortgage loans. Inquire with your lender on whether you can get a mortgage on an off-plan property. You will most probably receive a rejection or at best get an approval but with high interest rates and low loan-to-value ratio.

Those who can afford the risk of losing money in return for high profits from capital gain can make their own decisions irrespective of the learning in this book. It is their call. I am only giving advice that has served me and many others quite well. One of my close friends, in spite of all the advice I have given him, the fast-talking real estate agents have still managed to convince to buy two off-plan properties in downtown Dubai with the promise that prices will double in two to three years and a fortune can be made. When he called me with an excited tone of voice to congratulate him for this move, I couldn't say much. I wished him good luck. I do hope those two agents really do have a crystal ball so that my friend will not lose too much money.

Type

Having a clear picture of what type of residential property you are looking for in your defined location narrows down your search even further. The two broad decisions you will have to make here is whether you are looking for single-family homes or multifamily properties.

A single-family home, also known as a single-dwelling unit, is a structure with its own title deed that is intended to be occupied by one family. A multifamily residential unit is a structure with one title deed but with multiple and separate housing units, meaning each unit can be inhabited by a separate family. For example, a multifamily property can be a duplex, triplex, or even larger apartment complex, all under one title deed where each unit can be inhabited by a different family. Multifamily properties can be further classified into either small or large. Small multifamily properties are usually up to four units, whereas large multifamily properties are five or more units. Depending on the practice in your country, lenders often consider small multifamily properties as residential, whereas large multifamily properties are considered commercial, and therefore the mortgage application becomes less dependent on the applicant and more on the property financials.

Single-family homes are the most sought-after properties for home ownership by end users who want to occupy the property. For that reason, those houses tend to sell based on emotions and to command better appreciation. In comparison, multifamily properties are more often owned by investors who rent out the units for cash flow. Prices for multifamily properties are determined strictly by the rental income. Investors do not buy with emotions. They buy only if the numbers make sense. Due to their large number of units, purchasing multifamily properties requires that more capital be invested and therefore are usually more difficult for smaller investors who are starting up.

The figure below shows a quick comparison between single-family and multifamily properties.

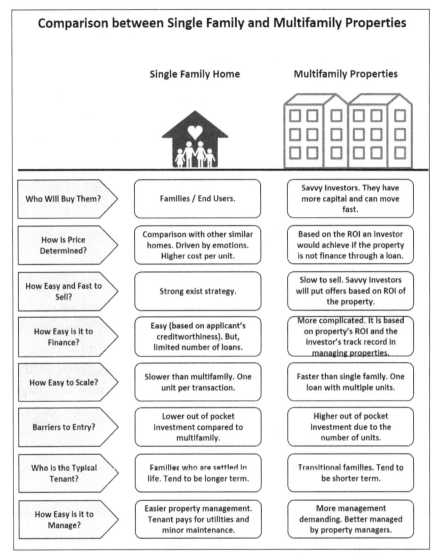

Figure 54—Comparison between single family and multifamily properties

The common wisdom is to start investing in single-family houses with less capital and less risk. Then you can grow into multifamily properties over time. In Papa Joe's words, "Get started with single-family investing and grow into multifamily investing." Your decision on what type of property to invest in depends on your current experience, capital strength, and investment goals.

Features

Property *features* are those basic descriptors used by any end user who occupies a property. Features describe the age of the property, built-up area (BUA), number of bedrooms, number of bathrooms, and number of parking lots. Features are what tenants will look into before signing the rental agreement. Assuming the property is in good condition, features will have a major impact on the rental rate and eventually on the investor's cash flow. The good thing is that those features enable investors to easily compare both the purchase price and the rent with other properties on a like for like basis.

Amenities

Amenities relate to the pleasantness or attractiveness of a property. They are the features of a property that provide comfort, convenience, or pleasure. Examples are a fireplace, central air-conditioning, a terrace, a view, a swimming pool, or a complimentary access to the community gym. Such amenities could be the competitive advantage that differentiates your property from others with similar features, and as a result may justify higher rental rates.

Condition

In the ideal scenario for the employee millionaire, given that each has a job and limited time to spend on repairing a property, investors want to find discounted properties that require no repair. Properties in good condition can be listed for rent from day one, which means your invested capital will start to generate returns as fast as they get rented out. On the other hand, many properties require minor cosmetic repair, causing a large discount from market price. Those fixer-uppers represent opportunities with discounted prices, which can have a big impact on the return on invested capital. An investor should have a good understanding of both the estimated cost of repair and the estimated time of repair before deciding whether a fixer-upper will be a good or a bad investment choice.

While properties requiring repair could indeed present great opportunities, investors should always be aware that the greater the required repair, the greater the discount, but the longer the time required to repair the property and have it ready for rent. This means an investor must weigh both the discount resulting from such a property and the lost rent due to time required for repair. When you do the math, you can make an informed decision. I recommend that investors who are just starting in rental property investments invest in properties that are rent-ready or that require minor cosmetic repair such as painting and other minor fixing. Investors who are experienced in construction, will let their experience guide them in buying properties with major cosmetic repairs and even sometimes some structural repairs. Investors with no experience in construction ought to stay away from major repairs.

I learned this lesson the hard way when I paid over $45,000 to fix a two-story duplex that required major structural repairs. My purchase price was at $245,000, which was 30 per cent less than the market value of $350,000. I ended up paying $290,000 for this property, which wiped away almost half of the savings from the 30 per cent discounted price. You might still think that I still saved around $60,000 on the purchase price. Yes, I did, but what if I was a new investor and did not have the $45,000 cash to repair the property?

An advantage of fixer-uppers requiring minor repairs is they will have fewer end users making offers on them. A better price might be negotiated with the seller if there are fewer competing offers. The other advantage is the forced appreciation resulting from the improved property condition. When such properties are restored and are rent-ready, they can command a rental income in line with the market for similar properties with good conditions. This means the investor will be securing an improved ROI with a higher rental rate and lower invested capital.

Investors in fixer-uppers should be aware that lenders may not be willing to approve a mortgage for properties requiring major repairs.

Days on the Market

When you start tracking properties being listed for sale, you will develop a sense of the average number of days similar properties sell in your selected location. It's a no-brainer that a property that has been listed for sale for quite some time (longer than what you are observing from other similar properties) may have an inherent problem that prevents it from being sold. Reasons could be related to listing price, type and quality of existing tenants, poor ROI, neighbourhood or street conditions, property condition, or any other headache the current owner is having. Sometimes, it might make sense to call those owners and seek to learn what problems they are having with it. You never know! Sometimes an existing challenge can be an opportunity for you to negotiate the price, fix the problem, and improve the property value.

Papa Joe's favorites are properties that aren't listed for sale. When I asked him why, he said: "Everything is for sale for the right price." His rationale is that when a property is listed, an investor will be competing with other buyers. With many competing buyers inquiring about the same property, the seller is often tempted to get greedy and increase the price to get the best price from the highest bidder. I have experienced more extreme situations in some of my transactions where the same property was listed by multiple agents, and an inquiry by a single potential buyer to those different agents was translated to the seller as multiple inquiries. As a result, this seller got greedy and started to raise the price from one day to the next. I walked away from the deal and then received a call from the seller's agent in a few days, asking me if I was still interested in proceeding with the old price. Having seen the seller's frustration with selling it, I ended up buying the property for about 15 per cent less than what the seller was originally asking for.

Level One Investment Criteria Worksheet

Being able to see all level one investment criteria in one document allows investors to compare properties on a like for like basis. This kind of comparison allows investors to narrow down their search to level two.

The level one investment criteria worksheet provides a helicopter view of all those criteria on a single spreadsheet, which can be downloaded from www.employeemillionaire.com/resources.

For such a worksheet to serve its intended purpose of comparing properties on a like for like basis, it is recommended that you fix the following criteria: location, construction, and property type. Why is that important? It will make a lot of sense to compare properties within a location that you have selected. It also makes sense to compare properties within that location based on their construction and type. It is neither fair nor accurate to compare an off-plan property to another one that is ready. It also doesn't make sense to compare a three-bedroom condominium to a three-bedroom standalone house with its own garden. Prices, features, and amenities will differ widely between locations and types of properties. This means separate worksheets are to be filled in by location, by property type, and by construction status.

Below are the different headers in this worksheet. I recommend you download the worksheet and take advantage of the formulas it has to enable you to better compare the properties you will be listing in the same worksheet. The sheet has comments to guide you on filling in each of the fields.

The headers of the level one investment criteria worksheet:

Country	
City	
Community	
Property Type	
Construction	
Days on the Market	Date of Reading
	Date of Listing
	Days on Market
Features	Number of Bedrooms
	Number of Bathrooms
	Number of Parking Lots
	Age (years)

	Built-Up Area (BUA)
	Plot Area
Amenities	Pool
	Gym
	Garden or Children Play Area
	View
Listing Price	Listing Price
	Price / BUA
Rental Income	Annual Rental Rate
	Rent-to-Price Ratio
General Comments	Remarks / Contact

To recap, a level one investment criteria worksheet for a selected location, similar property type, and similar construction status allows comparison of the remaining criteria (features, amenities, condition, and number of days on the market) in relation to each property's respective listing price. This worksheet automatically computes the median listing price. Therefore, it becomes easy to identify properties that are listed at or below median listing price. The worksheet automatically highlights those properties in green for easier identification. The next step is to consider pursuing further to level two those properties with a listing price at or below the median price.

In his efforts to explain the pitfall of using averages when comparing listing prices, Papa Joe clarified that whenever one property is listed at an extraordinarily high or low price, the average is skewed higher or lower as a result. Therefore the average becomes a less reliable metric as compared to median.

The median listing price, on the other hand, is the sale price in the middle of the data set when you arrange all the sale prices from low to high. The median sale price, then, represents the figure at which half of the properties in the area sell at a higher price and other half at a lower price.

LEVEL TWO INVESTMENT CRITERIA: WHAT WILL I CONSIDER FOR A VIEWING?

In level one you were looking at the investment criteria of a large number of properties without ever needing to step a foot out of your home or office. This is quite normal. You cannot expect yourself to go out and physically check on such a large number of properties.

In level two, you will need to analyse all the data obtained in level one to narrow down your list to fewer properties that qualify a physical viewing. The common practice is that you may look at the data of a hundred listed properties in level one and narrow down your list to around thirty potential properties for viewing. The single most important criterion for level two of the path to purchasing is *rent-to-price ratio*, which is the ratio of the gross monthly rent divided by the listing price of the property in question.

As mentioned earlier, the investor's purchasing decision property will be based solely on a property's financial performance, and to be more specific, on its cash flow. This is often referred to as the *back end evaluation criteria*, which will be covered in level three of the path to purchasing. A property with a positive cash flow would merit further investigation.

The property's cash flow is a function of its rent, operating expenses, and mortgage instalments. The rent shall be higher than both the operating expenses and the mortgage instalments combined for the property to generate positive cash flow. For cash flow to be computed, the numbers on rental rate, operating expenses, and mortgage instalments must be available on hand, but all this information will not be readily available at this stage. So, investors need to evaluate properties based on front-end evaluation criteria.

The data that can be made available before viewing a property is its listing price and potential gross rental rate. Such data is quite readily available on most property listing platforms or may be obtained from real estate agents. Savvy investors use both set of data, which are the gross monthly rent and the property listing price, to compute the rent-to-price ratio and follow the 0.8 per cent test as a pass or fail for viewing. This means that properties with a rent-to-price ratio of 0.8 per cent or higher are worthy to be considered for viewing.

$$Rent - to - Price\ Ratio = \frac{Gross\ Monthly\ Rent}{Property\ Price}$$

If rent-to-price ratio < 0.8 per cent → Fail

If rent-to-price ratio ≥ 0.8 per cent → Pass → consider for viewing

This ratio is quite simple to compute. Many investors perform such a math on the back of an envelope or using the calculators on their smart phones. This ratio serves as a front-end criterion. The higher the rent-to-price ratio, the better the potential cash flow from the property. Properties that pass the 0.8 per cent test will be considered for viewing.

For each hundred properties you would have considered on paper in level one, you will end up with about thirty properties that pass the 0.8 per cent test and therefore would classify for potential viewing. From here, you can contact your real estate agent or broker to schedule viewings for those shortlisted properties. Viewing those properties will allow you to see in reality whatever is registered on papers in level one. You will be able to get a good feel for the community, the street, the condition of the property, its features, and its amenities. From there you will need to make a decision on which properties you will make offers on.

LEVEL THREE INVESTMENT CRITERIA: WHAT WILL I MAKE AN OFFER ON?

Having seen quite a few properties, you will be tempted to move on and put offers on those select few where all the criteria in level one and level two apply. Before you get excited and make any written offer in the form of a letter of intent, it is important to understand two guiding principles (which Papa Joe used to repeat) for determining your offer price:

- The listing price, which is the seller's asking price, is not the real value of the property.
- The property value is based on its financial performance. This means, you determine the property value, which becomes your offer.

During our long mentoring session on that Saturday, Papa Joe wanted to make sure I differentiate price from value. He explained *value* as the amount of money that I am willing to pay for something, while *price* is the amount of money that I am asked to pay for it. He added that value can be perceived differently by different people. For an end user, the value perception can be emotional. Therefore, the offer for a property may reflect those emotions. In most cases, offers made on such emotional decisions are often much higher than what real estate investors offer for the same property. For real estate investors, the decision on the price they offer is based purely on numbers. No emotions are in play. In good deals the numbers work; in bad deals they don't.

With the difference between value and price settled in my mind, I couldn't wait for my next lesson on how to determine the value of a property based on its numbers. Before I was given the chance to ask Papa Joe to teach me, he described prudent investors as those who:

- Determine the value of a property based on its operational performance, *and*
- Validate the property value based on its financial performance.

Whereupon he proceeded to explain each separately.

Determining a Property Value Based on Its Operational Performance

To measure a property's operational performance, real estate investors always look its net operating income, which is computed by subtracting all annual operating expenses from the annual rental income.

$$\begin{pmatrix} Net \\ Operating \\ Income \end{pmatrix} = \begin{pmatrix} Rental \\ Income \end{pmatrix} - \begin{pmatrix} Operating \\ Expenses \end{pmatrix}$$

In Papa Joe's opinion, amateur investors often overlook or underestimate a property's operating expenses. As a result, they end up with negative cash flow and lose money instead of making money. When I asked him to enlighten me on the details of a property's operating expenses, he picked up his desk phone and called Ms Jing, asking her to come over to his office. In less than two minutes, a tall, elegant, smart-looking Singaporean woman entered his office. She walked proudly into the office and spoke confidently, introducing herself as the chief operating officer for the property management division in Papa Joe's company. When Papa Joe asked her to have few sessions with me on analysing properties based on net operating income (NOI), she opened her smartphone, checked her calendar, and gave me an appointment the following Saturday to meet her in her office. What I learned from Ms Jing's meeting on how to analyse rental properties is the focus of chapter 10.

When Ms Jing left, Papa Joe explained his reasons for calling her. "When you start your investment journey, you will have to work in your business and learn all the ropes of the trade. But when your investment portfolio grows, you will have to recruit the right professionals to work for your business." He clarified that because he works for his business, he is no longer involved in the transactional details, and because he wants me to go into this level of detail in the early phases of my investment journey, he would be connecting me with his team members who can each guide me regarding their respective areas of expertise.

After reassuring me that Ms Jing would be investing time teaching me how to look at a property's financials and arrive at its NOI, he wanted me to understand how real estate investors determine the value of a property based on its net operating income. He explained that the common wisdom is to determine the value of a residential single-family property based on comparative prices of similar properties in the same location, whereas the value of a multifamily residential property is determined based on its ROI (return on investment).

He shared a secret that made him a millionaire from investing in residential single-family properties before he started owning large multifamily properties. I liked the idea of learning Papa Joe's secret formula and was all ears. He whispered in a low voice, asking me to approach him from over his desk. He said: "Evaluate residential single-family properties based on both their comparative prices as the first filter and their ROI as the second filter. You will be an "AND" investor. Always look at *both* comparative prices *and* return on investment of a residential single-family property."

He then lay back in his chair, signaling to me that I could do the same. Speaking normally again, he explained that to determine a property's ROI, the investor has to look at its NOI as a percentage of its value. This assumes that the property will be bought for cash only, without a loan. The measure of a property's ROI is referred to as its capitalization rate. He took a white paper from the printer on the side of his desk and wrote the following:

$$Capitalization\ Rate\ (\%) = \frac{Net\ Operating\ Income}{Property\ Value}$$

He explained that a property value can be determined from both the net operating income and the capitalization rate (often referred to as cap rate). He wrote down the following:

$$Property\ Value = \frac{Net\ Operating\ Income}{Capitalization\ Rate\ (\%)}$$

I was excited to have a formula to determine a property's value. But upon reflecting on it, I figured out that NOI can be computed from the property's operating income and expenses, whereas I didn't know how to get the capitalization rate, so I asked Papa Joe to explain how to get it.

He said he'd been waiting for this question to jump out of my mouth as a sign that I was following him. He said: "Cap rate is the rate of return that a rental property will generate based on an all-cash purchase on its current market value." He insisted that I notice that the computation of cap rate uses property value, not listing price. In essence, cap rate is a ratio that measures the profitability of a rental property, assuming it is purchased on an all-cash basis, meaning without a mortgage loan.

I had to interrupt Papa Joe at this stage to ask him to explain why an investor would pay all cash for a property when a higher return on investment can be gained when a property is financed through a mortgage—as he taught me in previous mentoring sessions.

With his usual smart smile, he thanked me for asking this question that confuses many investors. He explained that the cap rate is meant to measure a property's financial performance based on its income (rent) and operational expenses. Whenever a mortgage comes into play, it will make it impossible to compare different properties since mortgages differ in their interest rates and terms. Therefore, different mortgage options will yield different returns on invested capital (or cash on cash return) even for the same property.

He asked me to take a step backward and look at cap rates, since the cash on cash return (CoC) was a measure we would be discussing shortly. After defining what the cap rate is, Papa Joe guided me on how investors decide on the rate they will be targeting for an investment in a rental property.

Investors often decide on the lowest cap rate that they will accept in order to make the investment worth their time, efforts, and invested capital. In that manner, when looking at potential investments, they compare the cap rates of those rental properties against their personal cap rate. They will make offers only on those properties with cap rates higher than their accepted cap rate.

Though things getting clearer, I was still struggling with how investors set a personal cap rate as a benchmark. Papa Joe gave me a new perspective by explaining that investors look at the cap rate as made up of two components: a risk-free rate of return plus a risk premium. As he explained this, he wrote down a formula.

$$\begin{pmatrix} Cap \\ Rate \\ (\%) \end{pmatrix} \rightarrow \begin{pmatrix} Risk\ Free \\ Rate\ of\ Return \\ (\%) \end{pmatrix} + \begin{pmatrix} Risk \\ Premium \\ (\%) \end{pmatrix}$$

He explained the risk-free rate of return is the theoretical rate of return of an investment with no risk of financial loss. All investments carry at least a small amount of risk, but the common practice is to consider earning interest on long-term deposits or investment in treasury bonds as a risk-free rate (or very safe investment).

He told me a story of two friends who each had $100,000. The first invested his capital in a safe investment—a treasury bond—and was quite happy with the 3 per cent yield (rate of return) he was collecting while doing nothing. The second person, although he could have done the same, was presented with an opportunity to invest in a rental property with a 7 per cent cap rate. To evaluate this potential investment, he would compare the cap rate of the property to the yield on the treasury bond. In that case, the difference between the cap rate of 7 per cent and the risk-free rate of 3 per cent is 4 per cent. This 4 per cent represents the risk premium, which is the additional return for the additional risk the second investor has assumed over and above the risk-free investment in treasury bonds. Such risks could relate to condition of the property, on-time rental payments by the tenants, demand for rental in the location of the property, and supply of comparable properties on the market to name a few.

To make sure I fully understood the relationship between treasury yield and interest rates, Papa Joe explained the treasury yield as the interest rate the government pays to borrow money. Treasury yields influence not only how much the government pays investors to borrow money from them, but also the interest rates people pay to borrow money to buy assets. This means that the cost of borrowing money, which is the interest rate, is closely tied to treasury yield. Papa Joe wrote down the following:

$$\begin{pmatrix} Cap \\ Rate \\ (\%) \end{pmatrix} \rightarrow \begin{pmatrix} Risk\ Free \\ Rate\ of\ Return \\ (\%) \end{pmatrix} + \begin{pmatrix} Risk \\ Premium \\ (\%) \end{pmatrix}$$

$$\begin{pmatrix} Cap \\ Rate \\ (\%) \end{pmatrix} \rightarrow \begin{pmatrix} Interest \\ Rate \\ (\%) \end{pmatrix} + \begin{pmatrix} Spread \\ (\%) \end{pmatrix}$$

The relationship between cap rates and interest rates is the least understood by investors. Cap rates often change over time for the same property without any changes to the property or to the location. This change is driven by changes in interest rates because investing in rental properties is largely impacted by the amount of debt that can be borrowed to purchase them. So the larger the spread between the interest rate (the cost of borrowing money) and the cap rate, the better the potential return on investment. This is the second aspect of determining the property value, which we will discuss next.

I still needed answers and guidance on specific cap rates in terms of numbers that I could follow, but Papa Joe was hesitant to give one answer. He clarified that his experience over more than 30 years proved to him that cap rates can go anywhere from 4 per cent to 12 per cent, depending on the prevalent interest rates, the location, and the property type. Apparently I did not like this answer and my facial expressions showed my discomfort. He explained that while cap rates of 4 per cent and 12 per cent are extremes, it is common to find cap rates between 6 per cent and 8 per cent. After challenging him on how he personally sets a target for cap rate, he shared that he adds a spread of 3 per cent to 4 per cent on top of the interest rate on the mortgage. For example, if an investor is preapproved for a mortgage loan with 3 per cent interest rate, the investor will target a cap rate between 6 per cent and 7 per cent to make the investment worthwhile. He explained how he personally sets his target cap rate by writing the following:

$$\begin{pmatrix} Cap\ Rate \\ Target \\ (\%) \end{pmatrix} = \begin{pmatrix} Interest \\ Rate \\ (\%) \end{pmatrix} + \begin{pmatrix} 3\% \\ to \\ 4\% \end{pmatrix}$$

This equation indicates that he sets a spread target between 3 per cent and 4 per cent on top on the ongoing interest rates. He asked me to explain what this suggested about his personal target cap rates. Thinking that it was a trick question, I wanted to keep my answer simple and safe. I replied that this suggests that the resulting cap rate will be a range with a difference of 1 per cent between the lower and higher end cap rate. He slammed the table very hard, but with a smile, signaling that I got the right answer.

He challenged my thoughts more by asking what lower and higher end target cap rates mean in determining property value. I thought it was another trick question, so I kept my answer simple and said that it means that we will end up with a range for the property value with a lower end and a higher end. I excitedly slammed the table and said that common sense suggests we offer the lower end of the property value, but we may negotiate up to the upper end value.

Papa Joe extended his hand towards me to signal a handshake and told me that I made him a proud mentor. To be sure we didn't lose this important point, he wrote again on the piece of paper:

$$Property\ Value = \frac{NOI}{Cap\ Rate\ (\%)}$$

He continued that the lower end of the target cap rate will lead a higher property value, while the higher end of the target cap rate will result in a lower property value. While the algebra explained that a higher denominator will result in a lower output for the equation (the property value), I couldn't understand the logic of why a property with a higher cap rate will lead to a lower determined property value.

Instead of giving me answers, Papa Joe propounded a problem: "If two cars, one with a 4-cylinder engine and the other one with an 8-cylinder engine, start from the same point, and travel at the same speed and in the same direction, which one will arrive at the same destination first?"

I saw the tricky part in this question, so I replied that both cars will arrive at the same time. Papa Joe agreed. "But which engine will be working harder to keep up with the other car?" he asked.

I replied that the 4-cylinder engine has to work harder to keep up with the same speed of the 8-cylinder engine, which might be cruising with less effort. With excitement, he confirmed that this is correct and asked me to rewrite the story by replacing cars with rental properties, engine capacity with property value, speed with NOI, and how hard the engine is working with cap rate. He gave me some time to resynthesize the story in my mind.

I told him: "Cap rate is a measure of the rate of the profitability of a rental property. The property with a lower value has to work harder (be more profitable) to produce the same NOI (in absolute terms) as compared to the property with the higher value."

He interrupted to say that I'd answered for myself why a property with a lower value has to have a higher cap rate to yield the same NOI as compared to a property with a higher value.

Next Papa Joe proposed a scenario where an investor wants to evaluate a property that is yielding an NOI of $12,000 per year. He suggested the ongoing interest rate be set at 3 per cent. He reminded me that the set target for cap rates is based on ongoing interest rates plus a spread target between 3 per cent and 4 per cent. Therefore, the investor may set a target cap rate between 6 per cent and 7 per cent, leading to a range of property value between $200,000 and $171,428 respectively. Obviously, the investor will offer the lower value of $171,428 and might be willing to go up to $200,000 in the negotiation process with the seller, if the initial offer was rejected.

As he explained things, I captured this idea on paper by drawing the following figure.

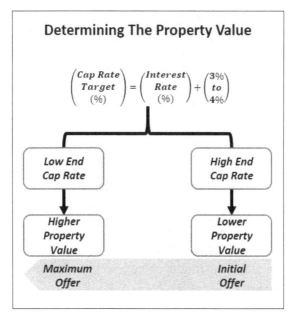

Figure 55—Determining the property value

I was excited and suggested that now an investor can be ready to make an offer to the seller. Papa Joe gave me the look that said to slow down. He reminded me that we still needed to validate the property value based on its financial performance, given that it would be bought on margin through a mortgage loan.

Validating the Property Value Based on Its Financial Performance

I have emphasised the importance of leverage in rental property investment in different sections of this book. Leverage increases the return on invested capital as compared to an asset purchased with only cash.

After walking me through the details of determining the value of a property in question, Papa Joe reminded me that the reason investors invest in an asset is to get returns, which are measured with what return on investment (ROI). In real estate investing, return on investment is also called *cash on cash*. It is the annual net cash flow (after all expenses and mortgage instalments) as a percentage of the investor's down payment. The higher the ROI, the better the investment for an investor. So after determining the property value, which is potentially the offer price, the investor has to determine the initial annual net cash flow of the property when it will be mortgaged. To do that, the investor will have to look at net operating income (NOI) less annual loan payments. Then the resulting annual net cash flow will have to be measured against the investor's invested capital (or the down payment) to calculate the ROI. If the ROI is favourable to the investor, this acts like an insurance that the price to be offered to the seller, if accepted, will result in a property that has both a good operational performance and a good financial performance.

I nodded that this made perfect sense, and I asked Papa Joe if he would guide me on what might be considered a healthy ROI or cash on cash to an investor.

He explained that return on investment can be categorized as *unhealthy*, *healthy*, or *wealthy*. Things had started to get even more interesting. He continued explaining how money can work hard for an investor or just be idle and dead.

Unhealthy ROI	This is dead or idle money, which may be losing value over time or at best keeping up with inflation rates. This is what people get when stashing money in the bank or investing in safe government treasuries. This is where savers become losers. They wake up one day to find their money still the same in terms of how much they have in the bank, but to realize the purchasing power of this money has become way lower than previous years. Any investment that yields a return that at best matches interest rates on mortgages is an unhealthy investment.

Unhealthy ROI % ≤ Mortgage Interest Rate %

Healthy ROI	This is the minimum ROI investors will accept when investing their money. The value in terms of percentage changes over time depending on prevalent interest rates and inflation rates.
	The general rule is to accept an ROI that is at least double the prevalent interest rates on mortgages.
	Healthy ROI % = 2 × (Mortgage Interest Rate %)
Wealthy ROI	This is where the investor's capital starts to work very hard and produce wealth building returns. This is where investors start to get double digits ROI and can even reach infinite returns.
	An investment that yields more than two times the prevalent interest rates on mortgages, with a minimum of 9 per cent, can qualify for an investment that produce a wealthy ROI.
	Wealthy ROI % > 2 × (Interest Rate %) … with a minimum of 9 per cent

Papa Joe's advice on qualifying ROIs as unhealthy, healthy, or wealthy has been a guiding principle on all my investments. It produced for Papa Joe wealth in multiple millions and helped me become an employee millionaire (and multimillionaire).

I follow this advice as a lighthouse. Whenever I evaluate any investment, I qualify its ROI before making any decision. In the few events where I went into the grey zones and allowed myself to be flexible on my criteria, my invested capital was dead at unhealthy rates. When that happened, it took me a lot of energy and time to get rid of low-performing investments.

To validate a property's value based on its financial performance, we need to evaluate its cash flow after all its expenses, including mortgage instalments, have been paid.

$$Net\ Cash\ Flow = (NOI) - (Annual\ Loan\ Instalment)$$

The projected loan instalment is a function of the offer price, down payment, interest rate of the loan, and length of the loan. With the help of many online mortgage calculators or the tools made available on www. employeemillionaire.com/resources, the monthly loan payments can be figured out by just entering the loan amount, the interest rate, and the term (length) of the loan. The annual loan instalment is computed by multiplying the monthly loan instalments by twelve.

Once the estimated annual loan instalment is available on hand, net cash flow can be computed by subtracting the annual loan instalments from NOI. Then the cash on cash, or the ROI, can be computed.

$$ROI\ (\%) = Cash\ on\ Cash\ (\%) = \frac{Annual\ Net\ Cash\ Flow}{Down\ Payment}$$

After allowing me some time to reflect on what has been shared with me, Papa Joe explained that with clarity on the cash on cash returns and the annual net cash flow, an investor can forecast how much money or profits can be made from the property before making an offer to the seller. The investor will be making an informed decision on the offer price. At the end of the day, the numbers have to work in good deals. The resulting investor's cash on cash from an investment in a property has to be at least healthy, and preferably at wealthy rates of return.

Papa Joe taught me to either walk away from a deal that produces unhealthy rates of return or to offer a lower price to make the numbers work and produce at least a healthy ROI. From his experience, many investors feel bad or shy about offering the seller a price that is way lower than the seller's asking price. They end up being flexible and offer a price in between their calculated offer and the seller's asking price. Papa Joe warned me not to fall into this trap and to always explain to the seller my thought process and how property value was derived. Most sellers will appreciate such an approach even if they may not agree on the offer price.

Once the value of a property proves to be both operationally viable (assuming no loan is involved) and financially healthy (assuming a loan is involved), the investor can send a letter of intent with the offered price and terms and conditions. The offer price is based on the determined value and never on the seller's requested or listed price. Chapter 11 will discuss negotiating prices and submitting offers in much more details.

LEVEL FOUR INVESTMENT CRITERIA: WHAT WILL I BUY?

In level three, the value of a property was determined following a process, and the lower end of the determined value range was offered to the seller as the purchase price. The objective of the letter of intent is to tie up the property and remove it off the market. This is where you start negotiating the terms and conditions of the deal, perform due diligence, and commit by signing the purchase and sale agreement. Both topics will be discussed at length in chapters 11 and 12.

The letter of intent is the first official communication from the buyer to the seller where the buyer maps out all the terms and conditions of the deal. Sending an offer gives the buyer the chance to test the waters with the seller. It gives an indication on the seller's attitude, level of motivation to sell, and willingness to negotiate.

My experience has led me to believe that dealing with tough, stubborn, arrogant sellers removes all the fun and excitement out of the deal. Although I continued the process on a couple of properties with such sellers, I rarely enjoyed the process or even the returns I enjoyed from such investments. I now try to stay away from such sellers. Papa Joe always taught me to stick to win-win deals and walk away from any deal where either of the parties will lose. This is why the seller's attitude is my first filter on what I might buy. After I judge the seller as a professional who has good business ethics and is willing to negotiate towards a win-win deal, I start looking into negotiating the purchase price within the property value band that was determined in level three as well as on the terms and condition of the deal. Judging a seller's attitude is more of a qualitative judgment based on what you may observe in the negotiation process.

Once the first filter on the seller's attitude is passed, the fun of hustling for the win-win purchase price and negotiating the win-win terms begin. The two major crossroads at this stage are whether a purchase price will be agreed upon and whether the terms and conditions of the purchase and sale agreement will be agreed upon. As a rule of thumb, never, never, *never* agree on a purchase price that is higher than the set maximum offer, which is the higher end of the computed property value, as determined in level three investment criteria.

Chapter Nine Actions Steps

Start prospecting for properties by following the investment criteria listed in this chapter. At first, it might feel like quite a long exercise, but with practice, all the investment criteria and their computations will become second nature to you.

Follow the steps in this chapter and use the tools offered on my website www.employeemillionaire.com/resources for each of the levels of the path to purchasing.

You should be able to shortlist the total number of properties that were considered to a handful that may qualify as potential great deals. Determine the value range of each of the shortlisted properties and, for each, determine your initial offer and maximum offer.

Do not make an offer until you read chapters 10 and 11.

The moment all this set of criteria became crystal clear in my mind, I understood why Papa Joe was so furious when he understood I was running like a busy fool looking to purchase rental properties without having any criteria. Having no criteria would have led me anywhere or even everywhere, but nowhere specifically, whereas having criteria has led me where I wanted to go. I urge you to define your set of criteria before you start making offers on properties.

CHAPTER 10

Analyse Rental Properties

Instead of sleeping an extra hour or so on that Saturday, I had to wake up early, as if it was a regular working day, so that I could make it on time to my scheduled meeting with Ms Jing. When I first met her in Papa Joe's office, she came across as an alpha woman type and I did not want to come across as a lazy pretending student who cannot even commit to an appointment. I prepared my cappuccino in a tumbler and had it on my way to Papa Joe's company.

When I reached the reception, I asked for Ms Jing, the chief operating officer (COO) of the property management division and was escorted to her office. When I arrived, she looked at her watch and stood up to welcome me, inviting me to join her at the meeting table in the corner of her office. While walking those few steps to the meeting table, I admired her attire and respected her confidence in the way she walks and talks. When we sat down, I assumed the same posture that she did. She opened her leather notebook, took her pen, and flipped to a new blank page.

With no time to lose, Ms Jing stated that they were in the business of real estate. As with any other business, the numbers in the financial statement determine the health of the business. I nodded in agreement. She said that each rental property under one title deed, irrespective of its number of dwelling units, needs to have its own financial statement. As a COO, Ms Jing's responsibility is to make each property profitable and to consolidate the financial statement for the total real estate business. To make sure I would follow her, she started with the big picture: Like any P&L (profit and loss) statement, in the business of real estate, we need to measure the income, the expenses, and the net cash flow. That cash flow can be positive (profit) or negative (loss).

Ms Jing stood up and walked towards the whiteboard adjacent to the small, round meeting table where we sat. She took the red marker and split the board in half by drawing a vertical line. She wrote "1- Property's Operational Performance" and "2- Property's Financial Performance" respectively on the left and right sides of the vertical line as a header for each of the sections. While she was writing on the whiteboard, I contemplated Ms Jing's command and sophistication. She interrupted my reflections and said with a loud voice: "When analysing rental properties, we analyse the property operational performance first and then its financial performance in relation to the investor's capital."

ANALYSING A RENTAL PROPERTY'S OPERATIONAL PERFORMANCE

Ms Jing said, "In analysing a rental property's operational performance, we examine the net operating income (NOI), which is computed by deducting all the property's operating expenses from its rental income."

$$\begin{pmatrix} Net \\ Operating \\ Income \end{pmatrix} = \begin{pmatrix} Rental \\ Income \end{pmatrix} - \begin{pmatrix} Operating \\ Expenses \end{pmatrix}$$

Since a decision on buying a property will be based on estimated rental income and estimated operating expenses, once the property is bought, a *good* property manager will make sure the actuals are at least in line with set targets (the initial estimates), whereas a *great* property manager will attempt to beat those numbers by increasing income or lowering operating expenses or both.

Rental Income

Determining the fair rental value of a rental property is critical, since the calculation of its NOI starts with having the rental income. The fair rental value is the rent a tenant is willing to pay to occupy the property for a set period of time. It can be determined by looking at current market rental rates for comparable properties. Comparable properties are those that have almost identical criteria related to location, type, features, and amenities (also referred to as level one investment criteria, which were explained at length in chapter 9).

To get rental rates on comparable properties, Ms Jing recommended asking real estate agents to do what they do best, scanning local papers, checking online property listings, and driving the neighbourhood scanning the For Rent signs and calling the landlord or landlord's agent pretending to be a potential tenant. When Ms Jing sensed I was a bit overwhelmed with the amount of research to be done just to get an estimate of the fair rental income, she reassured me that things are easier (and more fun) than what they may appear. Over time, after owning a few properties in the same target neighbourhood, this exercise will become easier since owning other properties in the same neighbourhood will make the investor an expert in this location and will help in making a better judgment of fair market rent.

When we were done with estimating rental income, Ms Jing asked what I thought a landlord's worst nightmare is when renting out a property. My answers related to tenants defaulting on their rent payments, tenants damaging the properties, and tenants calling in the middle of the night asking for their toilets to be fixed. With a beautiful and smart smile, Ms Jing told me that my concerns were relevant, but they become true concerns only once the property is rented out.

A landlord's biggest concern is finding the right tenants at the right time and at the right rent rate. Given the risk or probability of having any rental property occupied 100 per cent at all times, the smart investor must account for a vacancy rate in estimating the rental income. The longer the property remains vacant, the higher the risk the investor will shoulder the mortgage instalments from his or her own pocket as long as the property remains vacant.

This worried me, and I started to have second thoughts on investing in rental properties. I imagined fearful scenarios of not being able to personally pay the mortgage of vacant properties and receiving notices of foreclosure from the bank.

Ms Jing recaptured my attention. "We are in the business of real estate, and like any other business, sales—in our case, rent—is the lifeblood necessary for business survival."

The real estate agents and property managers on your team will play a crucial role in marketing rental properties to potential tenants. Choosing the right type of property in the right target location will improve the probability of finding tenants quickly who are willing to pay the right rent. It's a game of supply and demand, and following the property investment criteria explained in the path to purchasing (explained in chapter 9), will lead you to purchase properties that are sought after for rent at the right rental rate.

When I inquired about the vacancy rate to be considered when forecasting the rental income, Ms Jing explained that vacancy rates are location specific. Therefore, real estate agents can make a fair estimate of vacancies in a certain location based on its current history.

I did not digest her reply, and it showed by my indirect questions, trying to get a number. Ms Jing was hesitant to give me a number, but my persistent nature worked like magic, and I got her to share with me that in Papa Joe's holding an average of 6–8 per cent is the acceptable level for all properties across cities throughout the world. In the absence of data on vacancy rates in some locations, it would be a decent guesstimate, to start with 6–8 per cent vacancy rate, and then adjust for future purchases based on personal experience.

Ms Jing explained that a 6–8 per cent vacancy rate means that the property is expected to remain vacant for about three to four weeks per year. This period is a fair estimate to account for tenants moving out, conducting repairs, marketing the property, and having new tenants move in.

Out of curiosity, I challenged Ms Jing regarding the reasons an investor should account for tenants moving out of the same property every year. She replied that it would be a big mistake to underestimate vacancies and end up paying mortgage instalments out of pocket. When buying a property, an investor should account for the average vacancy rates in a certain location, and then try to achieve as low vacancies as possible with good property management. In that case, the investor is in a position to exceed the estimated rental income, which will improve the NOI as a consequence. When I nodded in approval, she continued writing on the whiteboard the following:

$$\left(\begin{matrix}Rental\\Income\end{matrix}\right) = (100\% - Vacancy\ Rate\ \%) \times \left(\begin{matrix}Fair\ Rental\\Value\end{matrix}\right)$$

Consider an example of a one-bedroom apartment that rents at $1,000 per month. The annual fair rental value would be estimated at $12,000 ($1,000 per month × 12 months). If we assume an 8 per cent vacancy, the rental income will be estimated as follows:

$$\left(\begin{matrix}Rental\\Income\end{matrix}\right) = (100\% - 8\ \%) \times (\$12,000)$$

$$\left(\begin{matrix}Rental\\Income\end{matrix}\right) = (92\%)X\ (\$12,000) = \$11,040$$

As this example shows, a vacancy of 8 per cent diluted the rental income by $960 ($12,000 – $11,040), which is almost one month of rent.

Operating Expenses

Determining a property's operating expenses will be tricky for the novice investor. It requires some hands-on experience, which is the area of expertise of property managers. Novices frequently underestimate those expenses and end up with the sour reality of higher expenses, resulting in low net operating income, which may lead to negative cash flow after the debt is serviced. Ms Jing quoted Papa Joe: "Rental properties with negative cash flow are large alligators eating the landlord alive." When cash flow is negative, the landlord will have to personally shoulder those expenses. Therefore, the property will take money out of his or her pocket.

I said I wanted to learn how to estimate operating expenses. These are costs that affect the day-to-day operation of the property and are considered necessary to keeping rental income flowing. In contrast, non-operating expenses, such as debt service and the landlord's income taxes, are not directly related to the property's core operations. Missing a mortgage payment, for example, will not affect the property's ability to produce income.

Ms Jing listed the following operating expenses on the whiteboard, then sat down to explain each one at length.

Operating Expenses
- Property taxes
- Property insurance
- Property utilities:
    o Electricity
    o Water
    o Sewer
    o Telephone
    o Heating and cooling
    o Garbage removal
- Master community fees:
    o Developer's community fees
    o Homeowner's association fees
- Property management
- Property maintenance
    o Repairs
    o Capital expenditures
- Marketing and advertising
- Administrative expenses:
    o Legal
    o Accounting

Property Taxes

Depending on the country where you live or plan to invest, property taxes can range from nil, like the UAE and some other countries in the Middle East, to a hefty sum of money. Before you make any investment in a certain location, always inquire with the local authorities about the property taxes so you can account for them in your estimation of a property's operating income. A great reference that lists the property taxes in most European countries is the International Union of Property Owners. On their website (www.uipi.com) they issue an annual report on comparative analysis of taxation. Other references can easily be found online for any country in the world.

In general, property taxes are calculated by the local tax authorities based on the value of the property or the assessed rental value, depending on the city where the property is located. Ms Jing explained that although such taxes are most often paid once a year, a good property manager will make provisions for those taxes and make those payments on a monthly basis in a reserve account so that all the required funds will be available and accounted for once property tax payment is due.

Property Insurance

Whenever a property is bought under a mortgage loan, the lender requires the borrower to carry mortgage insurance that covers the whole value of the mortgage. Mortgage insurance usually has two components: *life insurance* and *hazard insurance.*

Mortgage Insurance (often includes)
    Life Insurance
    Hazard Insurance

In their effort to minimize their risk, lenders often require borrowers to buy insurance that covers against both the borrower defaulting on mortgage instalments (due to death or serious illness) and property loss (resulting from damage). Hence, mortgage insurance may often include both life insurance and hazard insurance, and it would pay off the remaining balance of the mortgage.

Insurance premiums are often computed and charged annually, but payments are usually made monthly and may be packaged as part of the monthly mortgage instalments. Such insurance premiums can be estimated easily by inquiring with the lender or insurance companies.

Another type of insurance, which is better to have and never need than to need and not have, is *liability insurance*, which covers costs resulting from personal injuries. Although not mandatory, liability insurance can save the property owner lots of money in case of lawsuits resulting from personal injuries within the property premises. Premiums for liability insurance are also relatively simple to estimate by shopping around and inquiring from a few insurance brokers or insurance companies.

Mortgage insurance rates vary from 0.5 per cent to 1.2 per cent of the loan amount annually. The most common mortgage insurance rate is 0.5 per cent of the loan amount. Higher rates apply to borrowers with higher-than-usual risks. Lenders sometimes offer more competitive rates, as low as 0.3 per cent of the loan amount. With such a variance in rates, it is always advisable to shop around and get quotes that apply to your specific conditions.

Property Utilities

Property utilities usually means services such as electricity, water, sewer, telephone, heating and cooling, and garbage removal. For single-family units, all utilities are often the responsibility of the tenant. In some condominiums and large apartment buildings, where cooling and heating is centralized, the landlords of the individual units may be required to pay annual fees. In turn the landlord charges those fees back to the tenants either directly (through billing) or by accounting for the same in the asking rent.

In multifamily units, the landlord will be paying for the utilities of the common areas. Therefore, such costs need to be accounted for in the operating expenses. In such case, for the landlord to have a fair estimate of utility expenses, the practical way is to look at the most recent year's utility bills for the property, which can be obtained from the previous landlord.

Master Community Fees

Investors who purchase single-family homes that are part of a large master community or apartment building are required to pay annual fees towards either the developer's community fees or the homeowners' association fees. Such fees can be estimated by inquiring of the master developer or the community management company looking after the master development.

These fees account for expenses related to the common areas of the development, such as upkeep, maintenance, security, janitorial services, and pest control. Such fees do not account for costs related to the individual properties, which cost is covered under property management or property maintenance and repairs.

Single-family homes that are not part of master developments, condominiums, or large apartment buildings will most probably not have any master community fees. Still, it is always safe to ask before purchasing a property. Any surprises in operating costs will inevitably dilute the net operating income (NOI) of the property.

Property Management

Ms Jing recommended that novice rental property investors manage their own properties in the beginning. This will give them hands-on experience before they outsource this service in the future to professional property managers or property management companies. She also recommended that property management fees be accounted for in estimating operating expenses, even if the investor decides to do the job. This will make such a cost accounted for should the need arise in the future for professional property management to be contracted. Property management expenses can be estimated by asking a few property management companies for their fees to render the related services. In general, property management fees range from 5 per cent to 7 per cent of the annual rent. Such fees tend to be on the higher end for single-family units and on the lower end for multifamily properties.

Regardless of whether you will be contracting a property management company, establish a contact with one. Asking for a cost estimate for running the property on your behalf is never a bad idea. In fact, in their quote, the company will shed light on many areas of property management, which may serve as a checklist if you chose to manage your own properties yourself. Furthermore, in such meetings, a property management company sales pitch will share insights on proper property management and on lowering operating expenses.

Property Maintenance

Property maintenance expenses usually include both repairs and capital expenditures. Neither is easy to estimate. *Repairs* are both the corrective maintenance and preventive maintenance tasks that are performed in order to keep the property in a desirable condition. *Capital expenditures* relate to repairs that add long-lasting value to the property, such as a roof replacement, foundation work, or changing the whole pipe system of the house.

The age of the property plays a major role, since a house that is more than fifteen years old will likely require more maintenance than one built less than three years ago. In the same manner, a fifteen-year-old house that has been recently rehabbed will require fewer repairs than another house of similar age that has never been repaired. This suggests that estimating the cost of maintenance is a function of the age of the property and its maintenance history. Ms Jing said that in Papa Joe's company they follow this rule:

Property Age / Time Since Last Rehab	Annual Maintenance Cost
less than 5 years	5 per cent of annual rent
Between 5–15 years	10 per cent of annual rent
More than 15 years	15 per cent of annual rent

This rule for the estimated annual maintenance cost is an approximation that is averaged out over a long period of time, which means the estimated cost may not occur every year at the same rate. In fact, several months can pass without anything spent on maintenance, but then a big fat invoice will be received for a major repair.

The annual maintenance cost explained above also includes capital expenditure, which is basically those big ticket items that have to be changed over a longer period of time. Professionally managed properties will have a property manager who can keep a list of those capital expenditure items, their lifespan, the date they were last changed, the next scheduled replacement, and the cost of replacement. Ms Jing stood up and approached the whiteboard again and drew the table shown below.

Capital Expense	Lifespan (years)	Date Last Changed	Next Scheduled Replacement	Replacement Cost ($)
Foundations	50+			
Roof	25			
Exterior Paint	10			
Interior Paint	5			
Doors	20			
Appliances	10			
A/C	10			
Heating System	20			
Kitchen Cabinets	15			
Bathroom / Kitchen fixtures	15			
Tiles Floor	20			
Wooden Floor	15			
Water Heater	10			
Plumbing	30			
Windows	30			

The lifespan of the capital expenditure items listed above are standards used by major property management companies. This list refers to the most common items that are replaced. For a more complete list of capital expense items not listed above, visit the Fannie Mae website at www.fanniemae.com.

Ms Jing added that in the absence of any official document that proves when a capital expense was done by the previous owner, the astute investor or property manager will assume that the date an item was last changed is the date the property was built.

Given the wide range of replacement costs in different countries and even cities within the same country, investors should ask a few contractors for such costs. This will avoid surprises if an item requires replacement in the future.

Another point Ms Jing made was to account for capital expenditures monthly. This can be done by putting aside the estimated annual maintenance cost in a separate account. It can range from 5–15 per cent, depending on the property's age (as seen in the chart above). Whenever the need arises to pay for maintenance, the money will be sitting there.

On the medium-term horizon, it is always wise to forecast the big ticket expenses from capital expenditure by looking at a twelve-month horizon. You can do this by keeping an always up-to-date ledger of capital expenses (as per the table on the previous page) and account for any expense which next scheduled replacement date fall within the next twelve months. If you do, you will be able to manage cash flow better.

Marketing and Advertising

According to Ms Jing's experience, landlords who own a handful of single-family properties can best market their vacant properties through real estate agents who specialize in rental properties. The moment I learned that, the importance of having my team members on board (as discussed in chapter 7) became clearer to me. I asked about the rates that real estate agents may charge for finding tenants. Ms Jing wanted to explain common practices first. She promised me that once I understand the different types of relationships between landlords and real estate agents when it comes to finding prospective tenants, I can easily estimate how much I will be paying for having a rental property rented out. This made me 100 per cent tuned in, and I was all ears to listen to the lessons from my new mentor, Ms Jing.

Real estate agents, who specialize in rentals, make a living by earning a commission for having a rental agreement signed between the landlord and the tenant. Such commissions are usually negotiable and are in line with a generally accepted commission standard for the locality of the property. They are usually based on a percentage of the annual rent, which could range anywhere from 5 per cent to 15 per cent, depending on the city where the property is located.

The most common practice is that rental agents charge the tenants for their commission. In some cities, it is not uncommon for the landlord and the tenant to split the rental agent commission in half, or in some cases the landlord pays the commission in full for finding a tenant who occupies a vacant property. With such a large variance of common acceptable practices and norms in different cities, it is always wise to inquire about such practices, so that a realistic estimate can be forecast for marketing and advertising rental properties.

Regarding rental extensions after the expiry of the rental agreement: Some cities allow the initiating rental agent to charge a renewal commission when a lease is extended. This practice might be illegal in other cities. It is always advisable to inquire on the laws or practices related to rental extensions. With the help of the Internet, all such information is public knowledge that can be accessed online in no time.

Marketing and advertising the units to prospective tenants in multifamily properties may be handled by the landlord or the property management team. Below are some marketing and advertising channels most often used and proven to be effective:

Marketing Channels	Description
Online	Online advertising of rental properties on listing websites and social media sites comes at minimal cost or most often for free. Although the reach is quite high, many other landlords will be advertising online to the same audience, which makes the market more competitive in terms of rental rates and unique selling points that will attract the attention of the tenants. Those unique selling points are the location, features, and the amenities of the property.
Word of Mouth	In multifamily properties, spreading the news that you have vacant units through other tenants is the most effective and free word of mouth marketing. Many tenants would like to have their close friends or relatives live close to them, so they advertise well-managed properties to their close ones.
For Rent Sign	If the property is in a good location overlooking a high traffic street, putting a For Rent sign costs only a few marketing dollars and targets potential tenants looking to rent in a target community.
Bulletin Boards	Posting flyers on bulletin boards throughout your target community (e.g. grocery stores, gyms, or other community centres) is usually free and reaches out to prospective tenants in your target location.
Print	Advertising in print media (e.g. local newspapers, magazines, or bulletins) has a high reach, but it comes at a cost, which is higher than online marketing and without the

	visuals of the property.
Rental Agents	As with single-family properties, rental agents' commissions for multifamily properties vary from one city to another (from 5 per cent to 15 per cent of annual rent) and is often paid by the tenant. However, the accepted practices in different cities could be either both the landlord and the tenant split the commission, or the landlord shoulders the full commission.

Ms Jing referred to Papa Joe always preaching to his team not to get distracted by either of the extremes where the landlord pays nothing in marketing and advertising expenses or pays a full 15 per cent of annual rent. At the end of the day, the numbers will tally, and the wise investor will look at both the rent and total operating expenses in determining the net operating income (NOI), the value of a property, and eventually its return on investment after deducting the mortgage instalments. If the numbers make sense, then a property would be judged as a good investment opportunity.

Administrative Expenses

Administrative expenses include those related to services that will become more and more needed when a real estate business grows in the number of properties to be managed. The following fall under the administrative expenses category:

- Legal
- Accounting

As Ms Jing explained, a novice investor who owns only a couple of properties may require such services on a per-need basis. When the number of properties grows, an employee investor will have limited time to give the required attention to managing them. Administrative services may be outsourced, but then the business can better afford them.

To explain, Ms Jing started with the legal aspect of the rental property business. Rental properties are governed by laws meant to protect both landlords and tenants in most cities throughout the world. There are usually lots of forms to be completed. Below is a list of those most commonly used forms:

Forms	Concerned Parties
Marketing Agreement	Landlord and Rental Agent
Rental Application Form	Landlord and Tenant
Rental Agreement	Landlord and Tenant
Rental Condition Checklist	Landlord and Tenant
Eviction Note	Landlord and Tenant

Not all those forms and agreements may be legal obligations, but it is a good idea to fill them out. I have included those forms in my rental properties after facing challenges with rental agents or tenants. I address this in detail later, specifically in chapters 15 and 16, where I share some tips and general forms.

Accounting is another item that falls in the category of administrative expenses. As part of your team, an accountant will be able to give you both tax advice that is specific to your own financial situation and help with your rental property financials. An accountant's role becomes more important when the number of rental properties in your real estate business grows in number. Soon you will need professional management of accounts receivable and accounts payable to better manage your cash flow. As the number of rental properties grows, there will be more rents to be collected and deposited and more bills to be paid for each property. The best practice is to outsource accounting services to a third party company that has a professional team on board and the right software. Outsourcing accounting services will have accounting done professionally with a minimal retainer cost.

Ms Jing advised me to inquire about such retainer costs with accounting companies so that it becomes easier for me to forecast those expenses when estimating a property's operating expenses. In general, accounting companies charge per property, but the rates per property will be reduced when more properties are included within the same deal. This is when economies of scale will play in a landlord's favor with multiple rental properties.

Net Operating Income

So far in this chapter, we have discussed rental income, vacancies, and operating expenses. As explained earlier, net operating income (NOI) is computed by deducting operating expenses from rental income.

$$\begin{pmatrix} Net \\ Operating \\ Income \end{pmatrix} = \begin{pmatrix} Rental \\ Income \end{pmatrix} - \begin{pmatrix} Operating \\ Expenses \end{pmatrix}$$

An example can help to explain how NOI is computed. Earlier I shared a story about Joe Public, who is employed and receives $3,200 per month in earned income. After getting his finances in order, he managed to reduce his Debt-to-Income (DTI) to 38 per cent and got preapproved for a mortgage loan of $78,500. On a standard 80 per cent LTV, Joe Public could afford a property of up to $98,125.

He briefed some real estate agents about his target property and location. Joe Public analysed one of the rental properties, which he ended up buying for $95,000, a two-bedroom apartment located twenty minutes' drive from the city centre. He learned that his property could conservatively be rented out at $880 per month, which made him assume a fair rental value of $10,560 per year ($880 × 12 months). This property was located in a highly sought-after community, which makes finding tenants easier. But Joe Public wanted to be a prudent investor, and he still accounted for 6 per cent vacancy, after which the rental income ended up at $9,926.40. Below is how rental income was computed.

$$\left(\frac{Rental}{Income}\right) = (100\% - Vacancy\ Rate\ \%) \times \left(\frac{Fair\ Rental}{Value}\right)$$

$$\left(\frac{Rental}{Income}\right) = (100\% - 6\%) \times (\$10,560)$$

$$\left(\frac{Rental}{Income}\right) = (94\%) \times (\$10,560) = \$9,926.40$$

Then Joe Public wanted to estimate the property's expenses. He listed possible expenses in a table and started his quest to fill in the numbers.

Expense Type	Expense Details	Yearly Amount
Taxes:	Property taxes	$475.20
Insurance:	Property insurance	$380.00
Utilities:	Electricity	$0.00
	Water	$0.00
	Sewer	$0.00
	Telephone	$0.00
	Heating and cooling	$0.00
	Garbage removal	$0.00
Community Fees:	Developer's community fees	$0.00
	Homeowners' association fees	$750.00
Property Management:	Property management	$739.20
Maintenance and Repairs:	Repairs	$528.00
	Capital expenditures	$0.00
Marketing and Advertising:	Marketing and advertising	$0.00
Administrative:	Legal	$0.00
	Accounting	$0.00

Others:	Miscellaneous	$0.00
	Reserve	$0.00
	Total Operating Expenses	**$2,872.40**

On his first rental property investment, Joe Public's total operating expenses amounted to 28.94 per cent of rental income ($2,872.40 ÷ $9,926.40). The net operating income of this property was computed at $7,054.00.

$$\begin{pmatrix} Net \\ Operating \\ Income \end{pmatrix} = \begin{pmatrix} Rental \\ Income \end{pmatrix} - \begin{pmatrix} Operating \\ Expenses \end{pmatrix}$$

$$\begin{pmatrix} Net \\ Operating \\ Income \end{pmatrix} = (\$9,926.40) - (\$2,872.40) = \$7,054.00$$

With a forecast NOI of $7,054 and a target cap rate set by Joe Public at 7 per cent, he was able to compute the property value at $100,771.

$$Property\ Value = \frac{Net\ Operating\ Income}{Capitalization\ Rate\ (\%)}$$

$$Property\ Value = \frac{\$7,054.00}{7\%} = \$100,771$$

In order to prepare for negotiations with the seller, Joe Public did the same property value computation exercise on a target 6 per cent cap rate. The resulting number was $117,566. At this stage, he was ready with a property value range between $100,771 (as his initial offer) and $117,566 (as his maximum offer).

Joe Public was able to negotiate for a purchase price that was even lower than the lower end of the computed property value. He was able to purchase the property at $95,000. This is the focus of chapter 11.

As a potential landlord, if Joe Public had overestimated rental income and underestimated operating expenses, he would have ended up with overestimated NOI and an overvalued property price. He would have paid more than the fair market value and accepted the original asking price of $110,000. With proper computation of NOI and estimation of the real property value, he was able to negotiate the price even lower to account for unforeseen expenses.

▌ANALYSING A RENTAL PROPERTY'S FINANCIAL PERFORMANCE

Joe Public put 20 per cent down payment from his own pocket and financed 80 per cent from the bank. So at 80 per cent LTV, Joe Public took a mortgage loan of $76,000 at 4 per cent interest rate over a term of thirty years. The monthly mortgage instalment, which consisted of principal and interest, was $362.84. The annual loan instalment was $4,354.08 ($362.84 × 12 months). The instalment can be estimated using any online mortgage calculator. I have also included a mortgage payments calculator in the form of an Excel sheet on my website www.employeemillionaire.com/resources.

This investment would net Joe Public a cash flow of $225 per month, which is equivalent to $2,700 per year ($225 × 12 months).

$$Net\ Cash\ Flow = (NOI) - (Annual\ Loan\ Instalment)$$

$$Net\ Cash\ Flow = (\$7,054) - (\$4.354) = \$2,700$$

After investing in his first rental property, Joe Public was able to net $225 in the form of unearned income every month or $2,700 every year.

The golden question is whether this $2,700 unearned income from this rental property provides an unhealthy, healthy, or wealthy ROI. If you recall from chapter 9, the cash on cash returns or ROI, computed by dividing the annual net cash flow over the down payment, is categorized as unhealthy, healthy, or wealthy as per criteria in the table below.

Unhealthy ROI %	≤ Mortgage Interest Rate %
Healthy ROI %	= 2 × (Mortgage Interest Rate %)
Wealthy ROI %	> 2 × (Interest Rate %), with a minimum of 9 per cent.

Let's assume that Joe Public will be paying a total of 6 per cent in closing fees and title transfer. His total down payment from his own pocket will be the 20 per cent of total purchase price plus the 6 per cent of total purchase price to account for closing fees and transfer fees. At a negotiated purchase price of $95,000, the total money to be paid from Joe Public's personal pocket will amount to 26 per cent of this purchase price, which is equivalent to $24,700 ($95,000 × 26 per cent).

Let's compute now what will be the ROI on this property.

$$ROI\ (\%) = Cash\ on\ Cash\ (\%) = \frac{Annual\ Net\ Cash\ Flow}{Down\ Payment}$$

$$ROI\ (\%) = \frac{\$2,700}{\$24,700} = 10.93\%$$

An ROI of 10.93 per cent is more than two times the interest rate of 4 per cent, which Joe Public will be getting on the mortgage, and it is higher than 9 per cent. Therefore, it is considered a wealthy ROI.

This is where his money will start to work very hard and produce wealth-building returns. As such a rate of returns, Joe Public can get his initial capital in roughly 6.6 years. To estimate that, I used the rule of 72, explained in chapter 3. Below are the details of the computation.

$$T = \frac{72}{R} = \frac{72}{10.93} = 6.6\ years$$

Later I will explain how debt pay-down and appreciation will further improve the ROI on a rental property investment and reduce the time for capital payback. I saved this topic for after this chapter since, as Papa Joe taught me, decisions on purchasing a property should be based only on its cash flow performance. Any other benefits will be a cherry on top of the cake.

Do not fall into the trap of including capital pay-down and appreciation in computing your return on investment. You will be fooling yourself! Treat those as another added reward for investing your money and working hard to buy the right property and rent it out to the right tenant.

At the beginning of this section I referred to estimating monthly mortgage instalments by using either any online mortgage calculator or the Employee Millionaire mortgage payments calculator in the form of an Excel sheet on www.employeemillionaire.com/resources. I recommend you use any of those mortgage calculators to estimate the monthly mortgage instalments before submitting a written offer.

By this point you should have obtained a mortgage preapproval letter, which included the mortgage rate, the terms or tenure of the mortgage, and the maximum loan amount. You will need to estimate the actual loan you will be obtaining, which is 80 per cent of the price to be offered and shall not exceed the maximum loan amount mentioned on the preapproval letter. Any of the mortgage calculators will ask you to input the loan amount, loan rates, and the loan tenure in years. It is a simple as that: With those three inputs, you will instantaneously receive the monthly mortgage instalment, which consists of the principal and interest.

Please visit the www.employeemillionaire.com/resources website for a rental property evaluation tool, which helps you to factor in a property's rental income, operating expenses, and mortgage loan interest rate and terms to calculate its NOI, cash flow, and ROI by just filling in the property data that has been discussed in this chapter. Below is a snapshot of this tool.

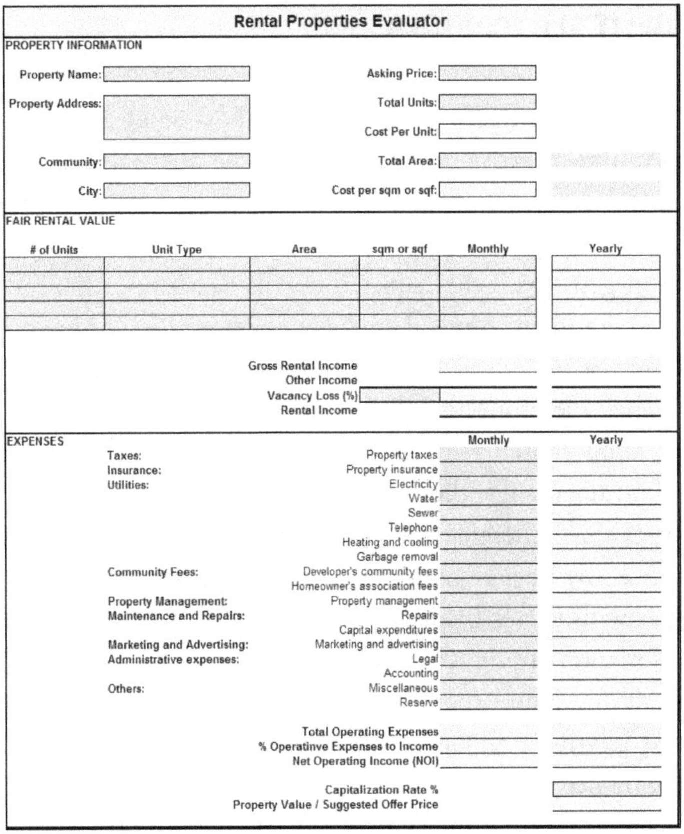

Rental Properties Evaluator

PROPERTY INFORMATION

Property Name:	Asking Price:
Property Address:	Total Units:
	Cost Per Unit:
Community:	Total Area:
City:	Cost per sqm or sqf:

FAIR RENTAL VALUE

# of Units	Unit Type	Area	sqm or sqf	Monthly	Yearly

Gross Rental Income
Other Income
Vacancy Loss (%)
Rental Income

EXPENSES

			Monthly	Yearly
Taxes:	Property taxes			
Insurance:	Property insurance			
Utilities:	Electricity			
	Water			
	Sewer			
	Telephone			
	Heating and cooling			
	Garbage removal			
Community Fees:	Developer's community fees			
	Homeowner's association fees			
Property Management:	Property management			
Maintenance and Repairs:	Repairs			
	Capital expenditures			
Marketing and Advertising:	Marketing and advertising			
Administrative expenses:	Legal			
	Accounting			
Others:	Miscellaneous			
	Reserve			

Total Operating Expenses
% Operatinve Expenses to Income
Net Operating Income (NOI)

Capitalization Rate %
Property Value / Suggested Offer Price

Figure 56—Rental property evaluator (Part 1)

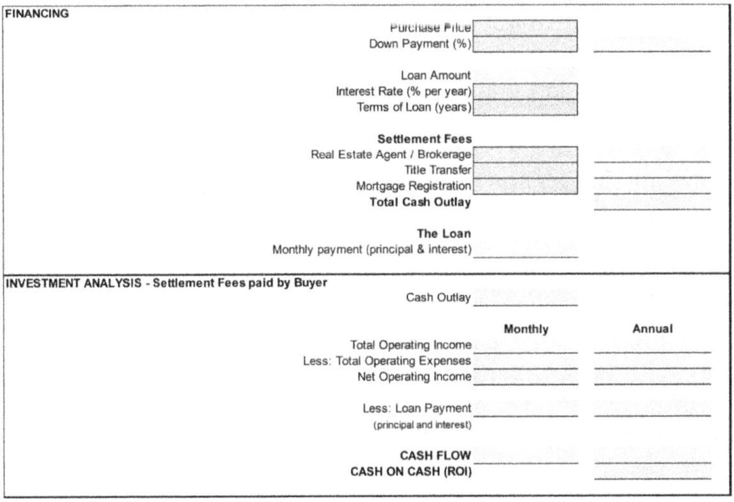

FINANCING

Purchase Price
Down Payment (%)

Loan Amount
Interest Rate (% per year)
Terms of Loan (years)

Settlement Fees
Real Estate Agent / Brokerage
Title Transfer
Mortgage Registration
Total Cash Outlay

The Loan
Monthly payment (principal & interest)

INVESTMENT ANALYSIS - Settlement Fees paid by Buyer

Cash Outlay

	Monthly	Annual
Total Operating Income		
Less: Total Operating Expenses		
Net Operating Income		
Less: Loan Payment		
(principal and interest)		
CASH FLOW		
CASH ON CASH (ROI)		

Figure 57—Rental property evaluator (Part 2)

PUTTING IT ALL TOGETHER

When Papa Joe needs to determine the value of a property that will enable him to arrive at a decision on the offered purchase price, he asks Ms Jing to give him both the fair rental income and a fair estimate of its operating expenses. In turn, she works with her team members in getting all the required details to arrive at the property's NOI (net operating income). Papa Joe will determine a property's value by dividing the NOI over his target cap rate. He will also determine the ROI when the property will be financed through a mortgage loan.

After a purchase is made, Ms Jing and her team deliver the estimated numbers since those will be set as their targets for managing the property. She reiterated the importance of getting those estimates correct since any deviation might mean the property was overvalued and that it will deliver below its targeted NOI, which is contrary to Papa Joe's mantra: You make money when you buy a rental property.

In analysing rental properties, neither Papa Joe nor Ms Jing ever mentioned anything about potential property appreciation. When I tried tricking her with a question related to analysing a property based on its potential future appreciation, she smiled and said that *buy and hold* investors buy rental properties based on the cash flow they generate now and in the future. They do not believe anyone can predict the future price of a property, and they do not believe in crystal balls. "Simply put," she said, "buy and hold investors treat any appreciation as the icing on the cake … or the cherry on top, but never as the goal."

Following that session with Ms Jing, long hours with a concentrated load of information, I passed by Papa Joe's office, as per his request, to brief him on what I learned. He returned a pleased smile and told me to see him in a few weeks when I was ready to submit some offers after analysing a decent number of properties. As I was exiting, he assured me: "Numbers don't lie. It's better to miss a good deal than buy a bad deal. Conversely, do not walk away from a good deal."

Chapter 10 Action Steps

After viewing a few properties that might be potential candidates for further investigation, run the numbers to determine which of them will make both operational and financial sense:

- You will need to estimate the annual rental income and each of the operational expenses to compute the net operating income (NOI).
- Set your own cap rate target (as explained in chapter 9) and determine each of the property's value range—your initial offer and maximum offer.
- From there, referring to the bank's preapproval letter, you can deduct the annual mortgage instalment from the NOI to determine the property's annual cash flow, which can be divided over your own down payment to obtain the cash on cash (per cent) return.
- Measure the cash on cash (per cent) return against the benchmarks of unhealthy, healthy, or wealthy ROI to determine the investment's attractiveness.
- Be ready to submit offers on those properties where the numbers work out well by following the advice in the next chapter.

CHAPTER 11

Negotiate and Submit Offers

Having learned how to properly analyse properties and estimate the real value to be offered to sellers, I was fired up and started reaching out to my team members. I contacted the real estate agents and shared with them my level one investment criteria, which are *location, construction, type, features, amenities*, and *condition*. In parallel, I started my own online search on the major property listing platforms for every single property that fit those criteria listed on the level one investment criteria worksheet (chapter 9).

From there I started filtering down each of those properties through the level two investment criteria, and each property that passed the 0.8 per cent test for the rent-to-price ratio was worth viewing.

I viewed about a dozen shortlisted properties in a span of five weeks and analysed each of them for its income, operation expenses, and NOI, which enabled me to determine the value of each of those properties.

After going through the level three investment criteria for each of those viewed properties, I was ready to make offers on a handful of them. To be exact, out of a total list exceeding 130 considered properties, only six passed all three criteria levels and qualified for written offers.

I was excited to contact Papa Joe for his guidance on how to negotiate and send offers, so I called him and asked him if we could meet for dinner in the middle of the week since waiting for the next Saturday could mean those properties might not be available anymore. Papa Joe admired my enthusiasm and passion to get into the game. He asked me to meet him at his favorite Greek restaurant at 9 p.m.

Papa Joe was a social person, and he always enjoyed connecting with friends and business partners over a nice meal. When we both arrived, we were seated at Papa Joe's favorite table. Without having to asking to what his order would be, a range of appetizers (his usual favorites) was offered on our table. While we were enjoying the great food, Papa Joe asked me to brief him on my search for rental properties and how I shortlisted those few properties that I wanted to make offer letters on. I explained to him how I set my criteria and how along each step of the process I started looking at a list of more than 130 properties and ended up with six properties that passed all my criteria.

Papa Joe congratulated me for not falling victim to the *captivity of passivity*. Analysis paralysis is a main reason most investors stop at the step of analysing properties over and over. They think they may get their estimates 100 per cent correct and therefore keep on overanalysing the deal until it's already gone.

According to Papa Joe, having gone through all those preparations and analysis put me in an excellent position to negotiate a good deal with any seller since having all the required numbers and facts about any property take the emotions out of the decision game.

OFFERS ARE DRIVEN BY NUMBERS, NOT OPINIONS

Papa Joe asked what my initial offer price on each of the six shortlisted properties would be. I shared with him the analysis done on each of them and the determined value range. I assured him that my initial offer would definitely be the lower end of the determined value range. Upon negotiation, I might consider stretching myself up to the higher end of the determined value range, but I would never go a penny more than what the property is worth. Papa Joe was pleased that I'd overcome such a steep learning curve and congratulated me for taking things objectively. To that he then added advice for novice investors like myself.

Have a Cushion to Fall On

According to Papa Joe, new investors with little or no experience usually overestimate a property value by either overestimating its rental income or underestimating its operational expenses … or both. Only experience will make an investor more meticulous about the numbers. For that reason, his advice was to take another 5 per cent off the lower end of the determined property value to act as a cushion for any overlooked number that might have led to an overestimated property value.

Low-Ball Offers Are for the Amateurs, Not the Investors

Papa Joe asked me to compute the difference between what would be my initial offer for each of the properties and the sellers' asking prices. He insisted that I take 5 per cent off my initial lower end estimated value for each. I used the calculator on my smartphone and said that the difference between my initial offer prices and sellers' asking prices for the six properties ranged between 15 to 25 per cent. The 25 per cent price difference between asking price and what would be my initial offer price worried me, and Papa Joe sensed this from my facial expressions.

He explained the difference between an initial offer price, which can be lower than the seller's asking price, and what might be considered as a low-ball offer. The latter are offers made by amateurs, not investors, who determine their offers based on facts and numbers. This does not mean there will not be hostility or mockery from sellers who believe their properties are worth far more than such offers. But being armed with the numbers will help explain how such offers were computed, allow for further negotiations within the determined property value range, or in extreme cases allow the one offering to walk away from a deal with stubborn, arrogant sellers.

Deals should always be win-win. Papa Joe taught me to walk away from any deal where *either* of the parties might lose. The seller's attitude is a good filter at this stage to feel whether negotiations will continue or both will part their own ways.

Negotiate within the Range of Computed Property Value

If the initial offer was rejected but the seller is open for a revised offer, the fun of negotiating for win-win deals begins. An investor computes the lower end and the higher range of the property value. Those two values act as the anchors of the whole negotiation process. As a rule of thumb, never negotiate on a purchase price that is higher than the set maximum offer, which is the higher end of the computed property value, as determined in level three investment criteria in chapter 9. Papa Joe recommended not to come back with a revised offer at the same meeting with the seller. It always helps to communicate that you will be running some numbers to determine how far you can stretch your offer.

Tying Up the Property

So far in the negotiation process, some non-written negotiations might have taken place between buyer and seller directly or through a real estate agent. No non-written agreement or arrangement ties up the property, which means the seller might still be open for offers from other buyers. At this stage, if the investor is comfortable with the numbers and the offer purchase price, a letter of intent is due to tie up the property and take it off the market once approved by the seller. The faster you can have your letter of intent signed by the seller, the better your chances you can close the deal at your offered price.

In some markets, the practice of a letter of intent is non-existent. Therefore a purchase and sale agreement will be the right document to tie up the property and to make it no longer available to any competitive bidder. We will discuss the process of signing a purchase and sale agreement in chapter 12.

In markets where a letter of intent is not a common practice, Papa Joe's advice was to "act like the leader and be a pioneer". When I came to Dubai in 2010 and started investing in rental properties, I was laughed at whenever I sent a letter of intent to the seller. Many agents challenged me because there it is not a common practice. I insisted on the process, and I never bought a single property without writing a letter of intent, which facilitated the whole purchase process.

The purpose of the letter of intent is not only to agree on the purchase price, but also to negotiate and agree on the terms and conditions of the deal before the final commitment through a purchase and sale agreement.

Why a Letter of Intent or an Offer to Purchase?

As mentioned above, a letter of intent helps in pre-agreeing on the purchase price and all terms and conditions of the deal that will appear in the final commitment—the purchase and sale agreement. This will make the process of signing a purchase and sale agreement quite smooth and swift.

In some markets, like Singapore and other parts of Asia, the letter of intent is commonly referred to as the offer to purchase. In this book, I refer to both a letter of intent (LOI) and an offer to purchase (OTP) as a letter of intent.

In his attempt to help me understand the difference between a letter of intent and a purchase and sale agreement, Papa Joe referred to the letter of intent a "pre-agreement for an agreement" and the purchase and sale agreement as an "agreement for disagreement". At first, he lost me with those definitions. He explained that a letter of intent lays down the basic deal terms like purchase price, down payment, earnest money deposit, due diligence terms, and timelines, as well as financing contingencies, all in a simple, standard format of up to two pages that does not require any legal advice from a lawyer or legal advisor. On the other hand, purchase and sale agreements involve many legal contingencies on how to solve disagreements as per local laws. A purchase and sale agreement can be tens of pages long, and its clauses are drafted in legal language and are more thorough.

Later that evening, over the delicious Greek appetizers, Papa Joe compared the letter of intent to a proposal for marriage and the purchase and sale agreement to the marriage contract. He explained the space in between them as the courting or engagement phase.

So a letter of intent is no different from a proposal to be sent to the seller. It serves to tie up the property until a purchase and sale agreement is signed. If well-designed and written, a letter of intent allows the buyer to legally walk away from the deal or to renegotiate the deal further if the due diligence steps reveals some information that was not available to the buyer early in the process. To ensure its fast delivery and receipt by the seller, it is best to have a letter of intent sent via email, fast courier, or through the real estate agent as long as a delivery receipt is signed acknowledge that the seller received the LOI.

In turn, the seller will review the LOI and usually replies with either an approval or a counterproposal on the offer price and the terms and conditions. In a few cases, sellers never respond to an offer they do not like, and it's OK to let go of a deal with a seller who is too arrogant to negotiate or reply. A counteroffer received from the seller is a good sign that the negotiation phase has just started and that the seller is interested. It will be a back-and-forth process until the LOI is signed by the seller. Only at this stage will the property be taken off the market.

Drafting a Letter of Intent (LOI) or an Offer to Purchase (OTP)

During our dinner over delicious Greek food, Papa Joe promised me that he would ask his team the next morning to send me an example of a letter of intent. His intention for that night was for me to understand what goes in a letter of intent and the different clauses of an LOI.

Papa Joe explained that an LOI mutually signed by both buyer and seller is not necessarily binding. Still, it needs to ensure the property is taken off the market until the terms and conditions of the purchase and sale agreement have all been agreed by both parties and in accordance with local laws. To have the property no longer available to other bidders, an LOI needs a good balance of being neither fully committed yet nor free to part ways, and this can be achieved with two important clauses: *earnest money deposit* and *contingencies*.

Earnest Money Deposit

In a fashion similar to a man in love who offers his dream wife an engagement ring to show the seriousness of his marriage proposal, an earnest money deposit offered to the seller shows the seriousness of the buyer to purchase the property. And earnest money deposit on a property is often referred to as a *good faith deposit* and is just an amount of money provided by the buyer to the seller when an offer is being made. A well-drafted letter of intent ensures the seller that such earnest money will be forfeited in favor of the seller in case the buyer does not live up to his or her end of the deal. A well-drafted letter of intent also allows for contingencies that let the buyer to legally back out from the deal without losing the earnest money deposit.

The amount of earnest money deposit is usually expressed as a percentage of the offered purchase price. This amount varies depending on common practices, which do differ by country and by city. In my real estate investment career in multiple countries, I have witnessed variations from 1 per cent to 10 per cent of the offered purchase price. In a seller's market, where there are many buyers bidding for a limited supply of properties, the earnest money tends to be on the higher end, usually around 10 per cent of the offered purchase price. In a buyer's market, where there are few buyers looking at many options from a large supply of properties, the earnest money can be as low as 1 per cent of the offered purchase price. In general, the higher the earnest money, the more the chances that the seller will agree on the offer and sign the LOI.

Earnest money is usually paid in the form of either a personal cheque, manager's cheque, or a wire transfer and held in a trust or escrow account, which is held by a real estate brokerage, legal firm, or a trustee. The funds will be held in the escrow account until either the day the deal goes through (and the title is transferred to the buyer) or the deal does not go through. When Papa Joe was trying to explain the possible scenarios that can play out with what happens to the earnest money, he took a white napkin from the table, unfolded it, took his pen from his jacket, and drew a table with four quadrants, as shown here:

	Deal Does Not Go Through	Deal Goes Through
Buyer Cannot Legally Back Out	Earnest money forfeited to the seller	Earnest money becomes part of the payment
Buyer Can Legally Back Out	Earnest money returned to the buyer (Contingencies)	

If the deal pushes through, the earnest money becomes part of the payment required for the complete purchase and transfer of title to the buyer. On the other hand, if the deal does not push through, the earnest money could either be forfeited in favor of the seller (in case the buyer does not have a legal reason to back out) or be returned to the buyer (in case the buyer has a legal reason to back out). Papa Joe wrote the word *Contingencies* and circled it in the quadrant where the deal does not push through and the buyer has legal reasons to back out. He said: "Contingencies are the legal provisions in a well-drafted letter of intent or purchase and sale agreement that allow the buyer to legally terminate a deal under clearly outlined conditions."

Contingencies

While nibbling on the delicious Greek mezes, Papa Joe took a piece of cooked carrot from one of the dishes with his fork and pointed them at me. He said, "While earnest money acts like a carrot to convince a seller to accept a buyer's offer, the contingencies allow the buyer to keep the carrot in his or her possession and legally walk away from the deal." Contingencies are provisions that outline specific conditions that can allow a legal agreement to be terminated without any liability on either of the parties. With the fork and carrot still raised over his plate, Papa Joe laid a couple of mint leaves over the carrot. He said that the more the contingencies there are in a letter of intent or an agreement, the less appealing is the earnest money deposit to the seller. Too many mint leaves over the carrot will make the carrot invisible and therefore not unappealing to a person who likes carrots. Likewise, for an offer to remain attractive to the seller, the number of contingencies should be limited to only a few that will really make or break a deal.

Usually, two main contingencies need to be included in any letter of intent or purchase and sale agreement, those relating to property inspection and appraisal, or to the lender agreeing to finance the property through a mortgage, or both. The two are related. The outcome of the property inspection may reveal some hidden facts on the condition of the property, which can lead a lender to be unwilling to finance the property due to the high risks involved.

Contingencies Related to Property Inspection and Appraisal

Viewing a property from the eyes of any person other than a professional inspector by walking it and looking at whatever your eyes may see can tell you only so much about it. A professional inspector will strip down a property and look at all its imperfections. A professional inspection of the property is due before the final commitment. An inspection contingency allows the buyer to back out from the deal should the report reveal things that may be a major cause of concern about the property.

An inspection contingency is usually time-bound within a specified time frame, after which the contingency is no longer applicable. For single-family residential units, a time frame of seven to ten days is an acceptable practice, whereas the process will take longer for multifamily properties. The time frame for property inspection allows for an appointment to be booked, time for inspection, and a couple of days for the report to be generated.

One of the many benefits of taking a mortgage loan through a bank is that the lender will enforce a property appraisal as a condition to finance the property. Usually a professional appraiser is nominated by the bank or else must be approved by the bank. An appraisal is less detailed and less thorough than an inspection report. It will be considered the bare minimum when purchasing a property. It is always worthwhile to pay the additional premium to obtain a more detailed property inspection report.

For investors who plan to buy the property from their own cash, the practice of having the property inspected or appraised is of utmost importance. A few dollars invested here may save the investor thousands spent on major maintenance that could have been revealed in an inspection or appraisal report.

A property inspection or appraisal report cites repairs that are needed on the property as well as the appraised value of the property. Both findings will have major impact on the decision whether to purchase a home. A typical report will include sections on paint, walls, windows, floor, roof, the electrical system, plumbing system, heating and cooling system, and the structural integrity of the property. The report will also give the appraised value of the property, which will be the benchmark used by the lender to make sure the property is worth at least as much as both the seller and buyer have agreed to.

Four possible scenarios can play out following a property inspection and appraisal report:

Inspection or Appraisal Report Finding	Recommended Actions
Major Structural Damages	Walk away! Back out of the deal. It's legal to do so since the conditions of contingency clause would not be met. There will be too many headaches and costs involved in rehabbing the property. This could be a reasonable investment option for other investors

who have the time and expertise in fixing up properties.

Most lenders will not finance a property that has structural damages. This imposes high risks on the property and on the lender.

Major Repair and Maintenance	Get quotes from three different contractors on the cost and time required to perform all necessary maintenance.
	If the costs and the time required for maintenance are not reasonable, walk away from the deal. It's legal to do so, since the conditions of contingency clause would not be met.
	If the costs and the time required for maintenance are reasonable enough, the price tag should be deducted from the offered purchase price. Proceed with the deal on condition that the lender will approve financing the property.
Minor Repair and Maintenance	Get quotes from three different contractors on the cost and time required to perform all necessary maintenance. This price tag should be deducted from the offered purchase price. Proceed with the deal on condition that the lender will approve financing the property.
All Clear	Proceed with the deal on condition the lender will approve financing the property.

As you may have realized, the contingency related to property inspection or appraisal is contingent on the bank or lender approving to finance the property. All the four scenarios described above were also contingent on the lender approving to finance the property.

Contingencies Related to the Lender Financing the Property

As explained previously, a lender wants to limit the risks of financing a property. The risks are twofold, related to the borrower (as covered in chapter 8) and to the property.

Two potential risks relate to the property: whether it has structural damages or major repair and maintenance (as covered in the previous section), or if its appraised value by a professional appraiser is less than the value that has been agreed to between the seller and the buyer. No lender will finance a property with an appraised value that is not greater than or at least equal to the sale price being agreed to.

Papa Joe asked: "What would you do if the lender decides not to finance the property that you have already put an earnest money deposit on?" His question took me by surprise, and I couldn't think of an answer. He answered that I would lose my earnest money if I do not have a financing contingency in place unless I have enough cash to finance the whole deal from my own pocket.

If the appraised value is equal to or greater than the agreed purchase price, then the conditions of this contingency would be met and the deal can move ahead from the perspective of this contingency. But if the appraised value is less than the agreed purchase price, there are four possible scenarios that can play out:

Contest the appraisal report and ask for a new appraisal to be conducted	In most cases, such a request to the lender falls on deaf ears. This request suggests that the appraiser nominated by the lender was not qualified or the report was wrong. In the eyes of the lender, there is already risk involved in the property, and very rarely will a lender accept a new higher valuation. In the rare cases a lender may accept such a request, the buyer will need to shoulder the cost of a new property appraisal.
Reduce the purchase price to match the appraised value	This is one of the most common scenarios that result from a low appraisal. Although it may be hard for some sellers to accept the bitter reality that their property is worth less than they wished or thought, for this scenario to work, the seller will need to have enough equity in their home that is at least equal to the purchase price. Otherwise, the seller needs to pay out of pocket to pay off the existing mortgage on the property as well as any related closing costs.
The buyer makes up the difference	This scenario could be a reasonable one in a sellers' market where there are few properties listed for sale. For this scenario to work out, the numbers still need to add up and the cash flow of the property must have an ROI that meets the investor's criteria. This scenario is often adopted by end users who wish to live in the property. Investors rarely follow this route.

If the investor has enough cash to cover a larger down payment and the property will still produce a cash flow with an ROI that meets the investor's criteria, the lender will then finance at a lower LTV (loan to value), which means the buyer will cover a larger down payment from his or her own pocket.

The buyer can walk away from the deal

If any of the above scenarios cannot play out in a win-win situation for both the buyer and the seller, the buyer can then legally back out of the deal since the condition on the contingency on appraised value will not be met.

In this scenario, the buyer would have incurred minimal cost related to property appraisal and applying to a mortgage loan.

In a sellers' market, where there are many buyers competing for a limited supply of properties, sellers may not agree on contingencies related to a property's appraised value. On the other hand, it will be highly risky for a buyer not to include such a contingency in a letter of intent or purchase and sale agreement since the down payment can be forfeited to the benefit of the seller if the lender will not agree to finance the property and if the seller does not have enough cash to cover the whole amount of the purchased price. A possible solution to such a situation is to include a contingency that the property's appraised value may be not less than 90 per cent of the appraised value. Such a percentage deviation from the appraised value could be 85 per cent, 90 per cent, 95 per cent, or any other number in this vicinity. In my experience, 95 per cent may be hard for a seller to accept by, and an 85 per cent means the buyer will need to make up for the difference. A 90 per cent is the most commonly acceptable number in a sellers' market.

When we finished our dinner that night, Papa Joe asked me to call him the next evening after I receive the sample letter of intent from his team members. He asked me to go through it, reflect on it, and then call him for a brief discussion.

What Should an LOI Include?

After a heavy meal the previous night, it was kind of tough to wake up the next morning. I dragged myself out of bed for a shower and a coffee before running to office—back to the rat race.

After a couple of meetings, lunch break was approaching. I checked my personal email on my smartphone, and voilà, an email from Papa Joe's secretary with the subject "Letter of Intent" was there in my inbox. I opened the email and found an attachment with a sample letter of intent. I had to finish some work in the office first and was looking forward to going for lunch all by myself so I could go through the letter of intent.

I ran to Starbucks on the lunch break, ordered a sandwich and a cappuccino, and opened my smartphone to go through the sample LOI. The letter of intent was short with a few clauses, each with its own title, as follows:

- Buyer's information
- Seller's information
- Property description
- Title deed condition
- Offered purchase price
- Earnest money deposit
- Remaining balance on closing
- Property inspection and appraisal contingency
- Financing contingency
- Final settlement
- Penalties

- Real estate brokerage commission
- Risk of loss
- Proration

At a first glance, what I assumed would be a simple, straightforward letter appeared a bit more complicated. But when I went through each of the clauses, I realized how simple and straightforward the content was. A document with simple language, without all the legal lingo, was not too hard to assimilate while having my sandwich and enjoying my coffee.

Later in the evening, I called Papa Joe to thank him for having the sample LOI sent over to me via email. It took him a few minutes over the phone to walk me through the different clauses of a letter of intent. In essence, an LOI should answer all the different W questions related to the deal.

- *Who* is making the offer?

An LOI must include the buyer's information. It is always smart to include "and/or assigned" next to the buyer's name if permitted by the local laws and practices. This allows the buyer (buyer one) to reassign the deal to another buyer (buyer two), who might be willing to purchase the property at a price that is higher than the negotiated price (by buyer one). This can allow buyer one to make a profit, which is equivalent to the difference between the higher purchase price offered by buyer two and the purchase price offered by buyer one. Although such a quick profit may not be the objective of an investor in rental properties, it may result in a handsome profit should buyer one decide that the deal is not worth moving forward with. This strategy is often referred to as *wholesaling*. I have not explained this strategy at length in this book on purpose since my objective is to allow you to own rental properties, achieve financial freedom, and become an employee millionaire.

- *To whom* is the offer being made? An LOI must include the seller's information.

- *What* is being bought? An LOI must include the property description, with its address, built up area, plot area (in case of townhouses or villas), and features. Some LOIs may include the amenities of a property. It is also important to mention that the title deed must be transferrable, free and clear of all liens and encumbrances.
- *How much* money will be offered as the purchase price? An LOI must include the offered purchase price, the earnest money deposit, and the remaining balance on closing. An LOI must also include clauses on proration of rent, other income, and expenses pertaining to the property, where applicable.
- *Where* is the buyer getting the funds? An LOI must clearly mention the kind of financing that will be used for the purchase—cash or financing through a lender. In case it is conventional financing, it is always advisable to mention whether the buyer has been preapproved for a loan.
- *When* is the closing date? An LOI must include the date of final settlement and title transfer to the buyer.
- *What if* the buyer or the seller back out from the deal?

An LOI must include clauses of contingencies related to property inspection, its appraised value, and its approval for financing by the bank. Those contingencies may allow the buyer to legally back out of the deal. On the other hand, an LOI must also include penalties on both the buyer and the seller in the event either backs out of the deal without any legal justification.

- *Who pays for what?* An LOI must have clarity on who is paying for commissions (of real estate brokerage or agency) as well as for closing costs.

After my brief phone call with Papa Joe, I went through the sample LOI again, this time with much more clarity. Below is a sample LOI that I often use for all my property investments. In some situations, some of the clauses will be omitted or simplified. But I never compromise on the clauses of contingencies. I have included on the Employee Millionaire website the sample LOI form, which is editable and ready for use. I have also included the lighter, simpler version of the LOI, which included the crucial clauses that a prudent buyer will never offer to purchase a property without including them in the LOI. Please visit www.employeemillionaire.com/resources to download the editable forms of the LOIs. Below is a snapshot of the LOI. It assumes a 10 per cent earnest money deposit. It can easily be edited to any other number depending on the local practices in your market.

Date: DD MM YYYY

From: Buyer's information ; and/or assigned.

Letter of Intent: Purchase of Property Description .

Dear Name of Seller ,

The purpose of this letter is to express our intent to purchase subject property with a title deed that is good and transferrable, free and clear of all liens and encumbrances.

We have outlined the terms and conditions of the purchase below:

Property Description: Subject property is located at address , with built-up floor area of #### square feet, herein described as "the Property".

The Title of Deed: The title to the Property shall be a good, transferrable title, free and clear of all liens and encumbrances.

Buyer Information: Full legal name with government identification number .

Offered Purchase Price: #### (in letters). However, should the third party valuation report show any maintenance required on the Property, the average quoted maintenance works of three (3) contractors will be deducted from the Offered Purchase Price.

Earnest Money Deposit: Upon signing this Letter of Intent, subject to Seller approval of this offer, the Buyer will pay an amount of #### (in letters), equivalent to 10 per cent of Purchase Price, in the form of a cheque to be held in escrow with Escrow Agent Name until transfer date. In a similar fashion, the Seller will pay an equivalent amount of #### (in letters) in the form of a cheque to be held in escrow with Escrow Agent Name until closing date.

Neither Earnest Money Deposit Cheques of Buyer nor Seller will be cashed in the favor of the other party except in the case of failure to complete the deal, as described under the *Penalties* clause.

Remaining Balance: #### (in letters), equivalent to 90 per cent of Offered Purchase Price at closing upon transfer of Title of Deed to the buyer.

Inspection Period: Buyer, at its sole and unfettered discretion, shall be allowed a ten (10) working day period from opening of escrow to review all property documentation, rent leases with existing tenants, obtain third party reports, and otherwise approve the property. If Buyer determines that for any valid reason the Property is not suitable for Buyer's use, such Letter of Intent shall terminate, Buyer's and Seller's earnest money shall be returned, and neither party shall have any liability or obligation to one another.

Financing: The buyer confirms that they have received a valid bank pre-approval to purchase a property subject to the lending criteria and other terms and conditions of the lending bank.

Final Settlement: Final Settlement, otherwise known as date of transfer of Title of Deed to the Buyer, is set at Thirty Five (35) days following the date of signing the Purchase and Sale Agreement, or at such time as mutually agreed upon by the parties hereto with good faith to accommodate any time required by the Developer, government agencies, and the Lender to process and deliver documentations pertaining to this deal.

Brokerage Commissions: Both the Buyer and Seller have engaged Real Estate Agency Name (herein, "agent") as the agent, and both agree that it the Buyer's / Seller's obligation to pay agent a ### (#) per cent commission based on the purchase price at the time of settlement.

Penalties: After signing the Purchase and Sale Agreement, the Buyer is liable for penalty of #### (in letters) in case the Buyer fails to complete the deal for any reason other than (1) a permitted termination pursuant to the property appraisal report or (2) the offered purchase price exceeds the value detailed in the property appraisal report by more than ten (10) per cent or (3) Seller's failure to perform Seller's obligations under this Agreement. In a similar fashion, in case the Seller fails to complete the deal for any reason other than the Buyer's failure to perform Buyer's obligations under this agreement, the Seller is liable for penalty of #### (in letters) and also reimburses Buyer for all costs reasonably incurred in connection with preparation of the proposed settlement, including but not limited to attorney fees, surveys, lender appraisals and processing fees, and title searches.

Risk of Loss: All risk of loss to the Property shall be borne by the Seller until the date and time of settlement.

Proration: Rents and other income and expenses pertaining to the Property will be prorated as of the final settlement date.

The terms expressed in this Letter of Intent will become null and void if not accepted within seven (7) days from the date of this letter. If you accept our proposal, we will proceed to enter into a Purchase and Sale Agreement within seven (7) days of acceptance.

During this period Seller agrees to discontinue any third party sale negotiations.

Sincerely,

Buyer's Name and Signature

Seller's Name and Signature

Real Estate Agent: Name, Registration Number, and Signature

The content in this sample LOI is self-explanatory. The previous sections in this chapter have attempted to explain the clauses of an LOI that require clarification, so that you can be better informed when making offers.

TIPS FOR WIN-WIN OFFERS

Papa Joe is a strong advocate of win-win scenarios for both the buyer and the seller. One of the best pieces of advice he ever gave me was to walk away from any deal whereby either I will win and the other party loses or I lose and the other party wins—or both parties will lose. Investment should be both fun and profitable, but most importantly, business ethics must never be compromised.

In win-win negotiation, the negotiating parties should take into account each other's interests. To achieve that, the most important resources—time, and money—should be exploited to the mutual interest and benefit of the negotiating parties. The offer to purchase and the negotiation process should be transparent enough to ensure clarity on the whole purchase process with clear timelines and understanding of who is going to pay what amount to whom. Such clarity will not only help the buyer guide the seller on the purchase process, but also will make the buyer be perceived as more professional than the rest. Such peace of mind can also distinguish a buyer from the rest of the crowd. Let's examine each of those resources—time and money—vis-à-vis having the buyer's offer to purchase accepted by the seller.

Time

Usually a seller would like to close as soon as possible to be done with the deal. The shorter the timelines in each step of the process, the better the chances a seller can favor an offer to purchase over other sellers. The seller wishes to receive the money the soonest and with the least amount of headache.

Here are some tips to speed up the deal:

- Send an offer as soon as you run the numbers. Don't lose time. Don't overanalyse the numbers and fall a victim of "captivity of passivity", as Papa Joe called it. Analysis paralysis makes novice investors analyse the numbers over and over without taking any action until the property is taken off the market or sold. Work smart (by analysing the numbers) and fast (by attempting to be among the first who make an offer on the property).

- Be clear on timelines of the purchase process from opening of escrow till closing date. The clearer and the more reasonable those dates are, the better the sense the seller will have of when the sale money will be pocketed and the burden of selling the property be taken off his or her shoulders.

- Sellers favor buyers with cash or preapproved financing over those who have not applied for a mortgage loan. Cash signifies the buyer has all the funds ready, which means no time spent on bank bureaucracies and an earlier closing date. A buyer with preapproved financing also indicates speed, given that half of the financing equation—of qualifying the borrower for a loan—has been solved. From a buyer with preapproved financing, the seller will get a sense of the available funds and a reasonably fast closing date. On the other hand, a buyer who wishes to purchase using a mortgage loan but hasn't yet applied for a loan means a potential risk to the seller, since the buyer still has to prequalify for a loan, which takes time and might end up with the loan application being rejected due to the buyer's financial situation. In offering on a property, never waive the financing contingency unless you are a cash buyer. If you are a preapproved finance buyer and you get tempted to waive the financing contingency to show the seller a faster closing, you might end up losing your earnest money if the bank will not finance the property for reasons related to the property. Chapter 13 discusses the topic of financing in further details.

Money

Money is the number one reason for a seller to sell a property. Sellers often need the cash—for whatever personal reasons. Some sellers know the true value of their properties, but others are either ignorant of the real market value or arrogant and hence will ask for a high premium compared to the fair market value. Some sellers are in no need of the cash, but would welcome a sale that brings them a high ransom and therefore ask for a selling price that is higher than the market value and wait until an ignorant buyer knocks on their doors. This can take a long time. In essence, in each real estate transaction, sellers have different motivations for selling their properties. What matters for them is the payoff. Some sellers are highly motivated and would like to take the burden of their properties off their shoulders, so they might accept offers that are lower than their asking price. Other sellers are less motivated to sell, so they wait longer until they find buyers who are willing to offer reasonable purchase prices close to their asking price.

Below are tips on offering a purchase price that will increase the chances of having an offer approved:

- Your purchase offer should be in line with the determined property value, as covered in chapter 9. Your initial offer should be at the lower end of the computed property value though you can go up to the higher end of the property value in the negotiation process. Both ends of the determined property value will still lead to a property that produces a positive cash flow after all expenses are paid. Remember to always run the number to compute the NOI, cash flow, and the ROI. The higher end of the determined property value must never lead an ROI that is less than a healthy ROI (two times the mortgage interest rate per cent).

- Do not lowball an offer by offering an arbitrary purchase price that is way lower than the lower end of the determined property value. It is OK to offer a few percentages points—up to 5 per cent—below the lower end of the determined property value to act as a cushion to accommodate expenses that were not forecast in calculating the property's NOI. But do not think it's smart to lowball an offer. I have met many investors—or wannabe investors—who think it is smart to lowball an offer way below the seller's asking price without any clue on how the offer was computed. They count on luck to find a highly motivated seller who urgently needs the money. Most often, those people end up not investing at all. Rarely, they might overpay for a property after thinking they were smart by just offering a purchase price that is 30 per cent, 40 per cent, or 50 per cent below the seller's asking price, without ever thinking that the seller was just overstating the asking price.

- In a hot sellers' market, where there are many buyers bidding for few available supply of properties, offering your best up front might be the right strategy, which means offering the high end of the determined property value as your initial offer ... and as your last offer. Your maximum offer up front sends a message to the seller that you are serious and not playing the negotiation game. If the seller counters your best offer and tries to make you go higher, just be assertive and say no.

- Offer more earnest money. The higher the earnest money, the more serious your offer appears in the eyes of the seller. In markets where the earnest money is expected to be below 5 per cent, be bold and offer 10 per cent. In markets where it is customary to offer 10 per cent, be bolder and offer 15 or 20 per cent earnest money. Never exceed 20 per cent, which is the down payment that will come out of your pocket to finance the deal on common 80 per cent LTV mortgage loans. Whatever the amount of earnest money you decide to offer, make sure that you have those contingencies in place to protect your deposit should you later decide to back out for reasons highlighted in the contingencies.

- Pay the seller's closing costs. Depending on the current practices in your market, it may be customary that the seller is required to shoulder all or part of the real estate agent commissions as well as other closing fees related to title transfer. If the seller has accepted your offer, which is still lower than the higher end of the determined property value, look into offering to pay part or all of the seller's closing costs—as long as the numbers work for you.

Discover the Seller's True Motivation— Time, Money, or Both

In the early stages of the win-win negotiation process, when submitting an offer letter, it may be tricky to determine the seller's true motivation—time, money, or both. It always plays to your advantage to investigate through the real estate agent and through any direct communication with the seller on what the seller's true motivation is. Is the seller looking for the absolute highest price, while not in a rush to sell? Is the seller in need of a fast closing and willing to compromise on the selling price? Real estate agents, by nature, usually are talkative and would not mind—or might actually like—sharing stories about the seller and the reasons for selling the subject property. In one of my coaching sessions with Papa Joe, when he saw that I needed guidance on how to negotiate with sellers after discovering their true motivation, he drew the *seller's motivation matrix*, a useful guide I still use even after negotiating on hundreds of deals.

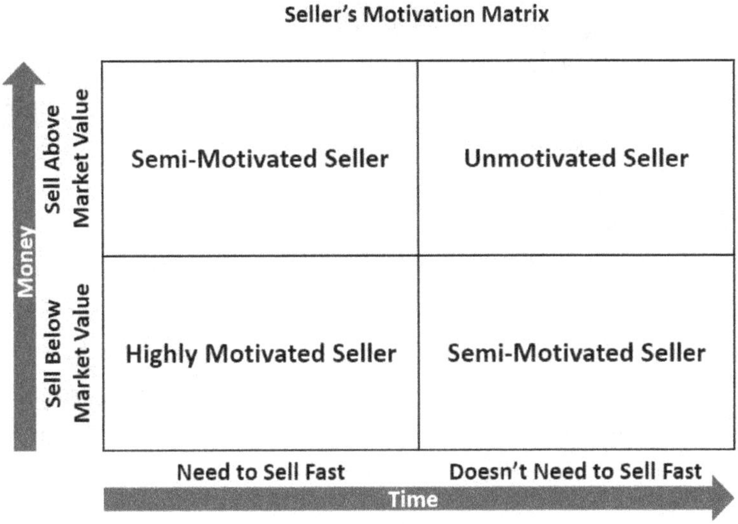

Seller's Motivation Matrix

Figure 58—Seller's motivation matrix

As you may have concluded, motivated sellers may be willing to compromise on their asking price as well as on closing date as long as they sell their property. On the other hand, unmotivated sellers are looking for the highest possible selling price and are in no hurry. In between the extremes lie the semi-motivated sellers who can compromise on either time or money. Discovering the seller's true motivation is an art that can be learned by practicing negotiations over and over. The more you engage with real estate agents and sellers, the more skilled you become in this art.

In a sellers' market, one strategy I often use to discover a seller's true motivation is the *dual offer strategy*. This works by giving the sellers two offers in the same letter of intent. The two offers are the two extremes of the determined property value. It works as shown below:

Dual Offer Strategy

- Offer a purchase price at the lower end of the determined property value and on all-cash basis. This ensures the seller a pay-off in the shortest possible time.
- Offer a purchase price at the higher end of the determined property value and with bank financing. This ensures the seller your higher offer, but it requires time to go through the bank financing process

The dual offer strategy requires the buyer to have enough cash to pay for the property in the event the lower offer was accepted on an all-cash basis. Don't worry. After investing in many properties, getting enough cash to finance such deals won't be a big issue. Even if purchased on an all-cash basis, a property can be (and ought to be) refinanced through a mortgage loan at a later stage. The topic of financing a property will be covered at length in chapter 13.

TAKE ACTION AND SUBMIT OFFERS

Making an offer is often uncomfortable. This is where non-serious investors drop out of the rental property investment game. They overanalyse the numbers and never arrive at a number they can offer to make a purchase. They fall to what Papa Joe calls the *captivity of passivity*. In a circle of colleagues, we used to refer to this analysis paralysis phenomenon as *intellectual masturbation*. People stuck in this stage fantasize about owning properties, but never go out and do what needs to be done to really own them. They wind up left out of the game. One day in the future they will realize the opportunities they missed.

My advice is to get off the sidelines and take your own fate in your hands. If you want to own rental properties, prepare by educating yourself before submitting offers. If you do not overcome your fears by presenting offers, you will not move towards becoming an employee millionaire with your rental property investment career. Whenever my feet get cold on any project I am working on, I think of a quote from Rabindranath Tagore I saw as a poster in a colleague's office: "You can't cross the sea by merely staring at the water".

After submitting offers in writing with a well-crafted letter of intent, where all the necessary conditions will protect you, it will be time to go through the process of due diligence. From there you either back out from the deal or negotiate further.

The next chapter tackles the details on due diligence, the nitty-gritty details of negotiations, and committing with the purchase and sale agreement.

Chapter 11 Action Steps

After running the numbers and determining both your initial offer and maximum offer for each of the shortlisted properties, kick off the negotiation process with the seller.

Submit written offers in the form of letters of intent as shown in this chapter. Be careful that you never compromise on the contingencies clauses.

Once your offer is approved by the seller by signing the LOI, be prepared to start the due diligence process, as detailed in the next chapter.

CHAPTER 12

Perform Due Diligence and Commit

It was funny that I felt I was ready to jump in and send an offer to purchase my first ever one-bedroom rental property before I was properly educated on how to analyse a deal and determine the real value of a property, based on which I can submit an offer. Then, when I was properly educated, it took me some time to take a leap of faith and submit a letter of intent.

It appeared that the more I knew, the more I analysed, and the more I *over*analysed to an extent I felt like I still needed more numbers to analyse. It was not until Papa Joe motivated me to overcome the *captivity of passivity* state of mind that I took a deep breath and hit the send button on my email with the letter of intent attached. It took the seller about eight hours to reply with a bit higher counter-offer. After understanding his true motivations, I managed to negotiate a bit on time and money until we arrived at a win-win common ground where the numbers worked well for both me and the seller.

The clock started to tick, and although the letter of intent was clear on the contingencies, I felt I needed a guiding hand to lead me throughout the process. I called Papa Joe as soon as I had agreed with the seller and asked him for guidance. Without hesitation, he asked me to connect again with his expert team member on this topic, Ms Jing.

It was around 8 p.m. that evening, and without giving any consideration that the time was after business hours, I called Ms Jing on her mobile. It appeared that she had saved my number from our previous encounter, when she taught me about analysing a property's income and expenses. With her usual positive attitude, in spite of apparently being in a family gathering with loud voices of children and babies in the background, she congratulated me on taking the necessary steps and proceeding to that level in my education. She asked me to meet her first thing in the morning in one of the residential towers owned and managed by Papa Joe's company.

After thanking her and closing the phone, I realized that my excitement led me to forget that I had to report to my job the next day. I didn't want to lose momentum, so I texted my boss, who was in Singapore, to inform him that I needed to take a day's leave the next day, and I apologized for the short notice. I received a confirmation by a return text message.

I had mixed emotions of excitement and fear of proceeding further with the deal. I started to worry about losing my earnest money deposit of 5 per cent. My fear even led me to worry that I might not be able to rent the property and pay for the mortgage loan instalments. At the same time, my *big why* list and my set objectives have always played a major role in reminding me to stay on course and proceed with the plan I created for myself.

My thoughts raced in all directions that evening. My own imagination beat me with up a doomy picture followed by a gloomy one and then over, again and again. I felt tired and just wanted to sleep. While in bed, I read my letter of intent and decided to focus on first things first. It was time now to perform due diligence on the property to determine whether the conditions related to the contingency property inspection and appraisal would be met.

The following morning, I freshened up with a cold shower, prepared my coffee, and drove to the amazing thirty-two-floor condominium tower owned by Papa Joe. When I arrived at the tower management office, I introduced myself to the property manager, Robert, who apparently was expecting me. A few minutes later, Ms Jing arrived on time and was pleased to see me there a few minutes before our appointment. As if there was no time to lose, Robert led the way to our meeting room, where Ms Jing asked him to spend a few hours with me to guide me on the due diligence process, then excused herself to tour the tower for her audit on how well the property was being managed. We agreed that she would come back around time for us to go to lunch and for me to brief her on what I'd learned about due diligence.

WHAT IS DUE DILIGENCE?

When we entered the small meeting room, Robert courteously welcomed me again and offered me a seat. He started by saying that a property that might appear as a great deal on the outside and on initial viewing may have hidden problems, major or minor, which might make the deal fall off the cliff.

While Robert went on with introducing what due diligence is about, my memory took me back about twenty years in the past to when my father was cheated when he bought a car without having it checked for physical damages or mechanical flaws. Because he trusted a car salesman he had never met before, my father ended up paying dearly for a car that had to be repaired to hide the many defects and damages following a major accident. It cost him a fortune to have the car repaired almost every other week until he was fed up and sold it for less than half the original price he paid a few months earlier.

Robert said: "You need to perform due diligence to investigate a property's hidden flaws." I opened my notebook (as usual) to assure Robert that he had my full attention.

Before going further with our meeting, Robert told of his experience in real estate and that he worked as a certified property inspector for over fifteen years before switching gears to property management when Papa Joe offered him a job on his team. Robert's experience enabled him to speak with authority and confidence on the topic of due diligence.

Robert appeared to have been fully briefed by Ms Jing on my previous coaching session with her on forecasting a property's performance. He explained that part of due diligence is to *verify* a property's income and expenses before committing to a purchase and sale agreement. Due diligence allows the buyer to discover whether the data used to evaluate the deal is all correct. Otherwise, the buyer reserves the right to either kill the deal or negotiate the purchase price to accommodate for any cost of required repair and maintenance.

Due diligence is about doing a thorough physical and financial inspection of a deal to make sure the deal meets the set of criteria that was forecast based on the information and data that were made available by the seller or the seller's agent. In other words, it helps ensure that the data provided by the seller to evaluate the deal is correct. This includes everything from the rental income, operating expenses, potential maintenance, and repair expenses.

There are three possible outcomes following a due diligence:

1. Ask the seller to make the necessary repairs.
2. Request a discount in purchase price.
3. Exit from the deal altogether as a result of what is found during the inspections.

TYPES OF INSPECTIONS TO MAKE DURING DUE DILIGENCE

Although a multifamily property inspection requires many more details and time, there is a minimum level of inspection that must be performed even on a single-family home. What is covered in this section includes mainly the types of inspection required on single-family homes, which is the focus of this book.

Three different types of inspection during due diligence go hand in hand simultaneously:

1. Physical inspection
2. Document inspection

3. Financial inspection

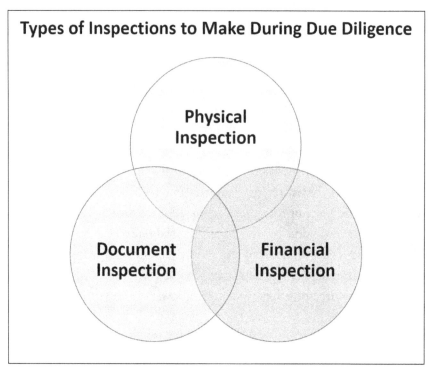

Types of Inspections to Make During Due Diligence

Figure 59—Types of inspections to make during due diligence

Physical Inspection

The physical inspection of a rental property is about uncovering things that may become a problem in the future. Those potential problems may have major financial implications on the buyer, which could be avoided if discovered before the final commitment. Any major foreseen expense can be brought on the table in the negotiation process.

At that stage, even before you have submitted your letter of intent to the seller, you should have walked through the property. Likely your eyes are not trained like those of a professional inspector, who can reveal problems that are hidden below the nicely-painted walls. As an investor, your inspection can help you identify potential upgrades such as new kitchens, baths, light fixtures, and appliances that can make it easy to rent the property. The inspection report of a professional inspector will cover these areas (in no particular order of importance):

- *Safety and fire inspection* in line with local regulations. An inspector will look into smoke detectors and undersized electrical breakers among other safety features required by law.

- *Roof inspection* that will report its condition. This is very important in locations where heavy rain can cause serious water leakage inside the property.

- *Structural inspection* will reveal any structural damages that could impose serious risks on the property or would carry a high price tag to repair.

- *Electrical system inspection* provides a thorough examination of the entire electrical system, ensuring all electrical wiring meets legal safety standards. The report will provide a checklist of required repair and upgrades to comply with the safety standards. The inspector will examine the kind of wiring, test all the outlets, and make sure ground fault circuit interrupters are properly installed. They will also check the electrical distribution board for any safety issues.

- *Plumbing system inspection* describes the condition of the interior water supply, drain, waste, and vent piping materials. It also examines the condition of water heating equipment and fixtures such as sinks, showers, tubs, and toilet seats for possible leaks. You never want to purchase a property that requires major plumbing repairs, which is usually quite costly.

- *Heating, ventilation and air conditioning systems (HVAC) inspection* provides an estimate of their age and checks whether they function properly.

- *Paint and walls inspection* checks cracks in the walls and whether those cracks are a sign of structural damage or building faults. Many of those cracks could be nothing serious, whereas a few could mean problems. Cracks can be covered by a good paint job. This makes them quite difficult for the untrained eye to identify.

- *Environmental inspection* may be required in certain countries to make sure there are no environmental hazards, such as asbestos insulation on heating lines or lead-based paint, which can be a threat to the local environment.
- *Appraised market value of the property* is an integral part of this report and one of the major requirements by the lender to ensure that the property is worth more than the mortgage amount to be lent to the borrower.

The typical inspection lasts two to three hours. Robert recommended that a potential buyer should be present for the inspection to get a firsthand explanation of the inspector's findings and ask the necessary questions. The inspector will also determine the fair value of the property, which will be reported to the bank.

A typical report will include all the areas covered in this section, with photos to illustrate the finding, and a professional opinion whether each problem is a safety issue, major defect, or minor defect. The report also determines which items need replacement and which should be repaired or serviced. This makes it easier to determine the cost of repair and maintenance by asking a few contractors to quote for the job.

The physical inspection needs to be done by a third party company, usually nominated by the bank or the lender when the property will be financed by a mortgage loan. In case of an all-cash purchase, the third party company is hired by the buyer. In all cases, the buyer pays for the fee related to physical inspection. During inspection, the inspector is obligated to report any existing or potential issues that are observed.

Once physical inspection is completed, the buyer usually goes back to the seller and either gets more clarity on some of these items, asks for certain things to be remediated, negotiates for a discount, or in case of structural and other major problems, walks away from the deal.

Document Inspection

This is one the most straightforward parts of due diligence. In the inspection clause of the letter of intent, the buyer usually requests specific documents to be reviewed. The most common documents include the title deed of the property, copies of rental agreements, a recent real estate tax bill, and a copy of the insurance policy. Document review should not take more than a day or two to be accomplished once the documents have been received by the buyer.

It is understandable if some sellers hesitate to share the documents requested by the buyer for inspection purposes before the purchase and sale agreement is signed. The buyer can offer to sign a non-disclosure agreement (NDA) to ensure the seller that all documents will be treated with utmost confidentiality.

If this solution does not work, it is OK for both the seller and the buyer to sign the purchase and sale agreement before the whole due diligence process is done, as long as all the contingencies set in the letter of intent are included in the purchase and sale agreement. Such contingencies will allow the buyer to either negotiate for a reduced price or exit the deal without any penalties if the findings of the due diligence merit such actions. Any hesitation from the seller to produce any of those documents, even after the purchase and sale agreement is signed, can signal a red flag that further investigation is required to reveal some more data about the property.

Here are the most common documents that should be inspected:

- *A copy of the title deed* to verify the ownership of the property. Any cautious buyer would like to verify that the seller actually owns the property and has the right to sell it. The verification of the property ownership data is usually done by the real estate agent, the lender, the lawyer, online, or by inquiring with the local relevant authorities. The real estate agent will always guide the buyer on the common practices in the market where the property is being purchased. If not sure who will be verifying the property ownership, a seller can ask the real estate agent or the bank that will be financing the deal. In their attempt to combat real estate fraud, which is a common problem, many cities impose this responsibility on the real estate brokerage firm working on the deal. I have heard of stories where a buyer hands over a sizeable cheque for the earnest money deposit to the supposed owner and then finds out that the property was owned by someone else. To those crooks, the large amounts of money they receive by conning good, willing buyers could be the jackpot that moves them to flee from those cities and search for a new country or city to start over with their fraudulent activities.

- *Title inspection* is also very important to make sure the title deed has no liens or encumbrances, which can break the whole deal. A lien is a legal claim made by a person or entity against a property to secure the payment of a debt. The most common lien is an existing mortgage on the property, which guarantees the lender it will be paid back before the property gets sold. This kind of lien is so common that it is expected if the seller has bought the property by financing it with a lender. Upon buying the property, the buyer or his lender will pay off first the existing mortgage on the property. Once the seller's lender gets paid back, the lien is released on the property, and then the buyer or his lender will pay the balance of the purchase price to the seller. This whole process will be explained in further details in chapters 13 and 14, which focus on financing the property and transferring the title. There are other types of lien attached to the property that are not related to an existing mortgage, for examples where the seller owes money to some other people or entities. This kind of lien signals major risks, and it is probably best to stay away from such properties. If the buyer will be financing the deal, the lender will not agree to finance such properties.

- *A signed rental agreement* to ensure the rental rate, duration of the contract, security deposit amount, and the agreed responsibilities of both the landlord and the tenant. As the new owner, the buyer will inherit all the terms and conditions of the rental agreements. Knowing the rental rate and security deposit are important in the computation of the final settlement to be paid to the seller under the proration clause of the letter of intent. This means the balance of the rent as well as the full amount of the security deposit will be handed over to the buyer on the date of transfer of ownership.

- *The recent real estate tax bill and proof of payment* to both contain estimates of the actual real estate tax to be forecast in the operation expenses as well as evidence that the previous tax bill has been already settled. This might not be applicable as of the writing of this book in many of the countries in the Arabian Gulf and some other countries. The signs show that the days of tax-free real estate are in a countdown already.

- *The liability insurance policy* on the subject property is always attached to the property, not the owner. This means the new owner will be liable to pay the premium for the liability insurance on the property from day one of ownership. The responsibility is automatically transferred to the new owner. On the other hand, any existing mortgage insurance will automatically be cancelled when the existing mortgage of the previous owner is settled. The new owner will be assuming a new mortgage insurance if the property is to be financed by a lender.

- *Existing service agreements*, which can be signed by the previous owner, are usually contracted for the property. This means such service agreements will be automatically transferred to the new owner. Examples of service agreements on single-family properties are general maintenance and landscaping contracts.

- *Local municipality documents* to confirm the property is zoned for its current and intended use and that it is registered as a rental property.

- *Homeowners association (HOA) or master developer rules and regulations* will highlight the declarations of covenants, conditions, and restrictions. In essence, such documents explain all the dos and don'ts about the property. An investor in rental properties will be highly deceived and will not achieve any returns if the property cannot be used as rental in accordance with the HOA or master developer rules.

Financial Inspection

When you analysed the property's rental income and operational expenses to compute its NOI (net operating income), many of the numbers were forecast to the best of the buyer's knowledge based on the available information and based on some common industry practices. The financial inspection part of the due diligence allows a thorough financial analysis based on the real numbers before the final commitment and signing the purchase and sale agreement. If the numbers still add up and the real picture is similar to or better than the forecast one, the buyer can move on with the deal.

In essence, a financial inspection allows the buyer to validate all the numbers, from rental income to operational expenses, which were previously shared by the seller or their agent.

During our meeting, Robert pulled out a small piece of paper from his jacket, unfolded it, and laid it on the table. My eyes gazed towards the paper like a thief trying to steal information. The papers had a few bullet points that Robert used as a guide for our discussion. Those bullet points turned out to be a checklist of the financial numbers to be checked and verified by the buyer. Robert proudly said that he came to our meeting well prepared in spite of a short notice given by his boss, Ms Jing, the night before. I thanked him for his efforts and the time he invested with me. In my thoughts I was thanking God for the blessings he gave me by making my path cross the path of mentors and coaches who have enlightened my way to invest in rental properties. Below are the numbers that Robert recommended I look at when conducting a financial inspection of a rental property.

- *Rental income review* verifies the property's income. Ask for copies of the rental agreements, which will be signed by both the landlord and the current tenant. A rental agreement can be a simple one-page document in some cities, and it can be lengthy elsewhere. No matter how long and detailed the rental agreement is, three financial items that a buyer needs to note are: what tenants pay in rent, their security deposit, and what they are responsible for. The last item has financial implications on the operational expenses. For example, in some rental agreements, the landlord is responsible for all repairs and maintenance. In others, the tenant is responsible for minor maintenance and the landlord for major tasks. The topic on rental agreements will be thoroughly discussed in chapter 15.

- *Property taxes or real estate taxes* can be verified by looking at the last year's real estate tax invoice and payment. The prudent investor will also inquire with the tax collector to confirm the taxes. This information is public and can also be found from credible websites.

- *Property insurance* is straightforward to figure out. As discussed earlier in this book, there are two major types of insurance: liability insurance (optional, but recommended), and mortgage insurance (mandated by the lender when a property is financed with a mortgage loan). Mortgage insurance covers both life protection and hazard protection, and is usually a percentage of the loan amount. It is quite simple to inquire with the lender or any other insurance provider on such rates and account for the monthly premiums to be paid as an operational expense.

- *Property utilities* can be verified by checking the last twelve months' utility bills. As discussed earlier in the book, for single-family units, all utilities are often the responsibility of the tenant. In some condominiums and large apartment buildings, where cooling and heating are centralized, the landlords of the individual units may be required to pay certain set annual fees. Depending on the existing rental agreement, such bills could be passed on to the tenants either directly (through billing) or by accounting for the same in the asking rent. This is why it is always smart to check the tenant responsibilities clause in the rental agreement. In multifamily units, the landlord will be paying for the utilities of the common areas. Such cost needs to be accounted for in the operating expenses. In such case, the utility expenses can be verified by checking last year's utility bills. This twelve-month period reveals fluctuations throughout the four seasons.

- *Master community fees* can be easily obtained by asking for the last year's bill. Such fees can also be verified by inquiring with the master developer or the community management company looking after the master development. Such fees may not be applicable for single-family homes that are not part of master developments, condominiums, or large apartment buildings.

- *Property management fees* may not be applicable in purchasing a single-family home. However, as discussed earlier, the smart investor will need to account for such an expense in the long run, even if the buyer is planning to personally manage the property. There could come a day when the number of properties an investor owns becomes too large to be managed, so the services of a property management company will be required. Although fees fluctuate between 5 per cent and 7 per cent, it is best to assume a 7 per cent property management fee in the operating expenses. If the property is currently managed by a property management company, asking for the agreement and the related invoices will be a good start to verify the expenses.

- *Property maintenance and capital expenses* are tough to verify. Although asking the seller for the historical maintenance bills will give the buyer an idea on the property's maintenance history, it is not enough in estimating the future maintenance bills. The findings of the physical inspection report will enable the buyer to pinpoint the required maintenance, which can be estimated by asking for competitive bids from three contractors. Such known maintenance cost on the current condition of the property is often used in the final purchase price negotiations. All other future maintenance costs can be estimated based on the property's age. The rule in the table below has been adopted and applied hundreds of times by Papa Joe and his team with a decent accuracy level.

Property Age	Annual Maintenance Cost
Less than 5 years	5 per cent of annual rent
Between 5–15 years	10 per cent of annual rent
More than 15 years	15 per cent of annual rent

Once the financial numbers explained in this section have been crunched, the buyer can either validate the profit projections made before submitting the offer or prove them to be wrong. If the numbers are far off and the buyer has included a contingency clause in the letter of intent, a price adjustment can be negotiated with the seller.

When Robert was done generously sharing his wealth of experience with me, and while chatting about the beautiful Philippines islands and some beautiful vacation spots, we heard the high-heeled rhythmic footsteps of Ms Jing coming our way across the corridor towards our meeting room. It was time for my lunch with her.

Before she entered our meeting room, Robert gave me a sound piece of advice, which I wrote down as soon as I had the opportunity. His advice was to trust the seller or the seller's agent about the information they share, but verify its accuracy. He summed it up in a few words: Be diligent when doing due diligence.

Ms Jing thanked Robert for his time and asked me if I was hungry. I was starving after spending hours paying attention to Robert. I thanked him for his time once again and left with Ms Jing down the long corridor towards the tower's lobby. While admiring Ms Jing's way of walking and witnessing how the whole property management staff respectfully feared her presence, she asked me whether Italian food is a favorite of mine. I smiled and nodded, and she suggested I join her in her car so we could talk while stuck in crazy Manila traffic until we reached the restaurant. Her driver was waiting at the lobby entrance. We sat in the back of the car. She put her beautiful, expensive leather bag between us and asked me to brief her on what I learned with Robert.

The long time in the heavy traffic felt to me like a few minutes. I did most of the talking, sharing what I had learned so far about due diligence. I enjoyed our discussion and appreciated her perspective on the points I shared. As we approached the restaurant, she asked me about what steps I planned next, after the seller approved my offer. She reminded me that the clock was ticking and that I had a few days to exercise my rights under the contingency clause in the letter of intent. To make sure I understood, she clarified that if I do not report back to the seller within the time allotted for the due diligence, the contingency clause related to the property inspection may become void. Even if the property had some maintenance issues or it was appraised at a much lower price than the offered purchase price, I could lose any opportunity to renegotiate the purchase price or even legally back out from the deal. What she said worried me, and she could sense my discomfort with being under pressure. She suggested we step out of the car and walk to the Italian restaurant where we could continue our chat over our business lunch.

DUE DILIGENCE MILESTONES

After we went through the menu and selected what to order from the wide variety of Italian dishes, Ms Jing told me of her fascination with Italian cuisine and Italy as a country and briefly described some amazing trips to parts of Italy. She brought us back to our topic by saying that among the most important traits of real estate investors are being attentive and being meticulous.

Such traits are to be exhibited especially during the due diligence process. This is the time to reveal everything pertaining to the property with a thorough investigation to reveal the good, the bad, and the ugly. It's the time when the buyer can get a clear picture of the costs required for property improvement and operational costs. It's the last chance to either renegotiate the deal or walk away from it, as per the contingencies laid down in the letter of intent.

Ms Jing's few words helped me put the whole context of due diligence into a bigger perspective after going through too much detail with Robert earlier that day.

As if she was reading my mind, Ms Jing guessed that I could be feeling that the whole process is overwhelming since a thorough assessment of a property means that there is a long list of things to be looked at, which takes a long time to do. To add to my discomfort, she added that I could be feeling a lot of pressure since I did not have all the time in the world to perform due diligence. I could have anywhere between ten days for single-family homes to thirty days for multifamily properties. She allowed me to reflect on this challenge a moment and then told me that this is where I should use leverage—using other people's time by working with my team members. I started to feel more at ease, like the whole process could be performed within the ten-day period I had in the contingency clause in the letter of intent.

"The time to start due diligence is the same minute the offer is accepted by the seller," Ms Jing asserted. My eyebrow raised, drawing an exclamation mark on my face. She asked: "You might be wondering where to start and whom to contact?" Spot on! She read my mind. She opened her leather notebook so that I could visualize the whole process while she talked through it.

Due diligence is the inspection process that takes place after a buyer's offer is accepted and before taking ownership of the property. This is the buyer's time to inspect and investigate the property before either taking ownership of the property or exiting the deal.

Once all the inspection is done, there are three possible routes on how to proceed:

- If the finding of the inspection is all clear and the property was appraised no less than 5 per cent to 10 per cent (depending on what has been negotiated) of the offered purchase price, the buyer can proceed with the deal as per the agreed-on purchase price, without any further negotiations.
- If the finding of the inspection reveals some non-major repairs and no structural damages, and the property was appraised no less than 5 per cent to 10 per cent (depending on what has been negotiated) of the offered purchase price, the buyer can ask the

seller to make the necessary repairs or request a discount in the
purchase price.

- If the finding of the inspection reveals major repairs, structural
damages, or an appraised value that is more than 10 per cent less
than the offered purchase price, the buyer can exit from the deal
altogether as a result of what is found during the inspection.

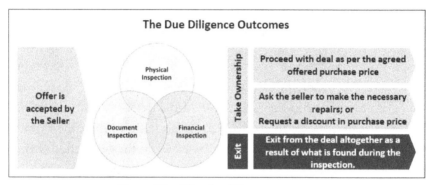

Figure 60—The due diligence outcomes

The whole reason for the due diligence process is to put an estimated
cost for each item in the list, so that the negotiation process with the
seller is based on factual numbers. You do not want to come across as a
buyer who is trying to undergo another round of hustling before signing
the purchase and sale agreement. The problems that were revealed
during the due diligence process can either result in a reduction of
the purchase price or be fixed by the seller before the transfer date.
Whatever may be agreed between both the seller and the buyer at this
stage will be stipulated in the purchase and sale agreement. If this is not
agreed upon in writing, once the sale is closed, the new owner will be
stuck with all those problems and will have to shoulder all the costs—
definitely not a wise move.

EXERCISING THE FINANCING CONTINGENCY

During the due diligence process, after the physical inspection and
property appraisal are performed by a qualified inspector, the bank or

the lender will respond with either an approval or a rejection to finance the property.

The next chapter covers the subject of financing the property. But it is important to highlight in this section some reasons for either the bank declining to finance the property or the buyer opting not to proceed with the deal.

The Lender's Possible Reasons for Declining to Finance the Property

As mentioned earlier in this book, lenders want to limit their risks. If the physical inspection reveals major structural damage or that the property's condition is a state of disrepair, most lenders will decline to finance the property to avoid the risks and headaches. In that case, buyers, especially with no experience in construction, should avoid trying to convince the lender to find a solution. The possible solutions here could relieve the lender from risk but levy a big risk on the buyer.

For example, the lender could require a conditional approval pending a second physical inspection to be performed after all maintenance is carried out. In such a scenario, the buyer may put time and money into improving someone else's property that might never be approved for financing by the bank. Even if the buyer can still convince the seller to perform all such maintenance, the buyer will be losing time and other opportunities. Both Papa Joe and Ms Jing recommended I never enter such deals as a novice investor to avoid being wiped out.

The Buyer Opting Not to Proceed with the Deal

The physical inspection report that the inspector submits to the lender will state the appraised value of the property. In the event the appraised value was way lower than the offered purchase price, the buyer reserves the right to either walk away from the deal or renegotiate it. The difference between the offered price and the appraised value is usually pre-negotiated and agreed upon in the signed letter of intent. This variation is usually between 5 per cent and 10 per cent.

THE FINAL COMMITMENT

The purchase and sale agreement is signed after the seller has agreed to the terms and conditions stipulated in the letter of intent. The timing could be either during the due diligence process or afterward, depending on the common practices in the market where the property is located. The timing does not make a big difference since the same conditions of the letter of intent, including the contingencies, will be transferred to the purchase and sale agreement, which is more legally binding. But as binding as the agreement is, with the right contingencies and language built into the agreement, the buyer can legally walk away from the deal, extend the dates, or renegotiate the offer based on the findings of the due diligence process.

The purchase and sale agreement, which may also be known as a *memorandum of understanding* (MOU) in some countries, could be drafted by the buyer's attorney, by the real estate agent, or it could be a standard template that is mandated by the local authorities. In many instances, the real estate agent will draft the whole contract. This is where all the conditions of the letter of intent will be written in more legal and formal fashion to protect both the buyer and the seller in the purchase and sale process. The purchase and sale agreement also spells out the responsibilities and obligations of each of the seller and the buyer, including how the seller will provide all necessary document and information requested by the buyer or the lender and the transfer date.

What goes into a purchase and sale agreement may vary from country to country and city to city, but there is a common language that is applicable to most countries and cities. You can download a template from my website www.employeemillionaire.com/resources. But always check with your attorney for necessary amendments to make the agreement more legally binding in your area. I will cover in this section some important language that you want to make sure is included in any purchase and sale agreement you sign. Below are clauses you cannot afford to live without. I will dwell on some explanations where required.

Buyer's and seller's information
Property description
Purchase price
Earnest money deposit
Final settlement
Seller's Obligations

The seller confirms the property has a registered title deed that is free of any liens and encumbrances and that the seller has the right and power to sell and transfer to the buyer.

The seller is required to warrant, to the best of the seller's knowledge, information, and belief that:

1. No condemnation proceedings have been instituted against the property.
2. There presently are not pending any special assessments against the property. Such a warranty must survive final settlement.
3. The seller is not aware and has not received any notice whatsoever that the property has or ever had any factor that may hinder rental or resale. Seller's warranties contained in this paragraph must survive final settlement.

On signing this purchase and sale agreement, the seller must not, either by himself or through his attorney or agent or representative, either directly or indirectly through any person:

1. market the property for sale to any third party;
2. enter into an agreement to sell or otherwise transfer ownership of the property or the seller's interest in the property to any third party;
3. increase the agreed purchase price of the property.

The seller warrants that all documentation given to the buyer is correct and furthermore indemnifies the buyer from any financial or other liability that may have arisen prior to completion of the purchase upon the transfer date.

Should the seller have outstanding mortgage liability, the seller agrees to request a liability letter from the seller's bank when requested by the buyer or the buyer's bank or finance company at the seller's expense. The seller is responsible for mortgage discharge fees, including of any other admin fees where applicable, to release any existing mortgage on the property.

The seller must provide the following necessary documents to complete the transfer:

1. The property's original title deed.
2. Original receipts of all payments as per the property's original payment schedule.
3. Any dues, penalties, or unpaid fees or maintenance fees due to the developer and utility companies must be settled before the transfer date. Evidence of payments must be provided.
4. All documents regarding warranties, guarantees, and assignments of all rights to these agreements.
5. Any other document or requirements stipulated by the developer including a *no objection certificate* (NOC) to sell the property.
6. Rental agreement (if applicable). The seller will issue the buyer a rent refund, with the amount pro rata from date of transfer.
7. Evidence of discharge and clearance of mortgage on the property (if applicable).

Buyer's Obligations

The buyer confirms receipt a valid bank preapproval to purchase a property subject to the lending criteria and other terms and conditions of the lending bank. Buyer will instruct their own bank to proceed with arranging a physical inspection and valuation of the property as soon as possible. The seller will make every reasonable effort to provide the necessary access to the property. The property inspection and appraisal fees are to be paid by the buyer.

The buyer agrees to pay the seller, either directly from the buyer's account or from the lending bank, the purchase price agreed upon in this agreement by manager's cheque or any other guaranteed method of payment.

The buyer is responsible for mortgage registration fees, including applicable admin fees, to register a new mortgage on the property.

Contingencies

The buyer, at its sole and unfettered discretion, shall be allowed a ten (10) working day period from opening of escrow to review all property documentation, rent leases with existing tenants, obtain third party reports, and otherwise approve the property. If the buyer determines that for any valid reason the property is not suitable for the buyer's use, the purchase and sale agreement will terminate, the buyer's earnest money deposit must be returned, and neither party will have any liability or obligation to one another.

Penalties

After signing the purchase and sale agreement, the buyer is liable for a penalty of #### (in letters) in case the buyer fails to complete the deal for any reason other than (1) a permitted termination pursuant to the property appraisal report, or (2) the offered purchase price exceeds the value detailed in the property appraisal report by more than ten (10) per cent, or (3) the seller's failure to perform the seller's obligations under this agreement.

Similarly, in case the seller fails to complete the deal for any reason other than the buyer's failure to perform the buyer's obligations under this agreement, the seller is liable for a penalty of #### (in letters) and also reimburses the buyer for all costs reasonably incurred in connection with preparation of the proposed settlement, including but not limited to attorney fees, surveys, lender appraisals and processing fees, and title searches.

Real estate brokerage commission

It must be made clear in the purchase and sale agreement who is going to pay for what.

Transfer and closing fees

It must be made clear in the purchase and sale agreement who is going to pay for what.

Risk of loss

The seller will retain legal ownership of the property until completion and accordingly bears all risk associated with ownership of the property until title transfer to the buyer.

Proration

The agreement must specify all proration for rents, tenants' security deposits, taxes, insurance, homeowners' association fees, and service charges.

Legal enforcements covering disputes

Making the final big commitment and signing on the purchase and sale agreement can be daunting to any buyer, especially in the early stages of their investment career. I remember the day I was going to sign the purchase and sale agreement on my first investment property. Whatever energy and motivation I had, whatever coaching I received, and whatever preparations I had made, I was trembling and scared on that day. I remember wishing I could have an accident on the way to meet the seller for signing to buy more time. When meeting the seller face-to-face to sign the purchase and sale agreement, I was trying to hide my sweaty hands and trembling pen. At the end of the day, I was signing on a property that was worth five times all the savings I had in my entire life. I started imagining all sort of doom and gloom scenarios that might lead me to lose all my savings and the property itself.

After a few deals, I gained confidence. Nowadays, my wife and I sign purchase and sale agreements while engaging in a hobby. We have developed our own templates for each of the cities we invest in. We got used to the process, which we follow faithfully. The whole process and the related forms became part of our language and programming. It is fun and we enjoy the whole action. When a few months pass by without our being engaged in a new purchase, we feel something is wrong and missing.

Chapter 12 Action Steps

After having your offer approved by the seller, approach the lender with either the signed LOI or purchase and sale agreement. This will signal the kick off of the due diligence process by your lender.

Depending on the outcome of the due diligence process, the deal can go on as agreed, can be further negotiated, or can be called off.

CHAPTER 13

Finance Your Rental Property

Contrary to what I had visualized to be an overwhelmingly long and complicated process, the whole due diligence phase, including the appraisal of the property value and the bank approval to finance, took no more than ten days. Thanks to my team members, it took me a couple of days to form a clearer picture on the property's required maintenance, its net operating income, and cash flow projections. I did whatever needed to be done to renegotiate the purchase price and the terms of the deal based on the finding of due diligence. I shook hands with the seller, and an addendum to the agreement that reflected the changes from the original purchase and sale agreement was signed by both parties.

From that point, the financing process kicked in. The bank's representative was in contact with me to coordinate the details of the property financing, including what would go out of my own pocket as cash and what the bank would finance.

The bank's portion had to split further between settling the existing mortgage on the property with the seller's lender and the net payment to the seller. My discussion with the bank's representative included my preparedness for closing fees and title transfer. There payments had to be in the form of manager's cheques, aka cashier's cheques. In order to be fully prepared and avoid mistakes in the financing process, I sought advice from none other than the expert on this subject matter, my dear Joyce.

Later that evening, I had no option but to wait till midnight Manila time to join the video call with Joyce after her office hours in Lebanon, which is in a time zone six hours behind the Philippines. During that call, I shared with her my excitement about being almost to the point of purchasing the property and I told her of my confusion regarding the financing process.

She smiled and thanked me for seeking her advice, which she never hesitated to offer. Joyce was able to share her wisdom, not only as a banker whose area of expertise was mortgage loans, but also from the perspective of belonging to a family of realtors that breathes real estate day in and day out. Once again I thought how blessed I was to have all those coaches and mentors coming into my life. I thanked God for his blessings and guidance.

PROPERTY FINANCING OPTIONS

Although my plan was to purchase a property through a mortgage loan on an 80 per cent loan-to-value, Joyce suggested we discuss both options regarding financing a property: all cash or mortgage loan. She teased me with the thought that financing a property through a mortgage loan can vary from 50 per cent LTV to the standard 75 or 80 per cent LTV, even to 100 per cent LTV. When borrowing 100 per cent of the property value, the investor makes zero down payment from his or her own pocket. The sweet spot varies by investor, depending on objectives, which could be cash flow or a high return on investment.

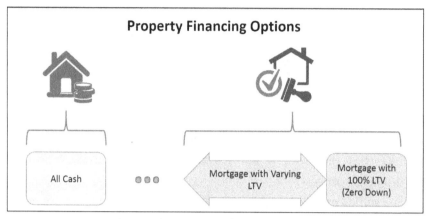

Figure 61—Property financing options

1. Financing a Property on an All-Cash Basis

The topic of purchasing a rental property on all-cash basis appeared to me as counter-intuitive to the benefits of leverage and investing for maximum returns. When we were about to discuss this option, I questioned who would purchase a property for all cash and receive lower cash-on-cash returns as compared to buying on leverage. I couldn't keep this thought to myself so threw it in the form of a question back at Joyce.

"I am a strong advocate of purchasing rental properties on leverage and maximizing returns on investment," Joyce affirmed. However, she wanted to share some scenarios when purchasing a property on all-cash basis might be the right option for some investors. Again, she managed to intrigue me, so I tuned in, and listened. For some investors, buying rental properties all cash could be just right for them.

Earlier in our video call, when Joyce mentioned the *all-cash* option for purchasing a rental property, I imagined the buyer carrying a case of cash and handing it over to the buyer. This idea appeared to be risky. Joyce clarified that *all-cash basis* is only a term used for purchasing a property out of the buyer's own funds. In reality, there is no cash money being traded. All the transactions take place in the form of manager's cheques (aka cashier's cheques) or bank wire transfers. The term *all cash* just means paying means of certified funds.

Reasons for Buying Rental Properties on All-Cash Basis

The most common reasons to purchase rental properties on an all-cash basis, if the person can afford it, are:

- *Avoiding risk of defaulting on mortgage instalments*, which could lead to the lender foreclosing on the property. Investors of that type are risk averse and think that although they have cash now, they are not sure what the future might hold for them.
- *Investing for a higher cash flow*, which means for a higher unearned income. For those investors, all that matters is how much net cash they receive per month. They understand that this high amount of net cash flow could not be the best ROI for their money, but they are quite happy with this equation. For them this could be their retirement plan, where fewer rental properties could secure them unearned income for life and without the risk or hassle of having a mortgage. For those investors, buying on all-cash basis is the right choice.
- *Paying all cash is a step before owning the property with no or little cash later.* This could be a short-term approach for investors who have the cash before financing through a mortgage loan at a later stage. Although this idea was out of my league at that time, Joyce managed to excite me about it and thought it might become useful one day. Indeed, this idea was useful to me, and I adopted this strategy on many of my purchases later in my investment career, when I could easily lay my hand on a lot of cash when I needed it. Excited about this strategy? The next section is dedicated to this topic.

Buying All Cash for Now to Own It with No or Little Cash Later

Joyce took us back to one of our earlier video calls, when she divided the whole financing equation into two halves. The first half is about the eligibility of the borrower, while the second is about the lender approving the property. Once the borrower's eligibility for a loan is confirmed, the lender issues a preapproval letter that has a subtle but important condition: The mortgage loan is computed based on whichever is lower of both the appraised property value and the agreed purchase price.

To better illustrate this point, Joyce asked me to consider a scenario of a property with a $100,000 appraised value done by a professional inspector nominated by the lender. If the investor has negotiated the purchase price for $80,000, which is 20 per cent below market value, by following clear and strict investment criteria and finding motivated sellers, the bank will compute the loan amount by applying the standard 80 per cent loan-to-value (LTV) on the lower amount of $80,000. For investors who would like to consider the discount they have obtained as their down payment in the form of sweat equity, paying all cash for the property and then refinancing it could be a solution.

Going back to our example, if the investor can afford to purchase the property on all-cash basis by paying $80,000 from personal funds, the same property can be refinanced directly afterward based on its appraised value of $100,000. In that case, following the 80 per cent LTV, the mortgage amount will be computed at $80,000 (80 per cent of $100,000). This strategy of paying all cash and then refinancing the property will result in the investor owning a property with zero or little down payment from his or her own pocket. I like this strategy, and I often use it nowadays. I can manage to get my hands on enough cash through tapping into savings, borrowing money on a short-term basis, or my favorite—financing or refinancing other properties I own.

Another advantage of buying a property on an all-cash basis is the ability to hustle for a lower purchase price by benefiting from the sellers' psychology towards their love of the word *cash*.

Sources of Cash

Joyce then shared a few important insights on how all-cash investors could get the cash they require to purchase a property. The most common sources of cash are:

- *Savings:* This is the simplest, easiest, and fastest form of cash. If the investor has enough cash in the bank, payments to purchase the property could be arranged via wire transfers or manager's cheques.

- *Short-term loan:* Many investors can qualify for personal loans or can tap into their existing line of credit to borrow money on a short-term basis. Other options are to borrow from hard or private money lenders, individuals and businesses aimed at financing investments for a return. The interest rates on such short-term loans are usually higher than mortgage loans, but this short-term higher cost in loan instalments is offset by the fact that such investors will be refinancing their properties shortly afterward at market value and end up owning properties with little or nothing out of their own pockets.

- *Financing or refinancing other properties:* This strategy is often overlooked by investors who currently own properties. Those investors can tap into the equity they have in their properties by applying for a mortgage loan on their currently owned properties. Such money will be relatively cheap money, since interest rates on mortgage loans are considered the lowest among any other form of loan.

Getting Cash by Financing or Refinancing Other Properties

An investor can borrow against some of the equity in a currently owned property. Equity is the difference between the current market value of the property and the current mortgage loan on the property. So if the property is currently owned free and clear, which means there is no existing mortgage on the property, the investor can finance the property and borrow up to 80 per cent of the market value of the same property, assuming the investor qualifies for an 80 per cent loan-to-value. If there is an existing mortgage on the property, the investor can refinance it by paying it off and replacing it with a new, larger one. The cash obtained from either financing or refinancing a property could be used towards the purchase of another rental property as either a down payment or as a full payment in cash.

There are other reasons why home owners could choose to finance or refinance the properties they currently own. Such reasons vary and include consolidating their debt into one loan to making use of the cash for other personal reasons (which reasons are beyond the scope of this book).

Drawbacks of Purchasing on an All-Cash Basis

Purchasing a property for cash only can have its advantages from a high cash flow perspective and more peace of mind from not owing any money to any lender, but it also has its own drawbacks. Although I love leverage in the form of good debt, I am not trying to convince you to use it. But I owe it to you to share some of the drawbacks of purchasing a property on all-cash basis.

- *Reduced return on invested capital:* Earlier in this book I demonstrated how leverage will improve the ROI as compared to purchasing a property on all-cash basis. But the upside of purchasing a property for all cash is the maximum net cash flow after all expenses are paid, which will translate into higher unearned income for the owner.

- *Fewer properties that can be purchased:* If a person has $100,000 in cash, this amount can all be used to purchase only one rental property worth $100,000 on an all-cash basis. However, with the use of leverage, on a standard 80 per cent LTV, five properties can be bought with a down payment of $20,000 on each of the properties. The latter example is oversimplified to drive home the point. In reality there will be other fees like commissions and closing costs, which can make the total number of purchases short of five properties, but definitely more than four.

- *Increased risk of litigation:* The more someone's wealth increases, the more this person is susceptible to litigations by other non-well-meaning individuals who are just greedy and looking for prey with enough fat. Investing in rental properties has its own risks and can make any landlord open for lawsuits by resentful tenants. Owning a property free and clear is a sign that the landlord has too much fat, and this makes litigators open their eyes wide for a hefty prey. On the other hand, when the title deed of a property shows a lien from a lender, which indicates that the property has a mortgage, it can keep lawyers far since they will automatically assume the landlord does not have much equity in the property as compared to owning it free and clear.

2. Getting a Mortgage Loan

Conventional loans are the most common standard loans that can be obtained from a bank or a mortgage broker. Getting a mortgage loan on a rental property is no different from getting a loan on a primary residence. Such loans do enjoy low and favourable interest rates, which makes them the most attractive types of loans. As a lender that wishes to manage risks associated with a mortgage loan, the bank will ask the borrower to put a sizable down payment of 20 to 25 per cent of appraised market value of the property. In turn, the bank will lend out the balance of 75 to 80 per cent of the property value to the borrower. This ratio of the loan to the value of the property is commonly referred to as loan-to-value (LTV).

WHY CONVENTIONAL LOANS?

Conventional loans are the most common form of mortgage loans for reasons known to many people. Their main advantages are these:

- *Most competitive interest rates* among loan types. Compared with any other loan for the same term, a mortgage loan with a lower interest rate will have a lower monthly mortgage instalment and therefore will result in a higher cash flow from the property.

- *Long terms* of up to twenty-five or thirty years on residential properties. Dividing the loam instalments over a longer period keeps the monthly mortgage instalments low and thereby improves the property's cash flow.

WATCH-OUTS OF CONVENTIONAL LOANS

It would be unfair to say there are disadvantages to conventional loans. This section is intended as a heads-up regarding what you may encounter down the road of conventional loans, especially when you start purchasing one rental property after another to achieve your objectives. This section will help you to ask the lenders or mortgage brokers in your market about current practices or regulations regarding conventional mortgage loans.

- *Conventional lenders might set a cap on the number of mortgage loans a borrower can have.* The limit on the number of loans varies from one market to another and from one bank to another. The most prevalent limit that is set by banks is anywhere between four to ten properties. The rationale for setting a limit on the number of loans is based on the assumption that the borrower's debt-to-income (DTI) ratio might go down below the approved threshold whenever the number of loans increases. An investor in rental properties can overcome this hurdle by proving to the lender that each of the properties financed with a mortgage loan is delivering a net positive cash flow to the borrower. This in fact will improve the borrower's DTI with the purchase of each additional property and therefore will improve the creditworthiness of the borrower. This is why it is so important to purchase each property below market value (at our target 20 per cent below market value) and rent it out to the right tenants to ensure a positive cash flow after all operating expenses are paid out and the debt is serviced. Another strategy to circumvent the loan limit set by the lenders is to apply for new loans from different banks whenever the borrower's limit is reached with a given bank.

- *The central bank* could set a cap on the number of mortgage loans a borrower can have. In some countries, the central banks regulate the total mortgage loans any individual can have at any given time, irrespective of the lending banks. In those highly regulated markets, the conventional lenders end up selling the loans to the central bank to get their money back and lend it over and over again to new borrowers.

- *The loan-to-value (LTV) might go down with an increasing number of mortgage loans.* Conventional lenders can manage their risks by lowering the LTV when the borrower has more than a set number of mortgage loans. The banks usually start with 75 to 80 per cent LTV on the first property. The LTV can go down to a range of 50 to 60 per cent when the same borrower has more mortgages. It is always wise to ask the banks what their practice is on LTV when you plan to have more than one mortgage. This can be one of your decision criteria on which lender can better fit your plans.

- *Even if the borrower qualifies for a loan, the bank can disapprove a property* due to its condition. Banks will likely not fund deals on properties that are not in good shape. Such a decision is based on the inspection report done in the due diligence process. Sometimes the seller can fix those problems before the bank reassesses the situation. In other instances, the problems are so big that the bank will consider the investment risky. Disapproving such bad property will protect both the bank and the lender.

CREATIVE METHODS FOR HIGHEST LTVS ON CONVENTIONAL LOANS

I love leverage—the leverage used towards the purchase of income-producing assets. Whenever I start doubting myself with the thought that each rental property I am buying with a mortgage loan is making me dig a deeper hole that I can never get out of, I remember Papa Joe's words on good debt: "You will become at least as rich as the amount of good debt you take in your life." I have this advice in the notes on my smartphone, and I make it a point to read it over and over, as often as it takes me to stay focused on my plan.

The more rental properties I can purchase with the maximum leverage, the more rental properties I can own. The caveat here is that the numbers have to work on each property I am planning to purchase with maximum leverage. My rule is simple: Each property shall deliver a positive net cash flow with a wealthy return on investment. As mentioned earlier in the book, an ROI is considered wealthy when the cash on cash returns are greater than two times the interest rate on the mortgage loan and with a minimum of 9 per cent.

With my good understanding of how leverage can work in my favor and with the investment criteria I've set, I love purchasing properties with little or no money down. I believe my hard work of finding and negotiating properties at an average of 20 per cent below market value becomes my right to be considered as my down payment in the form of sweat equity.

On the other hand, banks want to manage their exposure, and they will lend money up to a maximum of 80 per cent loan-to-value. The lenders base the value of the property on whichever is lower from the purchase price mentioned in the purchase and sale agreement and the appraised value from the property inspection report. Lenders are smart, and their rule can make my objective of purchasing a property with little or no money down almost impossible.

Thanks to all the mortgage brokers and loan officers who were on my team over the years, I have learned the tricks of the trade in overcoming such rules set by the lenders. Before you attempt to practice the creative methods in getting the highest possible LTVs—up to 100 per cent LTV—on conventional mortgage loans, make sure you inquire that it is legal to use any of the following creative strategies in your market.

- *Favourable sale* is a term used by banks in certain markets when the borrower buys a property below market value. In some markets, purchasing a property at a lower price gives you immediate equity, and some lenders have excellent policies that allow you to maximize the amount you can borrow when buying a property below market value. Things have gotten more difficult since the financial crisis of 2008, but in certain markets, some lenders are willing to loan 90 or 95 per cent of the appraised market value. They won't take the purchase price into account. If this strategy works in your market, then good for you. Just ask different lenders if they have such progressive loans, and you will be all set with the least amount of hassle.

- *Gift of equity* refers to a gift that represents a portion of the seller's equity in the property, transferred by the seller to the buyer as a credit in the transaction. This scenario can apply when the negotiated purchase price is less than the property's fair market value. The difference in the purchase price and the appraised value is considered a gift of equity. This strategy can be perfectly acceptable by some lenders in some markets, as long as the necessary documentation to prove the amount of the gift and confirm that no repayment is expected or required is filled out by the seller.

- *Trade for equity* happens when the buyer trades something other than cash for equity. This could be another property, land, a car, or any other valuable. This form of trading equity for down payment is legal and could be acceptable by many lenders. The creativity of both the seller and the buyer could border the grey area here, approaching what is considered to be illegal in some markets. The most common borderline creative practice is when the seller and the buyer conspire by agreeing on a higher purchase price than what is actually agreed upon. The higher purchase price will be at market value, which makes the lender still believe in this artificial purchase price and allows the buyer to get more financing and leverage. In such situations, the seller and buyer might end up having two sets of agreements, one for the purpose of loan documentation and another for the purpose of the actual agreement between them. In some other more creative situations, there will be only one purchase and sale agreement at the higher purchase price, but with a protection clause that mentions that the buyer has already paid the seller a non-refundable down payment—equivalent to the difference between the actual agreed purchase price and the higher one at market value.

- *Pay "all cash" at a discounted price and finance at market value* is a straightforward strategy that can work well for buyers who either have the cash available or can get access to the necessary cash. I covered this strategy at the beginning of this chapter.

A range of possibilities is available for you on getting the most possible leverage after all the hard work in getting a seller to agree to sell at a well-negotiated, discounted selling price. All you need to do is investigate what works best in your market, with your lender, for the seller, and for you.

OTHER TYPES OF LOANS

So far we have covered the most common type of loans—conventional loans—and how they might have their own limitations when the number of loans increases for the same borrower. An investor who has reached the maximum number of mortgage loans, which might be set by the bank or the central bank, and still wants to acquire mortgage loans at 70 to 80 per cent LTV, might need to seek other types of loans. This section explains the other types of loans from different types of lenders, in no particular order of importance or preference.

Portfolio Lenders

Most conventional banks are under a strict central bank's regulations. Central banks set the IBOR (interbank offered rate), which is the interest rate at which conventional banks lend to and borrow from one another or from the central bank in the interbank market. Central banks also offer home loans programs, generally referred to as *government insured home loans*, which are guaranteed by the government. Many conventional banks avoid the risks of holding mortgages, only profiting from origination fees and then quickly selling off the mortgages to other financial institutions or to the central bank. However, there is a category of banks known as portfolio lenders that operate in a different way. A portfolio lender is a financial institution that not only originates mortgage loans but also holds a portfolio of loans instead of selling them off in the secondary market. A portfolio lender makes money off the fees for originating the mortgages and also seeks to make profits off the difference between the interest received from loans and the interest paid on deposits. Because portfolio lenders lend their own money, the rules limiting the maximum number of mortgage loans set by the central banks may not necessarily be enforced on portfolio lenders.

It is not easy to recognize which of the banks or financial institutions are either conventional or portfolio lenders. The answer cannot be obtained by asking the loan officers whether their financial institution is a portfolio lender. Such answers can be obtained by investigating whether their financial institution does place a cap on the maximum number of loans any borrower can have at any one time.

Real estate investors can find portfolio lenders as strong partners for their growing investments. The interest rates on the mortgage loans may be a bit higher as compared to conventional loans. By all means make sure to run the numbers to determine whether the property will still have a positive net cash flow after all expenses, including mortgage instalments, are paid out. You will need also to determine the cash on cash returns to determine if the whole investment will remain a wealth-producing rate of return even with slightly higher interest rates.

Private Lenders and Hard Money Lenders

Both private lending and hard money lending are forms of private lending. The difference lies with the entity lending the money. In private lending, the lender is a private individual; whereas in hard money lending, the lender is a professional private institutional lender. For the sake of discussion, we will refer to both types of lending as private lending in this section.

Private lending is heavily dependent on relationships with family members, friends, or any other person who has enough cash to lend out for a profit. Such types of loans are flexible by nature, and the rules of qualifications are more lenient as compared to professional lending institutions. Loan-to-value in private lending can reach 100 per cent of the property value, and even more than 100 per cent to fund any maintenance and repairs required on the property. Private lenders want to put their money to work hard for them, so they lend it out to borrowers with a secured collateral (the property itself), at an interest rate that beats saving their money in a bank or investing in the stock market. The interest rate on private lending is higher than conventional lending and can reach up to 12 per cent. Investors may opt for this type of lending as a short-term approach until they qualify for a conventional loan with more competitive interest rates.

Partnerships

Partnership is two investors joining hands and leveraging each other's strengths to overcome each other's weaknesses. This works well with investors who have developed a solid reputation in finding and investing in great deals that reap wealth-producing returns. Such investors will draw money towards them like a magnet to fund future deals. On the other side of the coin will be investors with deep pockets or with access to cash who want to partner on investments that produce great returns. Both investors offer different things to the deal. In fact, they complement each other. One offers to manage the investment and the other offers to get the funds.

Partnership is not as straightforward as it may appear on paper. Partners should share similar principles on investments, and their objectives shall be aligned. Partnership is a long-term kind of relationship, and choosing the wrong partner could be similar to getting married to a spouse you don't get along or have anything in common with. I have heard many stories of successful partnerships as well as others that failed. I personally have never engaged in partnerships on real estate investment as of the writing of this book. I am not sure if someday I might have a different opinion. Only time will tell.

STEPS IN FINANCING A RENTAL PROPERTY WITH A MORTGAGE LOAN

I have discussed the property financing process throughout this book. The focus of this chapter is on financing rental properties, so this would the right moment to recap on the whole process.

Financing consists basically of two major phases, starting with getting preapproved for a loan as a borrower, followed by getting the property approved for the loan. The graph below allows you to visualize the whole process.

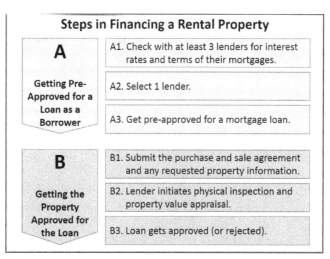

Figure 62—Steps in financing a rental property

Getting Preapproved for a Loan

Check for Interest Rates and Terms of Mortgages

The first step in financing is to start shopping around for a loan. I recommend that you check with at least three lenders to receive quotes for their interest rates and the terms and conditions of the different available loans. A good start is to check with large multinational banks, national banks, and smaller local banks. My personal preference is for small local banks for their flexibility and competitive rates. It is always wise to check with the bank where you currently hold a checking account.

Once you identify potential lenders, the next step will be to contact their respective loan officers to schedule an appointment. This is where the details of the different loan programs will be presented to you with all required paperwork. Based on your current financial situation, the loan officers will be able to give you a rough estimate of your eligibility for the mortgage loan.

Other options, like checking with private lenders, are also possible. But such loans come at higher interest rates and shorter terms, which makes them not the preferred type of lenders for most borrowers. There is no right or wrong answer here. This option could be the right one for you, as long as the math works and the numbers do add up to a successful potential investment with a positive cash flow and an ROI in line with your objectives.

Select One Lender

Once you have enough information on the different loan programs from different lenders, you can pick the lender that best suits your needs and with the most competitive loan program.

Get Preapproved for a Mortgage Loan

In this step, the lender will request all the documents related to your financial situation to determine your eligibility for a loan. This is when you as a borrower get prequalified for a mortgage loan. At the end of this step, you will receive a preapproval letter that states the approved loan amount.

Getting the Property Approved for the Loan

Submit the Property Information

With a preapproval letter in your hands, you will start prospecting for properties until you find one that meets all your investment criteria. In this step, you tie up the property and sign the purchase and sale agreement. At this stage, the second phase of getting the property approved for financing kicks in. The lender will request a copy of the purchase and sale agreement and possibly other documents related to the property.

The Lender Initiates Physical Inspection and Property Value Appraisal

The lender will start studying the property file and will initiate both a physical inspection and a value appraisal, which are done by a professional appraiser nominated by the lender. During this step, the bank needs to know that their investment is safe and that the property is worth more than the loan amount. The physical inspection also ensures the bank less potential risk on the property for the future.

Although this step is initiated by the lender, all the related fees are paid in advance by the borrower.

The Loan Is Approved or Rejected

After the appraisal is completed and the lender receives the report from the appraiser, the bank reviews the whole loan file, including the borrower's financial health, and makes a final decision whether to approve or reject the loan.

If the loan is approved, you will be notified in writing with the bank's final offer, which includes the details of the property, your down payment, the loan amount, the interest rates, the terms of the loan, the conditions for insurance, and the monthly instalments of the loan. Once you approve the bank's final offer, a closing date is determined. During this stage, the loan officer will work with you and guide you on all the steps and payments required for closing and the transfer of title in your name.

Chapter 13 Action Steps

Following the due diligence process, your lender will make a final decision on whether the loan will be approved or rejected.

If the loan is approved, the lender will send a written final offer.

Once you sign the bank's final offer, the loan officer will coordinate with you on the next step: the title transfer.

CHAPTER 14

Transfer the Title

All the hard work and the preparations in finding great deals, going through the due diligence process, and securing a mortgage has led to fruition. This is the long-awaited moment, the closing or final settlement, which is the date of the title transfer to the buyer's name. After receiving the final financing approval by the bank and signing on the bank's final loan offer, the closing date was well coordinated with all stakeholders: the seller, the bank's representative, the real estate agent, and of course the buyer. Irrespective of the number of properties I have purchased throughout my investment career, the step of transferring the title is often accompanied by a mixed set of emotions, ranging from excitement to concerns. Nothing is more exciting than the feeling of getting close to ending a long marathon and winning a prize that increases your wealth and produces unearned income. At the same time, before paying the seller, there is a tendency for buyers to second-guess their decisions and start feeling a bit of a concern whether all the math was done properly and whether the property will indeed enable them to achieve their objectives. I often find this mixed feeling of excitement and concern quite thrilling.

The exciting news about the settlement process is that both the buyer and the seller need to do little about transferring the title. In essence, settlement is a brief process during which all of the necessary paperwork will be completed and the transaction will be signed. During the closing meeting, the buyer receives the keys and the seller receives payment for the property. Deeds, loan papers, and other documents are prepared, signed, and filed with local property record offices.

Paperwork is often executed at the local property record offices or online. The end result is the buyer receiving the title to the property, the seller getting paid, the lender having the mortgage loan registered in the public records, the real estate agent getting paid, and the relevant government agencies collecting their transfer taxes or fees. All this paperwork and payments will take place in a matter of a few minutes and the buyer will walk out of this meeting as the new owner of the property.

This chapter will take you through all the required preparations for a smooth settlement.

THE FINAL PROPERTY WALK-THROUGH—THE RULE OF 24H

Before closing, the buyer has a final opportunity to walk through the property to assure that its condition has not changed considerably since the purchase and sale agreement was signed. This is when the buyer can also check whether any previously agreed maintenance and repair has been actioned by the seller and whether the work was done properly as per agreement.

The best time to conduct a final property walk-through is either on the same day of closing or the day before. Papa Joe follows the *rule of 24H* for any property he is about to purchase. This rule means that either the buyer or his representative will conduct the final property walk-through within twenty-four hours of the closing date. All the buyer has to do is set up an appointment with the seller to walk the property one last time before closing. This will allow the buyer to verify that the property is in the exact same expected condition as agreed upon in the purchase and sale agreement. During the walk-through, if the buyer finds any damage to the property, notices something has been removed, or notices any agreed repairs and maintenance not done, the buyer shall must it up with the seller immediately and may agree with the seller to postpone the closing date until issues are resolved.

GETTING PREPARED FOR CLOSING

A few days before closing, the real estate agent will be coordinating with the bank's representative to guide the buyer on all the preparations that are required on the date of closing. Below are the most important things a buyer needs to prepare for closing:

- Official government-issued photo ID that prove the identity of the buyer. A government-issued ID is also required for anyone else whose name will appear on the new title deed. Note that IDs need to match the names that will appear on the property's title and mortgage.
- Personal presence of the buyer and anyone else whose name will appear on the title deed.
- Original copy of the signed purchase and sale agreement.
- Certified cheques in the amount of the buyer's down payment.
- Certified cheques for the closing fees and mortgage registration fees.
- Certified cheques for the agent's commission, if applicable.
- Personal chequebook or some cash to pay smaller unforeseen fees that might crop up. Personal cheques are usually not accepted for large payments though they might be accepted for minor payments.

At the same time, the real estate agent will be coordinating with the seller on all the preparations that are required from the seller's end on the date of closing. Below is the list of the most important things a seller needs to prepare for closing:

- Official government-issued photo ID that proves the identity of the seller. A government-issued ID is also required for anyone else whose name already appears on the current title deed. Note that IDs need to match the names appearing on the property's title.

- Personal presence of the seller and anyone else whose name already appears on the title deed.
- Original copy of the signed purchase and sale agreement.
- The original title deed.
- Certified cheques for the closing fees and mortgage release fees, if applicable.
- Certified cheques for the agent's commission, if applicable.
- Personal chequebook or some cash to pay smaller unforeseen fees that might crop up.
- Keys to the properties.
- Access cards, if applicable.
- Proof of settlement of all utility bills, property taxes, developer's service fees, homeowner association fees, and any other contracted service fees as of the date of closing.
- Original rental agreement if the property is currently rented out to tenants.

As a buyer, preparing all the necessary documents and payments is crucial to a successful transfer of the title deed. Whereas the documents listed above are straightforward to prepare, getting the computation of the payments for final settlement right could be a bit confusing. When I was about to purchase my first property, I was mixed up in preparing for the certified cheques. I did the computations over and over so that I would avoid overpaying or underpaying the seller, the agent, or for any of the closing fees. I was aware that any discrepancy in the cheques could mean losing a day and then rescheduling the closing date until I could get the payments in order. The section below will guide you on how to prepare for the necessary payments that fall under the buyer's obligations.

SETTING UP SEPARATE BANK ACCOUNTS FOR YOUR RENTAL PROPERTY

As soon as your mortgage loan gets approved and a few days before settlement, the lending bank will disburse the mortgage loan amount into a new bank account that has been setup by the lender. The disbursed loan will not be yet at your disposal. In fact, as soon as the loan amount is disbursed to this account, the bank will automatically arrange for certified cheques to be issued on your behalf for final settlement.

Have your lender set up the bank account for you. It will make managing the finances of your rental property easier. As a rule of thumb, you should keep your rental property transactions, income, and expenses, separate from your personal expenses. In other words, mixing personal bank accounts with rental business accounts will just complicate your finances and bookkeeping. If your lender does not have the practice of setting up for you a separate account for the mortgage loan, then do yourself a favor and open a separate account to manage the new loan mortgage and the property income and expenses.

In managing your rental property and its finances, you will have ongoing transactions like rental income, operational expenses, and mortgage loan instalments. So it makes sense to have a current checking account. On the other hand, you will also be receiving security deposits from tenants, which are to be returned to them upon when they leave the property someday. So you will need to have those security deposits managed separately and saved in a savings account that will not be used for monthly operations of the property. It is simple to set up both the checking account and the savings account. I suggest you do so before closing and before loan disbursement. I also recommend that you open separate accounts—checking or savings— for each of the properties you purchase in the future, even if all their mortgage loans are obtained from the same lender.

In managing your rental property, you will be paying for operating expenses from your checking account. Therefore a chequebook would be useful. So it makes sense to request a chequebook at this point so that you are all set from day one in managing your rental business.

SCHEDULE OF PAYMENTS FOR FINAL SETTLEMENT

A few days before final settlement, the real estate agent will send you a document showing the detailed computations of both the seller's and the buyer's obligations in terms of payments. This will be an updated computation from what was previously provided when you signed the purchase and sale agreement. I always found such a document, which details all payments, quite useful in getting all the certified cheques in order and in arranging for any cash that might be needed for smaller fees. I always use it as a guide in organizing all the payment I am obligated to make.

In the few transactions where no real estate brokerage was involved in the deal, the loan officers of the lending banks were always of great help. In the rare event that I did not find adequate help from either a real estate agent or a bank's representative, I have used my own "Schedule of Payments for Final Settlement", which I explain in this section to help you prepare the certified cheques for payment to the seller, fees for the real estate agent, mortgage registration fees, and closing fees.

To better explain the schedule of payments for final settlement, I have summarized in the table below the most common payment obligations for both the buyer and seller. Note that not all fees or costs may be applicable on every closing. The schedule of payments makes you inquire on each of the payments so that you are better prepared with your part of the obligations on the closing day.

Buyer's and Seller's Payments Obligations	Buyer	Seller
Purchase Price	P	
Closing Fees	C1	C2
Mortgage Registration/Release	M1	M2
Real Estate Brokerage Fees	R1	R2
Total Payments Obligations	P+C1+M1+R1	C2+M2+R2

The buyer's and seller's payment obligations include the following:

- *Closing fees*, which are basically the recording fees that are paid to the government office that is responsible for recording real estate transfers in the city where the property is located. Fees vary widely from one city to another and usually depend on the purchase price or the value of the property. The local authorities may charge for taxes on real estate transactions, which are based on property value. Don't worry about the actual figures. Your real estate agent will guide you on such fees before the closing date.

- *Mortgage registration and mortgage release* are fees that become due on closing, as applicable. If the buyer is financing the purchase of the property with a mortgage loan, the mortgage will be registered with the local authorities for a fee. The government requires a mortgage loan to be registered so that all claims on the property can be checked by any future buyer. In the event the property was previously mortgaged, the seller's lender will release the mortgage only when the seller's lender gets paid for the balance of the loan. A release of a mortgage is the removal of the lender's lien on the property. The seller is liable for the mortgage release fee. Only when the previous mortgage is released on the government documents, can a new mortgage be registered. This process of mortgage registration and release acts as a protection for the lenders, the buyer, and the seller.

- *Real estate brokerage fees* are due on the day of closing. Depending on the practices in your area and whether both the buyer's agent and the seller's agent were involved in the transaction, both the buyer and seller may be responsible to pay commissions that become due on the date of transfer. Such commissions will not be any surprise to either the seller or the buyer since these should have already been agreed on when both parties signed the purchase and sale agreement.

- *Proration for any payment made by the seller or due by the seller* is often computed on a pro rata basis as of the closing date. The seller will produce all receipts of payments that prove that all utility bills, property taxes, developer's service fees, homeowner association fees, and any other contracted service fees have been settled. Any excess payment made by the seller for the period extending after the closing day will be paid by the buyer in cash or personal cheques on the day of closing. Similarly, in case the seller has failed to pay such fees, the seller will be liable to pay the buyer those amounts in cash or personal cheques on the day of closing. In case the property is being purchased while rented, the seller will need to hand over to the buyer any security deposit from the tenant, balance of the rent for the remaining period of the existing rental agreement.

- *The purchase price* is the price that has been agreed upon in the purchase and sale agreement. This is the largest amount due by the buyer and the buyer's lender on closing. The source of funds for payments to the seller and to the seller's lender (in case the seller has a mortgage loan on the property) is from the buyer and the buyer's lender. In preparation for payments for the purchase price, the buyer and the buyer's lender will agree before the closing date on:
  o What will the buyer pay?
  o What will the buyer's lender pay?
  o What will the seller's lender receive?
  o What will the seller receive in net?

Given that lenders may be involved at both ends of the deal, the buyer is interested in how much is going out from his or her own pocket as down payment. In a similar fashion, the seller will be computing the net amount that he or she will be receiving after the seller's lender gets paid first. Below are two simple equations and a figure that explains the different scenarios.

Figure 63—Purchase price payments to seller and seller's lender

$$\begin{pmatrix} Down\ Payment \\ from\ Buyer \end{pmatrix} = \begin{pmatrix} Purchase \\ Price \end{pmatrix} - \begin{pmatrix} Buyer'sApproved \\ Loan \end{pmatrix}$$

$$\begin{pmatrix} Net\ to \\ Seller \end{pmatrix} = \begin{pmatrix} Purchase \\ Price \end{pmatrix} - \begin{pmatrix} Seller's\ Outstanding \\ Loan \end{pmatrix}$$

THE CLOSING DAY

In spite of having all my documents prepared and my certified cheques arranged, I couldn't help thinking about what I expected to happen at the closing meeting the next day. On my first experience, I called in turn Papa Joe, my real estate agent, and the bank's representative to try to get from them more insights on the closing day. I always wanted to be prepared and on top of my game. And I do not want you to go through the same worries about the closing meeting. This section lays out for you what to expect to happen at closing.

- *Where will closing take place?* Depending on the country or city where the property is registered, the transfer of title may take place in either the title company office or the government office responsible for recording real estate transfers.
- *Who will be present at closing?* All stakeholders in the transaction are supposed to make an appearance at the venue with their government-issued IDs. The cast includes the seller, the buyer, the real estate agent (both the seller's agent and buyer's agent where applicable), seller and buyer attorneys (if applicable), a representative from the title company, and a representative from the bank or lender where the buyer is getting the mortgage loan.
- *What will happen during closing?* Both the seller and the buyer will sign a pile of legal documents and pay their respective share of the fees and closing costs. The seller will get paid, the new mortgage will be registered in public records, the title will be transferred into the buyer's name, and finally the buyer will leave as the new owner of the property, with a stack of important documents and the keys to the property. The whole process takes anywhere between an hour to two hours.
- *Are hiccups expected?* Experience has taught me to be prepared for the possibility that things might go off track at closing. For some reason, there is often someone getting stuck in traffic, a document is missing, a name is misspelled, or a certified cheque is issued with wrong information. By managing my expectations and allowing for a few hiccups during the closing meeting, I often dedicate a good two to three hours for the process to take place. This has always helped in managing my stress level when delays do take place. With the evolution of e-government processes and online submission of documents, there might often be system delays or technical issues. It is not a surprise when sometimes the process is not concluded on the same day and might take a day or two. If the transfer of title will not happen during the closing meeting, the buyer will receive a call when it is finished, and the real estate agent or a representative from the title company office or the government

office responsible for recording real estate transfers will hand over the keys and the documents proving the transfer of title into the buyer's name. Depending on the practices in different cities, the new title deed with the buyer's name might be handed over to the new buyer or kept in the safe with the lending bank. Whatever the process might be in your area, do not get worried. You will receive proper guidance from your real estate agent, the bank's representative, and your core team members.

Once the title gets transferred into your name, you will be the proud owner of a property that you have worked hard for a long time to acquire. After taking a few breaths to celebrate the success in purchasing the right property, a new chapter will start. You will need to get busy renting the property to tenants and managing its operations.

Chapter 14 Action Steps

Prepare for the title transfer into your name. In preparation for that important date, it is important to have the whole set of documents and payments arranged and in order to ensure a swift and smooth title transfer, without the need to reschedule or to delay any further.

CHAPTER 15

Rent Your Property

After closing on my first property on a Friday afternoon, I called Joyce and Papa Joe to make them the first to know about it. Both were happy for me. Joyce wanted to visit me in the Philippines to explore the country, get a feeling for my lifestyle, and to see the property. Papa Joe was proud of me for being transformed from a person who had only liabilities to a person who was starting to accumulate assets.

Over our phone call, Papa Joe reminded me that my new property would not be considered an income-producing asset until I managed to rent it out to the right tenant and the right rental income, which had to be more than the property operating expenses and the mortgage loan instalments. Papa Joe suggested we meet in an hour at a famous posh French café for a snack and a coffee.

The time was close to sunset. I arrived a few minutes early and waited for a few minutes until Papa Joe and a surprise guest arrived. In walked Ms Jing with Papa Joe. I immediately presumed our meeting would become an interesting coaching session by two of my favorite coaches.

After small talk over delicious French pastry and coffee, Papa Joe asked: "So you own it. Now what?"

I replied that I was definitely planning to rent it out as per the plan I had set.

"Good plan," he replied, "but how? Have you started yet?"

Ms Jing jumped into the conversation with the story of her first rental property. She did not want me to go through the same pain of not finding a tenant for weeks and months while paying the monthly loan instalments and the operational expenses from my own pocket—which was unsustainable.

Ms Jing silently reflected on how to present her thoughts in a way a novice to rental property investment could understand. She suggested we talk about getting the property rent ready first. Then we could go through the process of renting and managing the property.

GETTING THE PROPERTY RENT READY

The objective of owning a rental property is to generate unearned income to its owner. The money-making machine can generate income for life if well protected, insured, and kept in a good, rent-ready condition.

Insurance and Protection

Before tenants move in, a responsible landlord will protect his income-producing asset to avoid legal hassles and costly disputes with tenants. Any property is at risk of facing incidents like fire, floods, and water leaks. A landlord can get adequate insurance coverage that is specific to rental insurance coverage.

In chapter 10, we covered the type of mortgage insurance required by lenders, which covers the property up to the value of the mortgage. This kind of mortgage insurance usually has two components: life insurance to the borrower (the landlord), and hazard insurance to protect against property loss. With tenants occupying the property, the landlord needs to seek additional coverage, *landlord liability insurance*, which protects against:

- *Personal injuries to the tenant or tenant guest.* Such coverage provides protection against both medical and legal bills that arise from injuries on a rental property. Many laws hold the landlord liable for personal injuries that occur on the property, if proven that they resulted from the landlord's negligence in maintenance. With proper coverage of the medical and legal fees related to injuries, both the landlord and the income-producing asset are well protected.
- *Property damage* caused by tenant, tenant guest, or incidents like fire, floods, and water leaks. Such coverage is not limited only to the cost of repair of any damage, but also extends to the extreme case of covering for loss of income if the property becomes uninhabitable for the duration of the repair.

Landlord liability insurance is usually an add-on to the existing mortgage insurance or traditional homeowner's insurance policy. It comes at an inexpensive incremental cost, which is worth the cost to protect your rental business. Papa Joe also recommended seeking additional protection on the mortgage insurance for coverage on the value of the property instead of the value of the mortgage loan. This is another minimal cost for full protection against loss.

Does a Landlord Need an LLC for Protection?

When Ms Jing was closing on the topic of insurance, Papa Joe added his bit of advice on the topic of protection with LCCs, which is often confusing when it comes to owning single-family properties. LLC stands for *limited liability corporation.* These are intended to help landlords manage and contain the outcome of legal lawsuits against a landlord. The topic of owning properties under LLCs is confusing to many real estate investors. Real estate gurus always preach about LLCs and recommend them for real estate investors. But those gurus rarely clarify that LLCs can offer great protection for multifamily properties. When it comes to single-family homes, LLCs might not be the right option since lenders rarely offer mortgage loans for single-family properties owned by LLCs. Other challenges are the setup costs of an LLC and the recurring annual fees, which can be exorbitant in some countries to the extent it may lead to a single-family home operating with negative cash flow.

On the other hand, the number of individual rental units in multifamily properties can justify the LLC costs. Multifamily homes fall into the category of commercial properties, and the lending process is not dependent on the borrower as an individual but on the property's operations. Therefore, lending to an LLC is the common practice. One of the main advantages of LLCs is the *limited liability benefit*, which limits liability to the assets within the LLC—and not everything else the landlord owns. Another benefit of an LLC is its tax advantages, which vary from one country to another.

Before you decide whether an LLC is the right option for you, ask a lawyer or a CPA who can properly guide you. If an LLC is not the right solution for your case, remember that adequate insurance can offer you enough protection.

Having the Property in Rent-Ready, Habitable Condition

Before listing the property for rent, it *should* be in rent-ready, habitable condition. The best approach is always to negotiate with the previous landlord to have all the required maintenance and repair done before the transfer of title into your name. This section covers the alternative approach of not having the property rent-ready upon closing.

Despite the advice I received in my investment career, I fell into the mistake of trying to skim on the budget and rent a few of my newly bought properties without having them in rent-ready condition. Whatever was supposed to be a savings ended up costing me not only the cost of repair and maintenance, but also the cost of losing rent for longer periods or the cost of attracting the wrong type of tenants. Do not make the same stupid mistakes I made. Just learn from others' mistakes and move on.

The two most common bad consequences of not having a property rent ready before renting it out are these:

- Rental properties generally stay on the market for long periods if they are not fixed up and made rent ready. As an investor in rental properties, you will need the rental income to cover the property's operating expenses and its mortgage loan settlements. Any delay in having the property rented means paying all costs out of your pocket.

- Tenants who might agree to rent properties that are not rent ready are often what I call "headache tenants". They are the kind who take advantage of weaknesses in the property to hustle for discounts on the rent and for delays on rent payments. The headache starts from day one of negotiating on the rent or from the first day they move in. This annoyance tends to get bigger over time. Whether they are evicted or they willingly move out, it will be a big challenge to get them to make any repair to the property since they will play the wild card: We received the property in bad condition. On the other hand, when you hand over the property in rent-ready good condition, you leave little room for smart tenants who are into playing the game of "the property was not in good condition when we moved in".

Papa Joe's rule of thumb is: Fix it up first and get it rented second. I always attempt to have a property fixed up by the previous owner before closing. My second option is to always fix it up on day one of owning it. Every day counts. Every day that goes by without the rental income is a day lost. Once fixed up, I take all the necessary photos that prove its condition at the time of handover to the tenants. The tenants are also requested to sign a *move-in checklist* acknowledging the property's condition at the time of move-in.

RENTING AND MANAGING YOUR RENTAL PROPERTY

Once the property is rent ready, it will be time to get busy finding the right tenants. Renting a property consists of three main stages, with a pit stop between each of the stages.

- Attract
    - o Set the rules
- Manage
    - o Check against the rules
- Retain or evict

The following figure visually explains the whole process.

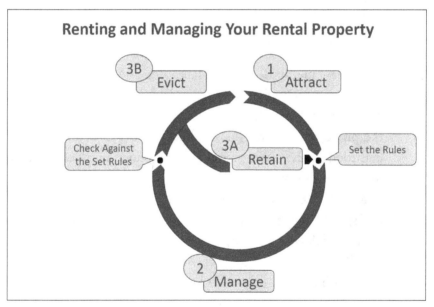

Figure 64—Renting and managing your rental property

Attracting Tenants

Attracting tenants is about finding the right tenant at the right time and at the right rent. Papa Joe warned me that any compromise on any of the three components will result in attracting the wrong type of tenants that will make my rental business suffer from losses and operational issues.

Both Papa Joe and Ms Jing were emphatic about attracting the right tenants. People around us in the French café were turning towards our table when the level of energy and excitement went up. Both Papa Joe and Ms Jing were providing their experience and stories while I was like a dry sponge, wanting to learn and take as many notes as I could.

Marketing to Potential Tenants

Finding the right tenant at the right time and at the right rent is all about marketing. There are different channels to market your property to potential tenants. The cost and the time required from your end will vary among them. I will outline the most impactful marketing channels in order of increasing cost and increasing time required by the landlord.

1. *For Rent sign.* This is one of the least expensive, most effective, and oldest methods, used by landlords and real estate agents long before technology made available alternative marketing channels with much wider reach. The sign should include the property's features (its size and number of bedrooms and bathrooms), the asking rent, and the phone number. What I like about this method is that it is targeted towards attracting potential tenants who are looking around for properties to rent in a specific neighbourhood. The For Rent sign is easy to place for a standalone single-family home or townhouses on their own lots. With a single-family unit within an apartment building or condominium, the unit owner may not be allowed to have For Rent signs displayed since it would mar the appearance of the entire building. The alternative approach for such a challenge is to inform the building management office that you have a vacant property for rent.

2. *Online property listing.* With technological advancement and the emergence of highly effective applications on smart phones, online property listing is becoming the most-used channel

among potential tenants who are scanning for properties to rent. In many markets, this method has overtaken conventional advertising in newspapers. A property listing in an online property listing platform can be free or at minimal cost. The beauty of such platforms is that they allow the end users (the tenants) to search and browse by any filter they choose. When you list your property on an online platform, fill in every single detail on your property, which will allow the tenants to find your property through the search filters. When a potential tenant lands on a page where your property is listed, the final decision to consider your property lies in having professionally taken photos that do justice to the property.

3. *Other tenants.* If you own other properties in the same neighbourhood or the same apartment building, your current tenants can be your ambassadors who can attract their friends or relatives. This is free or cheap marketing that works well. After all, who doesn't like to choose their own neighbor?

4. *Newspapers.* This conventional marketing channel is on the decline and is being replaced with online platforms. On the other hand, the older generation still likes to read the news with the format it has been used to most of its life. With the decline in newspaper readership, the cost of a classified ad is becoming competitive. It might be worthwhile to check the costs with your local newspaper.

5. *Real estate agents.* This is one of the fastest marketing channels. It comes at cost to either the landlord or the tenant, depending on the practices in a given market. The real estate agent cost can be shouldered by the tenant or the landlord or can be split between them. Real estate agents always have potential tenants on their lists and can have a property rented out in hours or a few days. I always use their help since their service comes at no cost or minimal cost for me in most of the locations where I own rental properties.

Screening for the Right Prospective Tenants

With a combination of the marketing channels discussed above, you will be receiving calls from interested prospective tenants. As a landlord who aims to select the right tenant, you need the right tools to screen the prospective tenants. Tenants that pass through all or most of the selection criteria filters are the ones who can qualify for a house viewing before a final decision is taken from both parties.

There are many approaches to screening prospective tenants, ranging from screening through the phone or asking them to fill out a rent application form. Given that most new landlords have a day job, landlords enduring long phone calls to allow them to screen potential tenants might not be the right option. I prefer and always ask prospective tenants to fill out a rent application form that includes the following vital information:

Applicant's Details:	Full name
	Copies of government issued IDs
	Contact details
	Emergency contact details
	Family size
	Number of occupants of the property
	Pets details, if any
	Smoking / non-smoking
	Any previous court judgment or bankruptcy
Rental History:	Previous two addresses
	Monthly rent, duration of tenancy, and reasons for leaving each
	Contact details of the two previous landlords
Credit Check:	Employment history
	Income verification
	Credit score

With a large smile on his face, Papa Joe shared weird stories about all types of tenants who fake the data in the application forms. In spite of many bad experiences he has encountered, Papa Joe's advice was to trust the information but verify it. Below are some pragmatic approaches to verifying prospective tenants' information provided in the rent application:

- Employment certificate from the tenant's employer stating income and length of service.
- Police clearance report that shows good conduct and no previous criminal history.
- Inquiring with the two previous landlords about the prospective tenant's rental payment history, housekeeping, and property maintenance.
- Third party tenants screening services, which are becoming widely used across many developed countries. This kind of service is still non-existent in many developing countries. The reports generated by those agencies are quite comprehensive, and the information is verified. A typical report will include tenant's information on:
  o Credit score,
  o Verified and authenticated employment reference,
  o Verified and authenticated current and previous landlord reference,
  o Financial suitability to rent with maximum affordability,
  o Verified and authenticated identification,
  o Good conduct reputation score that identifies criminal and negative social activity,
  o Any previous liability payment default.

Ms Jing jumped in to add a touch of wisdom drawn from situations she has faced with prospective tenants accusing her of discrimination. "This may become quite sensitive," she warned me, "and may lead to an unwanted legal course by some highly irritated applicants." Her advice on avoidance of discrimination covers from early in marketing the property until screening and final selection. According to laws in almost all countries, tenant screening and background checks must be performed without regard to race, skin colour, sex, ethnic origin, religion, disability, family status, or political affiliation. Any attempt to ask questions related to those areas of personal information may be judged as discriminatory, so just avoid those questions.

To protect yourself against discrimination complaints, even if no sensitive questions are asked, screen applications on a first-come, first-served basis and document the reasons for qualifying or disqualifying a prospective tenant.

I was tempted to share a standard tenant application form, but after thinking about it, I hesitated to do so for the simple reason that the form will vary widely with the laws and the practices in different cities. What goes into the application form was covered in this section. It is easy to find many rent application forms online, which you can follow and amend as per your needs.

Showing the Property to Prospective Tenants

After shortlisting prospective tenants, it will be time to arrange for property viewing. Nothing beats walking through the property before signing the rental agreement and handing rent cheques to the landlord. If you have decided not to engage the services of a leasing agent, arranging for viewings can be a challenge, especially if you are currently employed. In this case, property viewing is best arranged after working hours and on weekends. Given my limited time availability, I often schedule all viewings in a given time frame. This also creates a sense of scarcity and competition among prospective tenants, which allows the property to be tenanted in the shortest period.

Shaking Hands

After marketing the property, prescreening prospective tenants, and arranging for viewings, as a landlord, you will be able to select the right tenant who will pay the right rent and who will start the rental agreement at the right time. It just makes sense to give priority to screened prospective tenants who have agreed to pay the requested rent and to start the rental agreement as soon as possible.

After finding this tenant, you will need to ask for a deposit to hold the property vacant until the agreed-upon time to start paying rent. The prospective tenant needs to know that the property cannot be held indefinitely. A tenant who will not pay the deposit is likely still shopping around for other properties. This deposit ranges from 5 per cent to 10 per cent of the annual rent, and a deposit of one month rent is the most often used practice. If the tenant will not sign the rental agreement and make the rent payment before the agreed time, this deposit will be forfeited in favor of the landlord. On the other hand, if the tenant does sign the rental agreement and makes the rent payments as agreed, this deposit becomes the security deposit, which is required in rental agreements.

The figure below summarizes all the steps in attracting tenants.

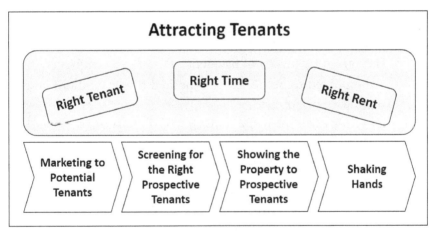

Figure 65—Attracting tenants

Setting the Rules and Signing the Lease Agreement

This is the pit stop that comes after attracting the right tenant, the time to sign the rent agreement. Different cities have different rules and regulations governing lease or rent agreements. Standard forms can be obtained from local authority websites, from real estate agents, from attorneys, or sometimes from local stationery stores. Don't be tempted to download lease agreements from non-trusted sources. They may be the wrong forms, which would make them not legally binding.

Rental agreements have standard clauses determined by local laws governing the landlord/tenant relationship. They also allow additional clauses to be agreed upon between the landlord and the tenant. Below is a set of rules that are meant to protect both the landlord and the tenant.

- *Lease term length.* Attracting tenants takes time, and some costs may be involved. For that reason, a landlord's interest lies in the longest possible rent period, which is often a one-year lease. The shorter the lease period, the higher the tenant turnover rate, and the higher the risk of having vacancy for a long time until the next right tenant occupies the property.

- *Rent amount and payment terms.* Any lease contract must clearly state the total rent amount and the terms of payment, which refer to the mode and frequency of payment. Although modes of payment may vary, the one that works best is usually payment by cheque, A batch can be issued in advance as per the agreed frequency of payments. Post-dated cheques (PDCs) are supposed to be cashed or deposited by the landlord on the dates written on them.

- *Rent amount increase on renewal of rental agreement.* After all your hard work attracting the right tenant, as a landlord, you wish to keep such tenants for the longest possible period. A well-drafted rental agreement will stipulate the conditions for renewal of the lease for another period of time. Pre-agreeing with the tenant on a preset rent increase for each renewal period will be the best strategy. The most common practice is to agree on a 5 per cent rent increase per year, if the local laws allow for that. In some highly regulated cities where landlords cannot increase as they please, it is a common practice for local authorities to set guidelines on rent increases. As a landlord, you will have to check and comply with the common practices and local laws in your area regarding rent increases.

- *Late fee description.* The rent agreement should clearly define penalties to be imposed on the tenant in case of late rent payments or rent cheques being rejected by the bank due to insufficient funds. Late fee penalties could vary anywhere between $50 to $200 for a few days of delay and even much more for longer delays. If the tenant does not correct the situation in matter of days, then the landlord can proceed with the eviction process (more on that later in this chapter).

- *Security deposit amount.* Any rental agreement must include a clause on security deposit, which could range from 5 per cent to 10 per cent of the annual rent. The most common practice is one month's rent to be taken as a security deposit and stored in a separate savings account. A security deposit is a refundable deposit that a tenant pays to their landlord (or a property management company appointed by the landlord) before they move into a property. As long as the tenant abides by the terms of their lease, this deposit should be returned to the tenant upon vacating the property on the expiry of the lease agreement. The landlord is allowed to keep all or part of a tenant's security deposit in any of the following situations: early termination of the lease, non-payment of rent, damage to the property, to pay any utilities and fees that the tenant neglected to pay, or to replace access cards and keys not returned to the landlord.

- *Repair and maintenance.* Whenever a rental agreement does not clearly define the property's move-in condition and also the rules of engagement regarding repair and maintenance, headaches from unnecessary late night calls and recurring expenses are bound to plague any landlord. Tenants are expected to keep the property in good condition throughout the term of the rental agreement. To better manage the tenants and expenses related to repair and maintenance, Ms Jing taught me four important lessons. These gave me more control, and I never deviated from them:

o A move-in condition report has to be signed in by both the tenant and the landlord before the keys are handed over to the tenant. Both parties shall make the property tour and record the condition of every corner of the property and take as much photos as possible to support the report. A sample "Move-in Condition Report" can be downloaded from www.employeemillionaire.com/resources.

o Two types of maintenance should be defined: *minor maintenance* and *major maintenance*, which are tagged to a dollar value as a threshold per occurrence, usually between $150 and $300, depending on what might be acceptable in a given location. The rental agreement must clearly state that all day-to-day wear and tear and *minor maintenance* (costing less than the set threshold per occurrence) is the responsibility of the tenant, whereas *major maintenance* (costing more than the set threshold per occurrence) is the responsibility of the landlord. This definition of major maintenance limits the landlord's responsibility to important structural maintenance, plumbing, electrical, mechanical, heating, or air conditioner-related issues. It is important to include "per occurrence" in defining the type of maintenance. Otherwise, tenants may abuse the set rule and lump several minor maintenance issues into one big-ticket major maintenance and ask the landlord to arrange for the maintenance and pay the expenses. It is also important to clarify that the landlord will require reasonable time, usually twenty-four hours, to take necessary actions on issues related to major maintenance.

o Any maintenance or repair work, major or minor, arising from incidents that are the tenant's own fault will be dealt with and paid for by the tenant.

- o A move-out condition report, which is the same format as the move-in condition report, should be signed by both the tenant and the landlord upon touring the property together on the expiry of the rental agreement when the tenant moves out. Any undone maintenance, which is the responsibility of the tenant, will be evaluated by a third party contractor, and the cost will be deducted from the rent security deposit.
- *General Rules.* Rental agreements will include clauses on the intended use of the property, the maximum number of occupants, smoking, pets, and responsibilities for utility payments.
  - o The tenant is not allowed to use the property for any commercial purposes or to sublet any of the premises.
  - o The rent contract shall specify the total number of occupants of the property.
  - o No repairs or alterations affecting the structure and integrity of the property are to be carried out by the tenant without prior permission of the landlord.
  - o Tenants are responsible for insuring their own household contents.
  - o No pets are allowed (if applicable).
  - o No smoking inside the property (If applicable and if enforced by local laws).
  - o The landlord is responsible for paying any developer's management fees, property management fees, and major maintenance fees.
  - o Utility bills and deposits (electrical, water, sewage, garbage removal, TV, telephone, Internet, and gas supply) and municipality housing fees are the responsibility of the tenant.
  - o The landlord is not responsible for any damages incurred from any accident or death or injuries while using the property or the facilities within the community or development.

    o   The landlord will give the tenant no less than two days' notice (except in the case of emergency) to enter the property to inspect, maintain, repair, alter, improve, or rebuild with the tenant's permission.

Papa Joe's advice on signing lease agreements with the tenants is to take the time to explain to them all the clauses of the agreement. Although it may take time, it will reflect a professional image as a landlord. Walking the tenants through every clause of the rental agreement will save landlords a lot of headaches coming from tenants complaining about ambiguities in the agreement. Also ask tenants to sign or initial each of the important clauses. This serves as a good protection against tenants' claims of overlooking important items in the contract.

Manage the Tenants

Property management is about managing its operating budget. A property's net operating income (NOI) is the difference between the property's income and its operating expenses (excluding mortgage loan settlements). To maximize a property's NOI, a rental property investor should improve the property's rental income and minimize its operating expenses. This boils down to managing both the tenants and the property. This section covers the topic of managing your tenants. Managing the property is the focus of the next chapter.

After attracting the right tenant, setting the rules, and signing the rental agreement, managing the tenants is the longest haul. Normally, rental agreements have a duration of one year, and they are meant to be renewed for longer periods as long as the tenant complies with the rules and does not leave the property for personal reasons. The clearer the rules in the rental agreement are, the more objective managing the tenants becomes based on clear black-and-white agreed rules of engagement.

Managing your tenants well is about setting the rules and agreeing on them before they occupy the property, but most importantly to make sure those rules are observed by both parties. Any leniency from the landlord in accommodating tenants not playing by the agreed rules will set precedents not only with the same tenant, but also with other tenants the landlord may have in the same development.

Early in my investment career, I made many mistakes in being lenient with my tenants regarding late rent payments or accommodating minor maintenance that was supposed to be the tenants' responsibility. Obviously, I was stupid and naïve. I ended up lowering my expectations with tenants, whereupon tenants ending up abusing my goodhearted inclination to have happy tenants. I started collecting one late rental payment after another, meanwhile incurring expenses on minor maintenance that were not my responsibility. You guessed it! This is a recipe for going bankrupt by owning rental property that requires financing from my own personal pocket instead of producing a positive net cash flow. It took lots of hard work to get back to the set rules and manage my properties' net operating income. In some extreme cases, I had to evict tenants who were unable to stick to the rules.

Managing your tenants boils down to managing both halves of the equation: collecting rents and managing maintenance requests.

- *Collecting rents on time and as agreed.* A rental property investor must follow the rental agreement to the letter in terms of having tenants paying the agreed rental amount and paying it on time. This means being tough in spite of listening to sad stories of the tenants and their financial challenges. You have to be fair to both the other tenants who comply with the rules and to yourself. As a rule of thumb, any attempt from the tenant to offer partial payment or to delay the rent payment will enforce the late fee provision of the rental agreement. Any repeated behavior from the tenant may warrant starting the eviction process.
- *Managing maintenance requests from tenants* can become tricky if the rental agreement does not clarify maintenance responsibilities and if the rental or property manager does not

follow religiously what has been agreed upon. It is important to be firm and tough in rejecting any maintenance requests that relate to either minor maintenance or day-to-day wear and tear, which are the responsibility of the tenant. Any leniency will set expectations that similar maintenance will always be the landlord's responsibility. Whenever a tenant sends a maintenance request that is not classified as major maintenance, the landlord or property manager should always refer to the maintenance clause in the rental agreement and never entertain such requests. On the other hand, if a maintenance request does qualify as major maintenance, unless it is an emergency, the tenant should allow at least twenty-four hours for the landlord to take necessary actions. With this in mind, as a landlord you will be training your tenants not to send unnecessary maintenance requests that will be declined. At the same time, you will be training them not to call in the middle of the night for major maintenance.

Check against the Set Rules

Throughout the duration of the rental agreement, the landlord (or a property manager assigned by the landlord) will be managing the tenants and having hands-on experience with them. Any deviation from the set rules will warrant the landlord taking necessary corrective actions with the tenant. Such corrective actions for any violations of the rules should be documented in writing with a proof that the tenant has been acknowledged. Modes of communicating important notices to the tenants can be email, a letter handed in person to the tenant with a signed acknowledgment receipt, registered mail, or through the legal route. If the tenant takes measures to rectify the situation, then the relationship between landlord and tenant can continue within the rules of the rental agreement. If the tenant does not take corrective actions, the landlord can start the eviction process.

Retain or Evict the Tenants

Upon checking a tenant's compliance to the rules agreed upon in the rental agreement, the landlord has two options:

- Retain the tenant and extend the rental agreement for another period. This is the most favourable outcome that can minimize risk of vacancies.
- Evict the tenant on or before the expiry of the rental agreement.

Eviction can be the result of any of the following:

- Late or no rental payments.
- Violating the terms of the rental agreement.
- Improper use of the property for reasons other than what has been specified in the rental agreement.
- Subletting the property without written approval from the landlord.
- Damaging the property.
- Causing health or safety hazards on the property.
- Conducting illegal practices such as with drugs or prostitution within the property or the neighbourhood.

As a landlord, you should never hesitate to take immediate action and evict a tenant by following the proper legal procedure in your city. Any of the problems above will have a detrimental impact on the property's net operating income and eventually its cash flow. This will ruin your whole plan of generating unearned income through rental property investment.

THE EVICTION PROCESS FROM BEGINNING TO END

Any landlord will run into the possibility of an eviction. It is always better to know how to go about eviction and what to expect through the process before you face a situation that merits an eviction. This section covers the main steps of the process. Note that specific laws vary by city, so be sure to check them to ensure you are acting according to the local laws.

Eviction of tenants has to follow legal steps. Any attempt to evict someone by yourself is illegal in most cities. Many landlords falsely believe they can kick a tenant out by force, remove their belongings, lock the tenants out of the property (by changing the locks), cut the essential utilities from the property, or harass the tenants as a way to make them leave the property. Any of those actions is considered illegal. A landlord needs to follow the rules of the *eviction process* in order to remove tenants from the property.

The eviction process is summarized in the following steps:

1. *Have a valid, legal, and documented reason to evict.* Tenants cannot be evicted for personal reasons. Otherwise the legal system will not rule in the landlord's favor. Most importantly, the reasons must be documented with enough proof to justify an eviction.

2. *Provide the tenant with a formal eviction notice.* With valid and documented reasons that permit an eviction, the landlord must provide the tenant a formal eviction notice, including number of days to vacate as stipulated by local laws. The eviction notice is a straightforward, simple-to-understand document that provides tenants with an ultimatum that will require them to fix the issue in order to avoid the eviction. The eviction note must state the reason of the eviction, a specific date for the tenant to either remedy the situation or vacate the property before an official eviction is filed with the local authorities. The landlord has to prove that the eviction notice has been received by the tenant by putting the notice on their front door, sending it through certified mail with a delivery receipt requested, or sending it through any entity that is approved by the local authorities for that purpose.

3. *Wait for the tenant to rectify the situation.* Once the eviction notice is received by the tenant, the landlord will wait for the tenant to take action to rectify the situation or move out within the number of days stipulated in the eviction notice. In practice, most of the issues get resolved at this stage. On the other hand, in the rare cases where the tenant does not take any action within the deadline, the landlord can proceed with filing for an eviction with the local authorities.

4. *Formally file for eviction.* If no corrective actions were taken by the tenant within the deadline of the eviction notice, the landlord can go the local authorities (local courthouse or public notary) to file for eviction and pay the relevant fees. Upon filing for eviction, the landlord must provide proof that the tenant has been given the proper amount of time by means of the eviction notice as local laws require. Thereafter, both the landlord and the tenant will receive a court notice to be mailed with information on the date and the venue of the court date.

5. *Prepare for the hearing.* After formally filing for eviction, the landlord will have to prepare for and attend the court hearing where both the landlord and the tenant will meet in front of a judge to determine the outcome. Before the hearing, the landlord will need to prepare all the documentation that proves the eviction case, which includes the rental agreement, any bounced cheques from the tenant, records of all payments by the tenant, records of all communication with the tenant, a copy of the eviction notice that was provided to the tenant, proof that the tenant received the eviction notice, and any other document that supports the case.

6. *The court decision*: Going to court can be stressful, but the preparation done before the hearing can remove most of the stress. By being honest and having enough documentation to prove the case, the judge can make an informed decision based on facts. If either the tenant or the landlord does not show up in court, some judges may automatically rule against the absentee.

7. *Evicting the tenant*: If the court case is ruled in the landlord's favor, the court will order the tenant to vacate the property in a set number of days. This court order will be sent by the court to both the landlord and the tenant. The tenant usually vacates the property within the deadline set by the court. If the tenant does not leave by the date set in the court order, the landlord can ask the local police to physically escort the tenant and all of the tenant's belongings out of the property.

8. *Post eviction actions by the landlord*: After the tenants move out of the property, it will always be wise to have the locks changed so the tenant cannot get back in later. Depending on the court decision, the tenant may also be required to compensate the landlord for any unpaid rent or damages done to the property. The landlord will have the property in rent-ready condition before a new tenant can move in. Such expenses may have to be shouldered by the landlord until the previous tenant pays for the compensation as ruled by the court. In extreme and rare cases where the previous tenant does not pay the money due, the landlord can file a claim in the court to get the payments.

Evictions can be stressful and time-consuming for both landlord and tenant. The key to reducing the probability of evictions in the future, lies in attracting the right tenants in the first place. This is why it is important to follow all the steps explained in this chapter in renting out a property.

This chapter has covered renting out your rental property and managing the tenants, the first half of the property management equation. The other half is about managing a property's operations, which is covered in the next chapter.

Chapter 15 Action Steps

After taking ownership of the property, get it rent ready as soon as possible, and arrange to attract the right tenant at the right time and at the right rental rate.

When the right tenant has been identified, set the rules and have the rental agreement signed by both parties.

Throughout the duration of the rental period, you will be managing the tenant and checking against the rules so that you a decide whether to retain or evict the tenant.

CHAPTER 16

Manage Your Property

Without any warning, Papa Joe changed his coaching style when the time was due for me to learn about property management. When I requested advice on property management, he reminded me of one condition for him to mentor me: I would work on any assignment he might give me without any expectation in return. I agreed to his rules then and have been committed to following his mentoring instructions ever since.

MY SIX-MONTH HANDS-ON EXPERIENCE IN PROPERTY MANAGEMENT

After getting my first rental property occupied by the right tenant paying the right rental income, it was time for me to learn the ropes of property management by rolling up my sleeves and getting into the action. Papa Joe offered me a non-negotiable six-month unpaid job in one of his apartment buildings as an assistant property manager. Given that I was already holding a permanent job, Papa Joe offered me simple job conditions: I was to work from 7 to 10 p.m. on weekdays, regular working hours on Saturdays, and I would meet Papa Joe once a month to share what I learned.

At first glance I felt my personal life had been sabotaged. I couldn't imagine not having time to rest. But I felt positive about this unpaid job. I envisioned that the payoff would come at a later stage, whenever I would need to put into practice all the experience I would accumulate in working as an assistant property manager. Indeed, the on-the-job training I received while reporting to a highly competent property manager saved me several thousand dollars in operating expenses, which I could have incurred due to ignorance.

Papa Joe texted me on a Sunday evening, advising me of my job details: the apartment building where I would be working and the name of my new line manager. Happily, I would be reporting to someone I had the pleasure of meeting and learning from on an earlier occasion.

The next day, after a long and hectic Monday at my nine-to-five job, I went for a one-hour break with coffee and a snack before heading to my new evening job. I sat in the coffee shop convincing myself that the six-month job would be relatively easy since I did not expect much to happen during evening hours. How mistaken I was!

I arrived on time to my new job and was warmly greeted by the property management team (the staff on the night shift), including Robert (my new boss). It was great catching up with Robert again a few weeks after my last meeting with him, where he generously shared his experience with me on due diligence. I knew I would learn a lot from working with him.

After introducing me to my new colleagues, Robert walked me through the main areas of the thirty-two-floor condominium tower. The first two hours of my first day on the job were dedicated to the property tour, with Robert explaining to me how his team gets busy throughout the day managing the operations of the property. To conclude my first day, Robert escorted me to his office, we sat down, and he shared with me the role of a property manager and his expectations of me in assisting him in managing the property.

THE ROLE OF A PROPERTY MANAGER

A property manager's main role is to manage the property's cash flow through managing its income and operating expenses. This suggests that the property manager's role revolves around attracting tenants, leasing the property, collecting rents, arranging for preventive and incidental maintenance and repairs, bidding for services, accounting, managing operating budgets, reporting the property's operations and financials, handling legal issues, and anything else necessary for managing a rental property.

To better help me understand the main responsibilities of a property manager, Robert drew a matrix that enabled me to visualize how a property manager manages both the tenants and the property so that both the rental income and the operating expenses are within the budgeted plan.

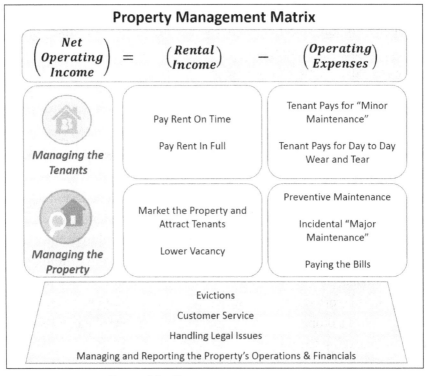

Figure 66—Property management matrix

The day-to-day job of a property manager is to manage the property's income and expenses according to the planned budget, which was the basis upon which the property was purchased. This is not a behind-the-desk nine-to-five job. It involves a lot of problem solving—and problems are not few when dealing with tenants, contractors, handymen, and staff. For multifamily properties, the list of the responsibilities of a property manager will be quite long. For single-family properties, which is the focus of this book, the list is more manageable.

Renting the Property

On top of the list of a property manager's role is to lower the vacancy and get the property rented out to the right tenants, at the right time, and at the right rental income. Once the rental agreement is signed, a property manager will keep on managing the monthly rent by ensuring the rents are collected on time and in full.

Renting out the property was covered in the previous chapter. Below is a quick recap on the property manager's role in renting the property and keeping it rented:

- Marketing to potential tenants
- Screening for the right prospective tenants
- Showing the property to prospective tenants
- Signing rental agreements
- Collecting rents on time and as agreed
- Managing maintenance requests from the tenants
- Retaining or evicting the tenants

Managing the Operating Expenses

Once the property is rented out and the rental income is kept well managed and under control, most of the time spent by the landlord or the property manager is managing the property's operating expenses.

Managing operating expenses revolves around the following responsibilities:

- *Maintenance*: One of the advantages of single-family properties is that the landlord is not responsible for maintenance of common areas or anything outside the property itself. Limiting the maintenance work—be it major or minor, incidental or preventive—to the property itself makes it easier to manage maintenance works. The most important starting point is to clarify in the rental contract the maintenance responsibilities between the landlord and the tenant. Having the landlord responsible for major maintenance only will limit maintenance work to either preventive maintenance or incidental maintenance. Preventive maintenance to rental property requires a thorough knowledge of the property, its needs for upkeep, contracting with service professionals, and budgeting to accomplish them. To stay on top of maintenance, a landlord or property manager has to schedule routine property visits to inspect appliances, plumbing systems, electrical systems, heating and air conditioning systems, and look for cracks in walls and pest problems. Below is the "Maintenance and Repair Hot List" that is bound to happen any time to any landlord:
    o   Appliances not working properly or out of order
    o   Air conditioning or heating system malfunctions
    o   Rusty hot water going out from water heater
    o   Water leaks in ceiling or under the windows
    o   Water leaks under the sink or bath tubs
    o   Water drip from faucets or toilets
    o   Toilet water leaks
    o   Clogged water or sewage pipes
    o   Electric distribution board or wiring problems
- *Paying the bills*: Maintenance works, services fees, developer fees, taxes, municipal fees, utilities fees, and any other expense related to operating the rental property have to be well managed by the landlord or the property manager. It's important not merely to pay the bills, but to pay them on time and within budget.
- *Managing the budget*: With rent collections and bill payments, accounting and cash flow management become major parts of

a property manager's role. This means that rental income and operating expenses will have to be posted and compared to set operating budgets. Two of my favorite coaches who have helped me in different aspects of my professional career had similar perspectives on identifying the measures of success and on tracking performance against them. Papa Joe often quoted Ken Blanchard: "Feedback is the breakfast of champions". Stewart B., my executive coach and mentor, consistently preached on the same topic: "If you want it to happen, measure it. If you want it to be repeated, recognize it". Managing budgets is all about recording income and expenses and tracking them against set budgets. If you contract the services of a property management company, recognizing and rewarding good performance will make the operational efficiencies repeatable and sustainable. Not tracking performance against set objectives is where many businesses and professionals fail. A few never set objectives or budgets, which means they never define success. Others who might have set their budgets, might fall victim to rarely tracking performance against them.

MANAGING THE PROPERTY AND THE TENANTS

At the base of the Property Management Matrix are the other roles of a property manager, which are:

- *Evictions*: No one likes evictions, but it is an inherent part of the rental property business. Evictions are mainly the outcome of late or no rental payments, violations of the terms of the rental agreement, improper use of the property, subletting the property without written approval from the landlord, damaging the property, causing health or safety hazards in the property, or conducting illegal practices within the property or the neighbourhood. The eviction process can be outsourced to property management companies or a lawyer. It doesn't need to take much of the landlord's time.

- *Customer service*: A rental property business is no different from any other business that needs to handle its customers. Being available for the tenants is the responsibility of the landlord or the property management company assigned by the landlord. Tenants need to contact the landlord or the property manager for emergency or major maintenance requests. The problem is that tenants have a tendency to consider any small thing an emergency. This is another reason why the rental agreement should clarify responsibilities of the landlord and the tenant.
- *Handling legal issues*: A rental property business has its own share of legal issues and contracts, which are not limited only to rental agreements and evictions. Owning and managing the day-to-day operations of a rental property are well governed by local laws. Landlords and property managers should become familiar with legal requirements for rental property ownership in their location.

MURPHY'S LAW

With all the good planning and controls in place, any small mistake, oversight, or deviation from the budget will have a ripple effect, with greatest impact on the property's net operating income. This can make a property operate with a negative cash flow, the exact opposite of why a rental property was purchased in the first place. In her business reviews with the many property managers of the different multifamily properties owned by Papa Joe, Ms Jing continuously reminded her team of Murphy's Law: Anything that can go wrong will go wrong.

During my six-month unpaid job as an assistant property manager, I was invited to attend two quarterly business reviews (QBRs), which used to take place at Papa Joe's head office. In this QBR, all the property managers had to present their respective properties' operations and finances. Ms Jing was great in questioning any deviation from the budget—line by line. She even asked questions to understand the better-than-budgeted results so that the best practices could be shared with everyone and repeated. In her efforts to keep the property managers' eyes on the ball, she was always referring to Murphy's Law in one way or another. Ms Jing discovered from experience that anything that can go wrong at property management generally does go wrong sooner or later, so frequent tracking of a property's performance is inevitable to keep it on track with the operating budget.

Many stories were shared in those QBRs, and each one demonstrated how things like attracting the wrong tenant, not collecting rents on time, not budgeting for the unexpected, or overspending on operating expenses versus budget can lead to detrimental effect on the property's performance. Attending those QBRs and listening to the stories explaining poor property financial performance have taught me to follow the same discipline in my rental property business. I track each of my rental properties' operating budget and financial performance at least once per month. It doesn't take too much time when I plan my time around this discipline. However small my business is, I follow this discipline so that whenever my business grows to new levels, I am all prepared with the right mindset, systems, and controls in place.

SHOULD YOU HIRE A PROPERTY MANAGEMENT COMPANY?

One major decision a rental property investor should take vis-à-vis managing the property is whether to self-manage the property or hire a professional management company. There is no right or wrong answer for either route. It is just a matter of the investor choosing how to spend time— managing properties or looking for other rental property investments.

I intentionally saved this section for the end of this chapter. I was worried that offering the option to outsource property management to a professional company sooner might make some readers choose the easy option and skip this chapter. In fact understanding what property management is and the role of a property management will help you identify what to look for so that you can hire the best property management company for your business.

Below is a checklist that will be quite helpful to go through when you are interviewing a property manager or a property management company:

- Their trade license or real estate license
- Property management fees
- Years of experience in property management
- Number of properties they manage
- Operating and financial reporting
- Policies and procedures regarding property management
- Forms and contracts used in property management
- References of at least three landlords who have been contracting their services for at least one year each
- How tenants' backgrounds and evictions are usually handled
- Vacancy rates of properties they are managing
- Length of time they usually take to fill in a vacancy with a new tenant

In addition to that list, I personally need to feel comfortable dealing with the property management company and its employees. I make it a point to visit their offices and meet the people who may be handling my properties. A visit to their offices can tell me a lot about the company's culture and the calibre of people I will be working with.

Whenever I sign a property management contract, I include the operating budget of each of the properties as an appendix to the contract. This becomes the basis on which their performance will be evaluated. Below are reasons that can make me consider discontinuing their services and start looking for another company to manage my rental properties:

- Failure to deliver on the operating budget that has been signed off by both parties.
- Failure to submit monthly operating reports.
- Failure to submit complete reports. Partial reporting is a sign of neglect or incapability.
- Failure to manage the tenants well and to collect the rent on time.
- Failure to conduct proper maintenance.
- Failure to pay bills on time.

These are simple and valid reasons to look for another property management company. But those conditions will be made clear in the contract we sign before starting the relationship. I do not allow room for surprises from either side. I agree on the rules of engagement in our contract and then follow closely on what was agreed on.

ADVANTAGES OF OUTSOURCING PROPERTY MANAGEMENT

Outsourcing property management offers numerous benefits to the owner such as the following:

- Less time to spend on managing a property, which allows for more time to be spent on doing other things or looking for new investment deals.
- A property management company has in place all the systems, processes, forms, and contracts in managing rental properties according to the local laws and regulations.
- Property management companies have established relationships with contractors who can perform maintenance faster and at lower rates due to their economies of scale.
- Property management companies can fill up vacancies at a faster rate than an individual owner can.

Outsourcing to a professional property management company can indeed be a powerful thing, allowing the owner to work on the business and not in it. As like almost anything in life, there are also disadvantages to outsourcing property management.

DISADVANTAGES OF OUTSOURCING PROPERTY MANAGEMENT

Fact of life: for every advantage, there is a disadvantage. A rental property investor should analyse both advantages and disadvantages of outsourcing property management before making a decision. The major disadvantages to be considered are these:

- Property management fees, which could range anywhere from 5 per cent to 7 per cent, is an operating expense that will inevitably lower the property's net operating income. In deciding whether property management fees are justified, a landlord should consider if time spent elsewhere is more rewarding in terms of income or whether a day job imposes the outsourcing of professional property management.

- With many properties and landlords to be managed at any given time by a property management company, lack of focus is another disadvantage of outsourcing property management. Such companies give more attention to the bigger players (landlords with more properties), and landlords with a smaller number of single-family units are sometimes given a second-class citizen kind of priority. This is why a landlord has to be fully engaged with the property management company and keep on demanding for updates and for the reports to be submitted in full and on time. If the landlord does not keep up the pressure, his properties will soon be moved down on the priority list of the property management company's staff.

Going back to the main question of whether you should hire a property management company or self-manage the property, I wish I could give you an answer that works well for you. What I advise is to weigh both the advantages and disadvantages of outsourcing property management before making your decision. My personal approach, which is the advice that was passed on me by both Papa Joe and Ms Jing, is to start with self-management myself until I learn the ins and outs of property management. This has made it easier for me to outsource property management whenever I required their services. This is only my recommendation. Each one of us has different circumstances, and the decision is quite personal.

CHAPTER 17

The Virtuous Cycle of Building Wealth through Rental Properties

When Papa Joe noticed that I was kind of cruising on autopilot with all the property management systems and controls in place, he asked me to visit him one evening in his apartment for a chat. He sat on his favorite brown leather single-seat sofa and offered me a seat. Separating us was a tall, beautiful, handcrafted, solid wood coffee table with a few books resting on top of the marble top. The book on top had one playing card inserted in it as a bookmark. All I could see was the back of this playing card, which appeared to be a well-designed premium card.

He started with what sounded like a serious conversation. He tapped me on the shoulder for the hard work and time I spent learning about investing in rental properties and applying the knowledge. But he showed discontent that I had put my foot on the brake and not started a new cycle. According to him, building wealth through investment in rental properties is a never ending-cycle. He reminded me of one of our earlier discussions when he told me that the more I invest in rental properties, the more I can invest in more rental properties.

He opened the book on top of the stack on the coffee table, took out the playing card bookmark, and kept the book open so he could return to the same page. All I could see was the back of the card. He said he had used the same playing card as a bookmark for all the books he has read for the last thirty years. Wanting me to guess what was on the playing card, he asked me what is the highest card in a deck of playing cards. This appeared to be another trick question since two options could be correct: the ace or the king. So I gave him both answers. He smiled and explained to me that the ace of spades is traditionally the highest card in the deck of playing cards in English-speaking countries. He turned the face of the playing card towards me so I could see the design of his special bookmark. It had a large, royal design in the shape of a spade, with ACE written on top. The stem of the spade was in the form of the letter T. The figure below is a reproduction from my memory of the design of Papa Joe's ace of spades playing card bookmark.

Figure 67—Rental properties wealth generators: ACE and T

Then he told me the secret he has used for the last thirty years to remind himself of the wealth generators of rental properties: ACE and T, which stand for:

- Appreciation
- Cash flow
- Equity Build-Up
- Tax Savings

RENTAL PROPERTY WEALTH GENERATORS: ACE AND T

Papa Joe admitted that he kept this lesson for me as the last. He wanted me to learn and appreciate the most important feature of rental properties: cash flow. He wanted me to be fully satisfied with my investment plan on the basis of the cash flow I receive from my rental properties. Other wealth generators—appreciation, equity build-up, and tax savings—are also important and have major positive impact on the wealth-building process, but he did not want me to fall into the trap of planning for appreciation, equity build-up, and tax saving in forecasting the return on my investment. He wanted me to understand clearly that cash flow is the main measure of ROI, whereas other wealth generators collectively act as boosters of wealth. I imagine cash flow as the main engine of a car and the remaining wealth generators as the turbo chargers.

Papa Joe had got my attention, and I opened my eyes and ears to a new lesson. Apparently, what I had achieved so far back then was only the beginning of my wealth-building process.

Appreciation

In its simplest definition, *appreciation* is an increase in the value of an asset over time. When explaining the topic of appreciation, Papa Joe's memory went back to some properties he had purchased fifteen and twenty years back that are now worth more than five times their original purchase price. He did not want to get into a discussion about economics and the loss of the purchasing power of printed money. But the fact that the prices of properties go up over time drives the message home well.

The reason he did not want me to purchase properties on the promise of appreciation is because in the short term, prices of properties can go up, down, or sideways. But in the *long run*, prices of properties have always gone up historically in all major cities in the world.

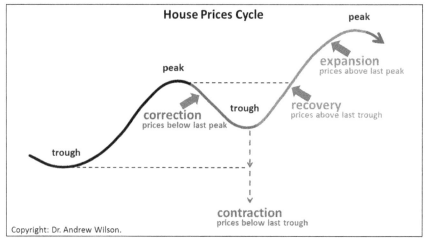

Figure 68—Wilson curve: House prices cycle

The price cycle of properties is well presented by Dr. Andrew Wilson, one of Australia's leading housing market experts, in the figure above. In principle, the house price cycle is typically depicted in four stages: a boom (peak), followed by a downturn (correction), followed by a recovery phase, which leads to an upturn (expansion) that sets us up for the next boom (a higher peak). According to Papa Joe, it is risky to purchase a property on the promise of appreciation and with the objective of flipping the property in a few weeks, months, or years. Markets always go in up and down cycles on the short term, which could make an investor wanting to flip houses lose money if the cycle was going downward in a correction phase. This is the simple reason why Papa Joe sees appreciation as the cherry on top of the cake, whereas cash flow is the cake itself.

The long-term increase of house prices over time is often referred to as *natural appreciation*, which can be visualized with the figure below.

Although house prices might go up and down in the short term, the overall direction has always been up in the recorded history of property prices.

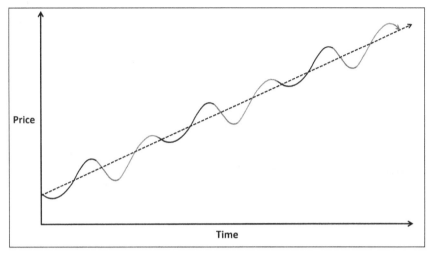

Figure 69—Long-term trend of house prices

Papa Joe also introduced me to the concept of *forced appreciation*, which is increasing a property's value by improving it such as by converting free, unused space in a home into an additional bedroom or bathroom. This strategy is used often by investors who make profit by improving houses and flipping them. This strategy might work well for some, but it is not the strategy that the employee millionaire will seek in building wealth and achieving financial freedom through rental properties, since this strategy requires a lot of time—and time is a scarce resource for employed investors.

Cash Flow

Cash flow has been the focus of most of this book. It is the most important wealth generator for rental property investors. In summary, cash flow is the amount of rental income left after the property operating expenses and its mortgage loan instalments have been paid. Cash flow is the result of good property management, where rental income is maximized and operational expenses are carefully controlled. Mortgage loan instalments also impact cash flow. The higher the property price, the higher its mortgage loan instalments and the lower the cash flow. So it is important to always purchase rental properties at the right price, which is at or below market value. Our target is 20 per cent below market value.

One of the most important lessons from this book is to purchase rental properties on the premise of the cash flow they generate as soon as they are purchased. Determining the cash flow of a property is fairly simple. By looking at like for like fair rental values, estimating operational expenses following best practices, and knowing the mortgage loan instalments, a rental property investor can deduct both the estimated operational expenses and the mortgage loan instalments from the rental income to estimate the property's cash flow.

Cash flow is the lifeblood of any rental property investor. It allows rental property investors to keep on growing their wealth by reinvesting in more and more rental properties that produce positive cash flow. This is at the heart of the virtuous cycle of building wealth through rental properties. We will come back to this later in this chapter.

Equity Build-Up

Equity build-up is the auto-pilot of wealth generation that is secretly working in the background. With each monthly loan payment, the remaining loan amount reduces and, in parallel, the investor's equity in the property increases by the same amount of the loan amount reduction. The beauty of this is that the income from the rental income, which is paid by the tenants, is used to pay the loan down monthly.

Papa Joe reminded me of one of his earlier lessons: "You will become at least as rich as the amount of good debt you take in your life". He refreshed my memory on how mortgage loans are designed in a way that each monthly loan instalment repays part of the principal and pays interest to the lender. However, loans are structured so that the amount of principal returned to the borrower starts out small and increases with each mortgage payment over time. Paying off the principal is what builds the borrower's equity in the property. So equity build-up starts quite slowly in the early years of the mortgage and then accelerates greatly in the remaining years of the mortgage loan. Equity build-up accelerates wealth building in the second half of the term of the mortgage. To refresh your memory on this topic, revisit chapter 3, where this concept has been explained thoroughly with many graphs and figures to help you visualize it better.

Tax Savings

Most governments encourage investors to own rental properties, since this helps to provide housing for the population. As a reward to investors who partner with the government in providing housing, those governments reward rental property investors through favourable tax treatments and thus encourage them to own more rental properties. Rental property investors are allowed tax deductions because they own rental properties. How tax savings work varies from country to country and sometimes from city to city. It is always advisable to meet with a CPA and discuss how this applies in your city.

Papa Joe referred back to his playing card and explained that ACE (appreciation, cash flow, and equity build-up) was deliberately designed on the *top* of the ace of spades and said that it was also deliberate to have the T (tax savings) at the *bottom* of the ace of spades. The message he was trying to convey is that investors should not plan to buy rental properties for the tax benefits they may offer. Tax savings may make a good deal even better, but will never make a bad deal good. He believes in tax savings as an added benefit to rental property investors, whereas the three other wealth generators are the true wealth-building ACE.

The Virtuous Cycle of Building Wealth

One of Papa Joe's favorite quotes is by an English writer, William Hazlitt: "The more things you do, the more you can do."

He explained that the purchase of the first rental property may have been the hardest in terms of know-how and getting the funds. After the first sale is closed and the property is producing cash flow, the purchase of the second property becomes easier for the simple reason of improved know-how and improved finances. Then a rental property investor can replicate the same process over and over to create what Papa Joe calls the *virtuous cycle of building wealth*. He gave me a few moments to reflect on this concept, and then he asked me to explain it back to him in my own words and understanding.

With his question, I felt like a bucket of cold water had been thrown at my face, like this was the big graduation exam by which, if I failed, I would disappoint my mentor, who had invested time and energy on my learning. Papa Joe courteously allowed me time to reflect on my thoughts by leaving me alone for a few minutes while he prepared tea and snacks for us. I took advantage of this time alone by opening my smartphone and jotting down my thoughts in the notes app. When Papa Joe came back with the tea and snacks, he sat down and was all ears to listen to my version of the virtuous cycle of building wealth.

I started with getting the investor's debt-to-income ratio (DTI) in order to qualify for a loan. Powered with a loan preapproval letter, the investor can negotiate and purchase discounted properties. Once the property is transferred into the investor's name, the focus becomes to rent the property and manage it well in order to improve its net operating income (NOI) and its cash flow. Then, with the investor's improved income (unearned income coming from the property's positive cash flow), the DTI is further improved and the investor can qualify for more loans to purchase more rental properties, which generate more cash flow, which will allow the cycle to be repeated over and over at an increasingly faster pace.

Papa Joe took a few seconds of silence. I felt like I messed up in my answer. As he relaxed in his chair, he congratulated me for making sense of it all. To get the idea to sink in my mind, he added his point of view on the virtuous cycle of building wealth by insisting that an investor's job is to acquire income-producing assets, improve their unearned income, get their invested money back (without selling the asset), and continue to acquire more income-producing assets. The more this cycle is repeated, the sooner financial freedom is achieved and the more wealth is accumulated. This is why Papa Joe does not flip properties and rarely sells his rental properties. Following this cycle, the investor's money is always moving and never parked in a bank or non-income-producing assets.

Below is a visual representation of how the virtuous cycle of building wealth works with rental properties.

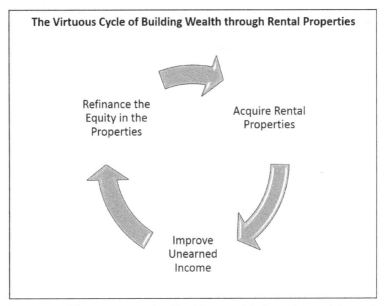

Figure 70—The virtuous cycle of building wealth through rental properties

With those words, Papa Joe urged me not to get lazy. He recommended that I stay in the game by continuing to look and purchase more rental properties. He reminded me not to ever fall victim to the captivity of passivity. I have followed his advice ever since, and thanks to the advice and pushing from Papa Joe, my life was transformed.

SHOULD YOU SELL YOUR RENTAL PROPERTIES?

Many people I have encountered throughout my life, in many corners of the world, believe that the way to wealth is flipping properties. They think that a real estate investor should buy low and sell high to turn a profit in the shortest possible period. That profit is either used to flip another property or pocketed. The investor's overlook is that the key to wealth is cash flow, equity build-up, and appreciation—and in some countries, tax savings. The unearned income from the positive cash flow generated from a rental property should be the number one reason for investing in properties.

Papa Joe was always inspired by Warren Buffet's famous quotes about investing for the long term: "Our favorite holding period is forever." He often also shared another quote from Warren Buffet: "Only buy something that you'd be perfectly happy to hold if the market shut down for ten years."

The strategy of buy and hold does not mean that one day you may either need to sell your property or find a great selling opportunity to sell it when the market is at an irrational peak. I have made large profits in instances when the market went crazy and prices of properties were skyrocketing. I was in the market, and I felt that the peak was irrational and unsustainable. I sold some of my properties at a close point of the irrational peaks and pocketed a handsome profit. I knew that property prices go into cycles and that the market was due to correct. My knowledge about the properties price cycle developed by Dr. Andrew Wilson enabled me to have a certain level of confidence about when to sell and when to buy. I knew I could never predict the market, and I was certain that I did not have a crystal ball, only a certain level of confidence gained by observing cycles and being in the game. I was not an observer from the sidelines.

In other instances, when I needed the money to purchase other properties, there was no reason for me to sell any of my properties. I have tapped into the equity of my other properties and obtained new financing from the bank. In this way, I ate a piece of the cake and still had the whole cake in my possession.

To answer the question of whether selling a rental property is the right decision, the short answer is: It depends. The longer answer is: It depends on your circumstances. If you need access to cash for personal reasons or to invest in other rental properties, then selling your rental property may not be your only option. A better option might be to tap into the equity you own and refinance your existing rental properties to get the cash you need. With this strategy, you will still own the income-producing asset and you will have achieved the objective of getting the cash you require. On the other hand, if your reason for selling is just to benefit from an irrational peak in prices that is eventually due to correct, then selling your rental property might be appropriate. But you should consider some consequences such as paying capital gains taxes.

Capital Gains Taxes

One important watch-out whenever you consider selling a property is the *capital gains tax* to be paid to the government. A capital gains tax is a type of tax imposed on capital gains or profits an investor realizes when selling an asset for a price that is higher than the purchase price. Capital gains taxes are triggered only when the asset is sold, not while it is held by the investor. Let's say the price of a property is appreciating every year. The investor does not owe a capital gains tax until the property is sold, no matter how long it's held.

Most countries' tax laws provide for some form of capital gains taxes on investors' gains, although laws vary from country to country. For example, in the Philippines, capital gains taxes are charged at a flat tax rate on the gross selling price. Some other countries are more investor friendly, and they levy no capital gains tax on the sale of residential property. A few countries with no capital gains taxes as of the writing of this book are United Arab Emirates, Singapore, Hong Kong, Switzerland, Cayman Islands, Monaco, Belgium, Malaysia, New Zealand, and Belize. Always check on the latest laws regarding capital gains tax before considering investing in capital gains tax-free countries.

Most countries with capital gains taxes consider the sale of an asset to be taxable if the asset was owned for more than a certain period, usually a year. Otherwise, the profit from the sale of the asset falls under earned income tax. But many European countries will not enforce capital gains tax if the property was owned for more than ten years. Given the differences in the laws between countries, inquire with a lawyer or the local authorities on the specific capital gains tax laws in the city where you either own or plan to own rental properties.

The Tax Foundation lists on its website (taxfoundation.org) the capital gains tax rates in different countries. The table below is extracted from the Tax Foundation website, last updated in 2015. It shows the capital gains tax rates in the OECD countries (Organization for Economic Co-operation and Development).

Top Marginal Tax Rate on Capital Gains, by OECD Country, 2015		
Rank	Country	Rate
1	Denmark	42.0 %
2	France	34.4 %
3	Finland	33.0 %
3	Ireland	33.0 %
5	Sweden	30.0 %
6	United States	28.6 %
7	Portugal	28.0 %
7	United Kingdom	28.0 %
9	Norway	27.0 %
9	Spain	27.0 %
11	Italy	26.0 %
12	Austria	25.0 %
12	Germany	25.0 %
12	Slovak Republic	25.0 %
16	Australia	24.5 %
18	Canada	22.6 %
19	Estonia	21.0 %
20	Japan	20.3 %
21	Chile	20.0 %
21	Iceland	20.0 %
23	Poland	19.0 %
25	Hungary	16.0 %
26	Greece	15.0 %
27	Mexico	10.0 %

28	Belgium	0.0 %
28	Czech Republic	0.0 %
28	Korea	0.0 %
28	Luxembourg	0.0 %
28	Netherlands	0.0 %
28	New Zealand	0.0 %
28	Slovenia	0.0 %
28	Switzerland	0.0 %
28	Turkey	0.0 %
	OECD Simple Average	18.4 %
	OECD Weighted Average	23.2 %
Source: Ernst and Young and Deloitte Tax Foundation Calculations.		

Deferring or Rolling Capital Gains Taxes

In some countries, such as the United States, Canada, and India, a taxpayer who wishes to avoid paying capital gains taxes upon the sale of a property may have the option to defer or roll those gains by replacing the property sold with another property of *like-kind* within a specific period of time without having to pay capital gains taxes that would otherwise become due on the sale of the original property. Other countries have similar rules, but they apply only for primary residences. Such laws are complicated and vary by country. You should always check with a CPA on any specific laws in your location.

It is important to highlight that in those countries that allow capital gains taxes to be deferred, they are never avoided indefinitely. Papa Joe put it in a few words: "Capital gains tax may be deferred, but it never means the sale of a property is tax free." In other words, as long as the investor is reinvesting the gains into a similar like-kind or higher value property, the taxes due are deferred or postponed. There might come a day when the new property will be sold and the gains not reinvested into similar or higher-value like-kind property. At that time the investor will be taxed. On the other hand, there is no limit for holding the property, which means taxes can continue to be deferred as long as the investor still owns the new property or engages in another exchange down the road when the new property is sold.

What to Do with the Money?

Once you either sell a property or get some additional financing on it, you will be facing another problem: What to do with the money?

Many will be tempted by what money can buy them, and they start purchasing liabilities, which defeats the whole purpose of increasing their unearned income and getting closer to financial freedom. For others, staying on track of achieving their objectives remains their focus, and they reinvest the money into other rental properties, which will enable them to achieve financial freedom. They will make their money work harder for them. This is what is often referred to as the *velocity of money* or what Papa Joe calls the *virtuous cycle of building wealth*, which I covered a few sections earlier.

I have been following the golden rule of keeping most of my cash invested in rental properties. This means that if I ever consider selling any of my rental properties for a decent profit, I will always have an alternative plan to reinvest the profits in another rental property, whether in the same city, another city, or even another country—one that I have already researched and in which I have prospected for discounted properties. In other words, my money is always working hard to generate unearned income and wealthy returns for me. I avoided learning the lesson the hard way, having to pay large bills of capital gains taxes and then parking the remaining profit in the bank with almost zero returns.

CHAPTER 18

Final Words

▌WHAT IS YOUR DASH?

My executive coach and great mentor, Stewart B., once asked me: "What is your dash?" Of course I did not understand his question. In fact, I thought it was a trick question. He paused for a few seconds to allow me some time to think and then gave me a hint to imagine what might be written on the tombstone of a person who died. I immediately made the correlation that he meant the *dash* that separates the date of birth and date of death of a person, which is the time a person spends alive on earth.

He asked me again: "What is your dash? When your eulogy is read, would you be proud of the things they will say about you and about how you spent your years from birth till death?"

He recommended I not answer his question then. But he strongly advised me to reflect on my dash and to think of anything I would like to change in my life now. I thought of this as an opportunity for any person to rewrite their dash. With those words, I came to realize that what matters the most is how we live and love during our years on this earth. It matters not how much wealth we accumulate for the sake of wealth, but we can think of wealth as an enabler to spend quality time with our beloved ones.

With the help of Stewart during several coaching sessions, I managed to clarify my purpose in life: Adding value to people's lives. This became the filter for every decision I make in my life, including writing this book.

When Stewart helped me identify my priorities in life, serving God, my family, and the community were on top of the list. Everything else became secondary or an enabler.

This is exactly how I see creating wealth and having plenty of money—as an enabler. Being wealthy and financially free can offer you choices in life. You can choose to retire early and spend more quality time with your family and serving the community; you can also choose to open a business you have always wanted to venture into; or you can choose to remain employed for a company you enjoy working with, especially if you have reached a senior position and if you really love your job. Whatever you choose, being financially free will allow you to have more conviction in your decisions. Gone will be the days where you will forced to stay in a job that you hate!

Thinking about what your own dash is will always be time well spent. I rarely have seen people giving their lives adequate thought and figuring out what their purpose is. On the contrary, I often see people taking ample amounts of time planning for their day-to-day things or their vacations. Don't get caught in the daily stuff. You will be better off to think of your life beyond material things. If you make it a practice to revisit your *big why* list every year and often refer to it to remind yourself of it, that would be a great start.

When I was writing this last chapter of the book, it was Christmas Eve of 2017. I tried to reach Papa Joe on his mobile in California, where he was retiring, to wish him a blessed Christmas and inform him that my book has come to an end. His daughter picked up the phone and informed me that he had passed away. He was a father figure to me. He helped me to transform my life. I believe his dash goes beyond all the wealth and success he achieved is his life. His dash was about teaching many others like me how to achieve the best in life and add value to people's lives. I miss Papa Joe. May God bless his soul and may he rest in peace.

SEEK THE HELP OF COACHES AND MENTORS

It is amazing how a coach can help you in figuring out the important things in life that you want to achieve and how a mentor can help you achieve those goals. While digging in my notes, I found a simple definition that differentiates a coach from a mentor. "A coach has some great questions for your answers; a mentor has some great answers for your questions."

The coaches I had the honor to work with in my life asked me many challenging questions that have triggered my thoughts and made me look for answers. In parallel, I have worked with great mentors who have helped me with the answers to the questions triggered by my coaches. I hope this book has achieved its objectives of enabling me to be both your coach at times and your mentor at others. My objective has been to share my learning and experience, which have enabled me to achieve financial freedom. Without the help of coaches and mentors, my mistakes could have been plentiful, and I might not have achieved whatever success I have so far.

You will need the help of coaches and mentors before and during your rental property investment journey, but equally so after reaching your short- and medium-term goals. You will need someone to hold you accountable for achieving your objectives. You will need someone who will help you unfold priorities you will have in your life down the road a few years from now. You will be amazed how your priorities in life will evolve throughout the years, especially when you grow in experience, skills, and in wealth.

Thank you for taking the time to read this book. I hope you will apply the concepts shared here in your rental property investment career. You can always visit www.employeemillionaire.com/resources to get the forms and templates that I talked about in this book. Please also feel free to contact me if you need any assistance, coaching, or mentoring in your rental property investment journey. I will be honored to work alongside you and witness your success in the future. I can be reached on <u>contact@employeemillionaire.com</u>.

▌WILL YOU TAKE ACTION AND CHANGE YOUR LIFE?

I will leave you now with a question, which I trust you will reflect on and hopefully make meaningful changes to your finances and to your life. Once you decide on what you want to achieve in life, don't get caught in "the captivity of passivity". Get out there and make it happen. Take action!

REVIEW REQUEST

Thank you so much for reading this book. I realize that there are millions of books out there and I want to express my infinite appreciation that you chose mine.

If you have enjoyed this book (and I think you did if you got to the end), please leave a review – this is one of the only ways authors like myself can find readers like you.

If you wish to write a review (and I hope you do), you can select this book from my Amazon's author page:

www.amazon.com/author/hjchammas

ABOUT THE AUTHOR

H. J. Chammas lives with his wife Joyce and their new born son, Ryan, in Dubai. Both are active real estate investors specializing in single family rental properties.

H. J. Chammas is a self-made "Employee Millionaire" who has achieved financial freedom by investing in rental properties throughout Asia, Dubai, and Europe. With over 10 years of industry and investing experience, he brings forward a blueprint for investing in rental properties in a simple and clear manner.

He is the founder and CEO of the Employee Millionaire, a company that empowers employees to achieve financial freedom and become millionaires with real estate investing.

To emulate Chammas' success in single family real estate investment, sign up for his program on www.employeemillionaire.com to learn the sound investing principles and avail of free templates and worksheets that makes rental properties investing almost on autopilot.

If you have enjoyed reading this book, please visit H. J. Chammas' author page on Amazon and review this book. Your opinion matters. You can also check his other books and audiobooks.
www.amazon.com/author/hjchammas

To keep updated with the latest articles that H. J. Chammas will be writing on the topic of rental properties, follow him on Facebook and LinkedIn.
www.facebook.com/EmployeeMillionaire
www.linkedin.com/in/habibchammas

More From
The Employee Millionaire

If you have enjoyed this book, we hope you'll take a moment to check out some of the other great material offered by *The Employee Millionaire*.

The Employee Millionaire **Video Coaching Program**

Dedicated to educating employees on leveraging their position of being employed to achieve financial freedom through rental properties investing, *The Employee Millionaire* offers a video program in the form of pre-recorded training modules packed with visuals and action steps that will hold your hand and walk you through the path to financial freedom… on every step of the rental properties' investment blueprint. This video program is equivalent to me coaching you from a distance and guiding you on taking actions.

www.employeemillionaire.com/VCP

Download your free resources from the link below:
www.employeemillionaire.com/resources

The Employee Millionaire **Inner Circle**

Join my Inner Circle where I will personally work with you one-on-one with your rental properties investments to help you on each step of the rental properties investment blueprint to achieve financial freedom. This is a 12-month program where we will be having video calls and where you will be asked to perform different tasks that will push you to go out there in the market and start investing in rental properties.

There are very limited openings for the Inner Circle. Apply now by sending me an email with the subject "Inner Circle."

contact@employeemillionaire.com

CPSIA information can be obtained
at www.ICGtesting.com
Printed in the USA
BVHW080634130722
641927BV00006B/39